"*Leading Strategically* is a practical and insightful guide to the core actions of effective leadership. I appreciate how City and Curtis expertly highlight the critical role of relationships, context, and history—often-overlooked factors that have been essential to my success as a leader. The case studies provide a compelling look at the complexity and opportunities of strategic leadership, making this book an invaluable resource for those dedicated to transforming schools and districts with intentional, strategic leadership."

—Kyla Johnson-Trammell, superintendent, Oakland Unified School District

"Written by passionate educators for passionate educators, this book will help you become the leader your students, *whānau*, and community need you to be. *Leading Strategically* provides the insights and tools to navigate challenges with clarity and purpose. *Kia kaha, kia toa, kia manawanui*—be strong, walk tall, be big of heart."

—Alec Solomon, principal, Whangārei Boys High School, New Zealand

"*Leading Strategically* masterfully bridges the knowing-doing gap in educational leadership. City and Curtis offer a compelling framework that demystifies strategic thinking and provides concrete tools for putting it into practice. As a professor preparing the next generation of system leaders, I appreciate how this book speaks to leaders at every level, offering practical wisdom to help them maximize their impact while sustaining themselves in the work."

—Shanna Peeples, National Teacher of the Year (2015) and Dr. John G. O'Brien Distinguished Chair in Education, West Texas A&M University

"*Leading Strategically* shows us how to marry leadership and a strategic mindset, a combination that is the essence of impactful leadership. The book is practical and pushes my thinking, making it accessible, invaluable, and a fun read. The case studies are real and rich, confirming that City and Curtis can walk the talk. I wish I'd had this book as a principal, principal supervisor, and central office leader. I'm glad I have it now."

—Gene Pinkard, president, Instruction Partners

"With insightful advice, clear analysis, and compelling case studies based on decades of experience, Liz City and Rachel Curtis have provided a timely and necessary guidebook to strategic leadership that will empower schools and school districts to reach greater heights. Our work is and has to be all about student success. *Leading Strategically* will help all of us keep that focus and support us to achieve more."

—Adrienne Battle, superintendent, Nashville Public Schools

"These two have done it again. In *Leading Strategically*, City and Curtis provide educational leaders with insights that are research-based, field-tested, and actionable. They offer realistic and inspiring examples to help leaders tackle sometimes seemingly intractable systemic challenges. A timely must-read."

—Meredith Honig, professor of education policy, organizations, and leadership and director of the District Leadership Design Lab, University of Washington

"Liz City has consistently given me the best leadership advice of my career, so I'm delighted she's made her insights more broadly available through this book. *Leading Strategically* demystifies leadership in a way that is remarkably actionable. The book will help you realize small wins today on your way to big leadership wins tomorrow!"

—Alejandro Gibes de Gac, CEO, Springboard Collaborative

"Once again, City and Curtis have offered an invaluable blueprint at a critical moment for the education sector. As we continue to contend with the devastating effects of the COVID pandemic and navigate an uncertain future, impactful leadership has never been more important or necessary. But how can we expect leaders to think expansively and act ambitiously while simultaneously doing more with less? This book surfaces that tension and others, and responds with real-world strategies and applications, demonstrating what is possible when leaders and their teams lead strategically."

—Saskia Levy Thompson, program director of Education for Economic and Social Mobility, Carnegie Corporation of New York

"Educational leaders have plenty of people telling them what they *should* do. Far rarer (and far more useful) is savvy, and practical advice about what it takes to actually get things done. That's what Liz City and Rachel Curtis are known for, and what *Leading Strategically* delivers in spades. Leaders should do themselves a favor and read this book, tomorrow."

—Rick Hess, senior fellow and director of Education Policy Studies, American Enterprise Institute

"Having worked with City and Curtis and witnessed their transformative approach to strategic leadership, I am thrilled to see their insights captured in this book. *Leading Strategically* helps leaders focus on what truly matters and take decisive action for lasting impact. With a clear framework and real-world cases, it equips practitioners to navigate complexity with focus, adaptability, and purpose."

—David Kauffman, assistant superintendent of Human Resources and School Leadership, Navarro ISD

"*Leading Strategically* is a must-read for education leaders who understand that lasting change starts with people. As a superintendent, I know that cultivating relationships is at the heart of everything we do—whether building trust with our staff, engaging families, or empowering students. City and Curtis provide a powerful framework that not only sharpens strategic thinking but also reinforces the critical role of relationships in driving meaningful progress based on the experiences of our students, staff, and community. This book offers the practical tools and real-world wisdom needed to lead with intention, foster collaboration, and create a culture where both educators and students thrive."

—Ivan Duran, superintendent, Highline Public Schools

"*Leading Strategically* is a vital guide for leaders focused on clarity of purpose, deep diagnosis, and continuous improvement. City and Curtis tackle each of these with an awareness of context and relationships, providing sharp insights, practical tools, and probing questions to drive learning and action. It's a must-read for current or aspiring leaders trying to maximize their effectiveness and impact and sustain themselves in the work."

—Julie Mikuta, copresident, Charles and Lynn Schusterman Family Philanthropies

"*Leading Strategically* captures the key practices that help great leaders best serve our students—whether they're teachers, principals, district staff, superintendents, or board members. Its blend of strategic insight, deep focus on context and relationships, and commitment to continuous improvement resonates powerfully. The book's questions, tools, and case studies translate big ideas into practical action, making it an invaluable resource for anyone leading in education."

—Tom Boasberg, superintendent, Singapore American School, and former superintendent, Denver Public Schools

"*Leading Strategically* is an invaluable resource for any leader looking to make a lasting impact. With clear frameworks, thought-provoking questions, and insightful case studies, City and Curtis guide the reader from understanding to action and offer practical strategies to make leaders more effective. This book is a must-have for anyone committed to fostering meaningful change and growing in their leadership journey."

—Ryan Wise, dean, Drake University School of Education

"*Leading Strategically* is a humanizing text, guidebook, and reflective toolkit that supports education leaders (and any leaders) to reflect and act upon strategy by keying into the inter- and intra-personal dynamics, from historical and contextual knowledge to cultivating relationships and harnessing power. The introspective questions, reflective journal prompts, mini case studies, and in-tune stance with the demands of leading and living in 2025 make the book relatable and easy to read from cover to cover or in sections. This book helps me consider my own leadership journey, with an awareness of my intersectional identities; and it is a great tool for self-discovery, team learning, and within classes and learning organizations."

—Samantha Cohen, Hurst Senior Professorial Lecturer, American University

Leading Strategically

Achieving Ambitious Goals in Education

Elizabeth A. City
Rachel E. Curtis

Harvard Education Press
Cambridge, Massachusetts

Copyright © 2025 by the President and Fellows of Harvard College

All rights reserved. No part of this publication may be reproduced or transmitted in any form or by any means, electronic or mechanical, including photocopy, recording, or any information storage and retrieval systems, without permission in writing from the publisher.

Paperback ISBN 9781682539880
Library of Congress Cataloging-in-Publication Data is on file.

Published by Harvard Education Press,
an imprint of the Harvard Education Publishing Group

Harvard Education Press
8 Story Street
Cambridge, MA 02138

Cover Design: Dave Kessler Design
Cover Image: Ostanina Anna via Shutterstock

The typefaces in this book are Gill Sans MT, Minion Pro, Museo Slab, and Myriad Pro.

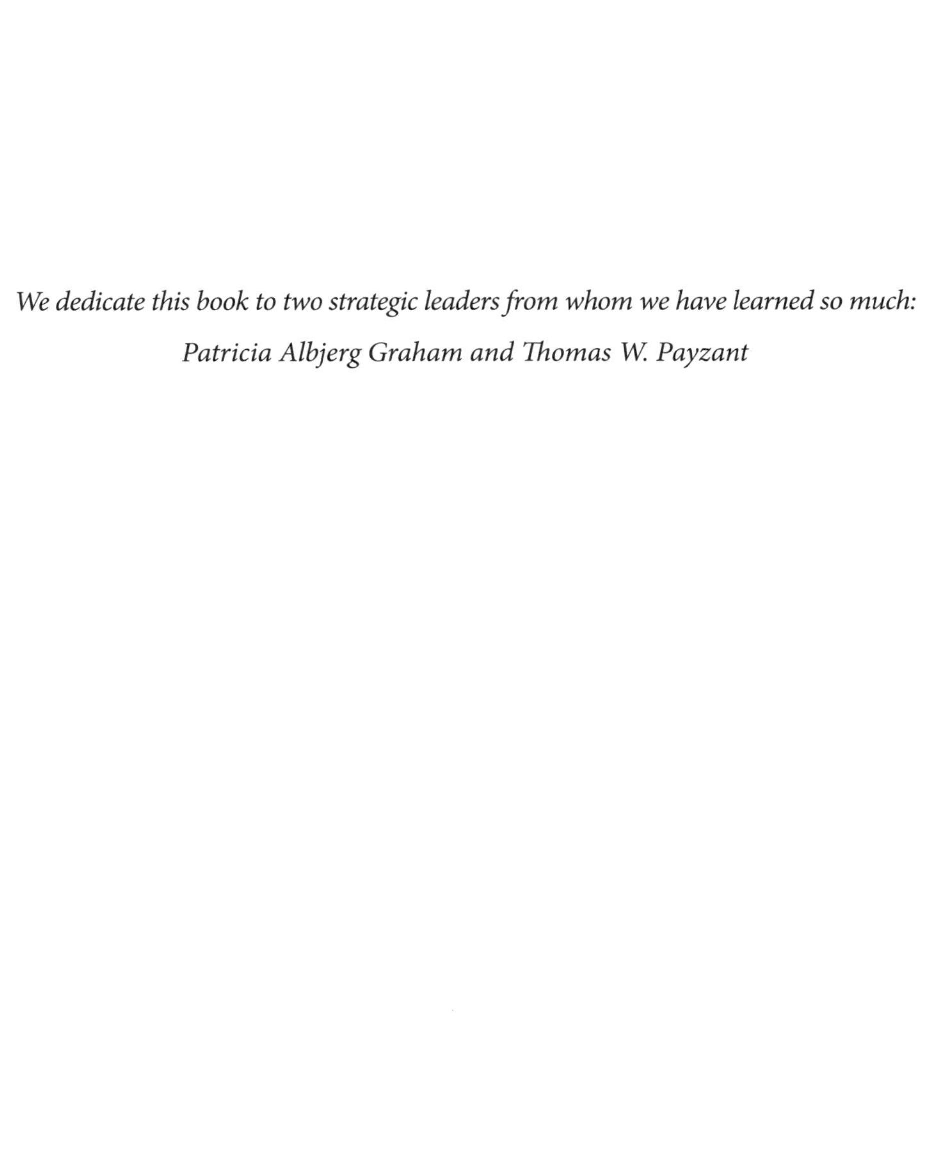

We dedicate this book to two strategic leaders from whom we have learned so much:
Patricia Albjerg Graham and Thomas W. Payzant

CONTENTS

FOREWORD

LIKE MANY OF MY PEERS IN EDUCATION, one of the most nagging challenges I face is the struggle to make progress toward what I feel to be important goals while dealing with a myriad of urgently immediate, but ultimately less important, problems and issues. As CEO of Baltimore City Public Schools, my days run the gamut from high level discussions on the Science of Reading or reducing chronic absenteeism to HVAC breakdowns in antiquated school buildings on a hot day. I've often said that I spend 80 percent of my time keeping the lights on, leaving only 20 percent of my day (on a good day) to focus on the big issues of providing a quality education for the young people of Baltimore City.

How do I balance the urgent issues of the moment against the big ideas and challenges facing my school district and public education? How can I most effectively use my time and my mental energy for maximum impact? Most important, once we've developed a plan, what is an effective strategy for its implementation and review to gauge the impact of our efforts? In the course of more than thirty years in the field of education, I have led a wide range of groups and organizations, ranging from an individual classroom to an urban public school district with 75,000 students, but I have never resolved the tensions inherent in these questions to my satisfaction.

It was a timely coincidence that I received the invitation from Rachel Curtis and Elizabeth City to write a foreword for their new book on leading strategically on the day I completed a three-day retreat with my cabinet members. Three days of reflection on district goals with respected colleagues and without the press of hourly interruptions had been a rewarding experience, but the questions raised in *Leading Strategically* shed a light for me on whether we had been consistently asking ourselves the right questions throughout our discussions.

Having known Rachel and Liz personally and appreciating their professional expertise, I was excited that they had collaborated on a long-anticipated complement to *Strategy in Action*—their well-received exploration of how to develop and implement a strategy for school improvement. I knew and respected them as talented practitioners with a deep respect for the complexity of the work of schooling and improvement and a commitment to making their work accessible and practical. When I read the manuscript of *Leading Strategically: Achieving Ambitious Goals in Education* I knew it had been well worth the wait. I also realized that the issues, techniques, and—most significantly—the questions they raised would have a positive impact on my team's approach to planning moving forward.

I was impressed by the way the book is designed and laid out to build knowledge, support action with questions, tools, and resources, and invite analysis to deepen learning through authentic mini-cases. The five elements of strategic leadership that form the foundation of the book comprise a concise, practical framework for the problem of balancing the demands of the big issues with the urgency of smaller ones, while following through to track how the outcome of what we planned to do actually compared with reality. In doing so, the authors bring an important message about how to create change and improvement in complex situations.

My personal favorite (although I found them all to be valuable) is Element 5: "Think Big, Act Small, Learn Fast"—through which effective leaders make "bets" on the right course of action to solve a complex problem, learn quickly from the results, and make necessary adaptations as they go, based on the results of each "bet." Of course, the effectiveness of this approach depends on an analysis of the plan's implementation. One of the great strengths of this book is its underlying emphasis on how the "planning" must convert to implementation, followed by a review of the actual impact of the plan versus our expectations, and the subsequent adjustment needed. Too often, central office teams and administrators think that simply developing a plan is sufficient, but the real challenge of leadership is to build *and implement* a plan for the work, then follow up with *analysis of actual results to facilitate adjustment*. Putting plans into place is not enough. Recognizing the reality of results and making adjustments is a critical aspect of leadership. As I reflected on this process, I realized I had applied variants of that principle in past situations, but without the benefit of the intentional systematic approach the authors describe.

Reflection is a critical component in this book. Readers are encouraged to stop at the end of each chapter or mini-case, reflect on a similar situation in their own careers, and write down their thoughts in the space provided. While it may sound obvious, I discovered that the conscious effort to stop and think in real time was both pleasurable and productive—leading me to wonder why I didn't do it more often.

I am looking forward to my next cabinet retreat, before which I will present copies of *Leading Strategically* to my department chiefs to serve as the basis for what I know will be a productive exploration of how we—and the members of our teams—can become more effective leaders. I also intend to present copies to all our principals as a professional development tool to be shared with their school-based teams.

Staff leadership is a cornerstone of my administration in Baltimore, along with literacy and student wholeness. Throughout my tenure I have encouraged all staff members to lead from their seats, with the knowledge and self-confidence that they can make a difference and contribute to the work of giving our students the tools and foundation for success. The habits of mind outlined in *Leading Strategically* apply to everyone in the organization: from the CEO to central office and school-based staff. The ability to discern what's important in the noise of a hectic day; how to cultivate productive relationships between individuals and organizations; how to identify and harness power—when to wield it, when to share it, when to cede it; and (of course) how to think big, act small, and learn fast. These are tools that will make all staff members more effective leaders. The authors' ability to show how all of these elements interact in the real world to create the complexity we operate in is an eye-opening, valuable experience.

Equally meaningful from my perspective, the focus on the importance of prioritizing the *context* of our efforts is critical: the need for all of us as educators to keep in view for whom our work, our plans, and their outcomes should be focused. Our leadership is in service to our young people, their families, and the larger community, which is the driving force behind our efforts to be the best leaders we can be.

As educators, we are at a pivotal point nationally. The big questions are: Can we continue to have public schools that the public sees as viable and valuable? Is public education perceived as a worthwhile investment? As our nation grapples with this foundational pillar of democracy, can we educate youth from all backgrounds and do it well? Our ability to find answers to those questions, to resolve those immensely complex issues and meet the incredibly difficult challenges they represent will play an important role in determining the future of education and our country. *Leading Strategically* does not provide all the answers; it does provide a valuable toolkit for developing the skills we will need if we are to find them.

Sonja Santelises, EdD
CEO, Baltimore City Public Schools

INTRODUCTION

THERE IS A FIFTEEN-YEAR STORY BEHIND THIS BOOK. It started in 2009, when we published a book called *Strategy in Action* to respond to a challenge that we saw again and again in our decades working as educators, and then as resources to leaders, schools, school systems, and nonprofit organizations.[1] Educators were working incredibly hard but not having the impact they hoped to have on students' learning and development. One underlying problem was a lack of strategy guiding all this hard work. When we say "strategy," we mean a plan for improvement anchored in a clear *why*, which includes a small set of carefully chosen actions that, when pursued together, create something more impactful than if each action were pursued on its own. Strategy is focused and coherent, doesn't try to be all things to all people, and is developed and pursued in a way that leverages experience and expertise and builds ownership, engagement, and capacity. *Strategy in Action* taught readers how to develop such a strategy. The book resonated with tens of thousands of readers and provided the foundation for strategy work in hundreds of schools and school systems in the United States and around the world. We have supported many of these schools and systems, and it has been humbling and inspiring to see the incredible work that educators have done with our ideas, making them richer and more powerful and realizing positive impacts for students.

In addition to our ongoing work supporting strategy development and execution in schools and school systems, we have each pursued our shared passion for leadership development. Between us, over the course of our careers, we have created and led many efforts: teacher leadership initiatives; principal preparation programs set in the authentic work of school systems; programs to prepare central office leaders; efforts aimed at preparing leaders for cabinet-level leadership and superintendent or chief executive officer (CEO) roles in school systems, nonprofits, state departments of education, and entrepreneurial ventures; and programs and networks to support new and experienced superintendents locally, regionally, and nationally. We have done this work from within or in partnership with organizations as varied as the Boston and Chicago public schools, the Harvard Graduate School of Education, Teach for America, the Massachusetts Association of School Superintendents, and the Aspen Institute.

As we have focused on supporting the development of leaders at different stages of their careers and growth and in a variety of roles and contexts, we have seen people struggle with a common set of dilemmas. These challenges relate to ideas of strategy but are about how people approach their work on a daily basis—the extent to which they are thinking and acting strategically. Common symptoms of this struggle include the following:

- Confusing the means and the end
- Focusing on technical and structural changes without considering the more complex, human-centered change required
- Creating long lists of things that need to be done without identifying and prioritizing the key drivers on the list and/or exploring the relationships between these things
- Designing high-potential work without including the people affected by it, those who need to implement it, or those who have the power to jeopardize it
- Considering work absent the context and history that surrounds it, which has much to teach about how to set work up for success
- Forgetting about people's need to feel safe and a sense of belonging to do their best work, as well as both the interpersonal and organizational relationships needed to do high-impact work

These symptoms manifest in a principal spending enormous time, energy, and social and political capital to ensure that teachers have common time for planning, without being clear about the most important work she wants teachers to engage in during that time and how to ensure that happens. Or a leader reorganizing his nonprofit's organizational structure without first understanding the history behind the current structure. Or educators running headlong toward a solution to a problem they've identified regarding families' engagement in their children's schooling without being in conversation and partnership with families to define the problem or being willing to share or cede power when developing a solution.

These efforts are consistently less impactful than the leaders intend, which makes the people involved feel less efficacious. As one's sense of agency and possibility is diminished, work that is fundamentally complex and challenging feels even harder. This combination is corrosive, affecting people's satisfaction and ability to sustain themselves at work. This, in turn, makes the work less sustainable. Think Sisyphus pushing a rock up a hill. We wrote this book to address this dynamic. We want to help people be more effective, in hopes that it will make the work feel more sustainable and encourage them to think expansively about what they can do on behalf of all children.

Moreover, our experiences have convinced us that leaders' ability to think and act strategically is essential for the successful development and execution of strategy. The more strategic leaders there are, the more likely it is that organizations will be guided by ambitious, coherent strategies that drive toward a rich vision. While we, as authors of a book on strategy development and execution, believe strategy is central to an organization's success, we also know that many people are in organizations where there is either no strategy or a weak strategy. We want to help these people have the biggest possible impact, both in their daily work and in the influence they can have on colleagues and the organization more broadly.

We have come to understand that a root cause of the problems we keep seeing is lack of knowledge, skills, and habits of mind of strategic leadership. When we drilled down another layer by asking why this lack of knowledge, skills, and habits of mind exists, we realized that this idea of strategic leadership had not been fully articulated, much less made accessible to educators. Our observations and analysis crystallized into a single question: *What does it mean to lead strategically from wherever you sit in an organization?* That is the question this book answers.

At a moment in our process of writing this book when we felt like we were chasing our tails a bit (an inevitable stage of book writing, at least for us), we each answered the question: *If you had to summarize the essence of leading strategically in two words, what would they be?* Rachel said, "Paying attention." Liz said, "Placing bets." While our answers give you a peek into each of our fundamental ways of walking through the world and leading—and why we love to work together—they also show you how we began to cultivate the ideas and arguments of this book.

"Paying attention" is about observation and discernment, about seeing and trying to understand people, their behavior, and their relationships. It's about understanding what is or is not actually happening in an organization (sometimes in contrast to what is espoused) relative to its aspirations and impact. It is about walking through the world with eyes, ears, and heart open, and then synthesizing what's been taken in to inform decisions about what to do (or not do) and how to do it (or not do it). Paying attention builds understanding of the context and needs of the organization and makes it possible to adapt leadership in response to both.

"Placing bets" focuses on getting to action. It acknowledges the level of uncertainty in any decision and encourages leaders not to be paralyzed by it. It's impossible to know for sure if something is going to work for everyone all the time, or even some people some of the time, even if it has worked before or in some other situation. Contexts are different, and conditions are always changing, as are people. "Placing bets" does not mean gambling with people's lives; it means understanding that trying comes before knowing. It's an acknowledgment that whatever is done will likely play out differently than planned or imagined, will not work for everyone, and will be full of learning that can be harvested to support continuous improvement.

This book is the one that we wish we had had when we were leading in schools and school systems every day. It would have saved us a lot of time, energy, and angst and made us much more effective. Our goal in writing this book is to turn the tide of education leaders expending so much energy for so little progress. By leading strategically, we believe that leaders can be more impactful. And that the combination of expending less energy and seeing greater progress will sustain leaders in this hard and profoundly important work. We hope this book supports leaders to lead with openness and curiosity rather than fear and anxiety, and to think in terms of possibilities rather than constraints, and abundance rather than scarcity. Such a stance makes the work more interesting and joyful, opens up possibilities, and models what we most hope for all children.

To answer our question, *What does it mean to lead strategically from wherever you sit in an organization?* we have synthesized all that we have learned about strategic leadership from our own work, the leadership of educators we have worked with, and multiple knowledge sources. We've had the privilege of working with and learning from brilliant teacher leaders, parents, principals, central office staff, superintendents, board members, and nonprofit leaders who exercise strategic leadership. Their wisdom is woven into this book, as is our conviction that strategic leadership can be exercised by people at any level of an organization.

This book is for any current or aspiring education leader who wants to be more impactful in making things better for children, their families, and their communities. We have written the book to be as relevant for a teacher who has recently assumed leadership among his peers as it is for a nonprofit middle manager who is trying to figure out how to lead substantive work from the middle of an organization, or a superintendent who understands that her two greatest points of impact are her work with her board and how she ensures the effectiveness of her leadership team and its individual members. Knowing that leadership doesn't happen in isolation, we have also written the book to support teams to become more strategic. The content of the book can serve as a curriculum for developing strategic teams made up of strategic leaders. Because one of the jobs of leaders is to make everyone around them more strategic, we have explicitly addressed how to build other people's capacity in the elements of strategic leadership that we introduce in the book.

We have tried to make this book accessible and practical. You don't have time for endless theory, and you don't want to finish the book without clear images of what leading strategically looks like in practice and steps you can take immediately to be more effective. And reading a book is more fun if you can engage with the ideas presented. To this end, the book is organized into two parts. Part I explores five elements of leading strategically that we have distilled from our decades of work. Part II shows the five elements in action and interaction with one another in mini-cases drawn from real situations.

The five elements that we focus on in Part I of the book include (1) discern, (2) cultivate relationships, (3) understand context and history, (4) harness power, and (5) think big, act small, learn fast (see Figure I.1). These elements are introduced next.

DISCERN

The discern element is foundational for all the other elements. Leaders and aspiring leaders commonly struggle to discern what's important through the noise of day-to-day demands and find it a challenge to carve out space to focus on that. The most common signs of this struggle are trying to do too many things, rushing to action without fully understanding the problem, and pursuing actions that are incomplete or ineffective. The ability to discern helps leaders figure out what is important, which in turn supports focus and intentionality—crucial skills of strategic leaders.

Figure I.1 The Five Elements of Leading Strategically

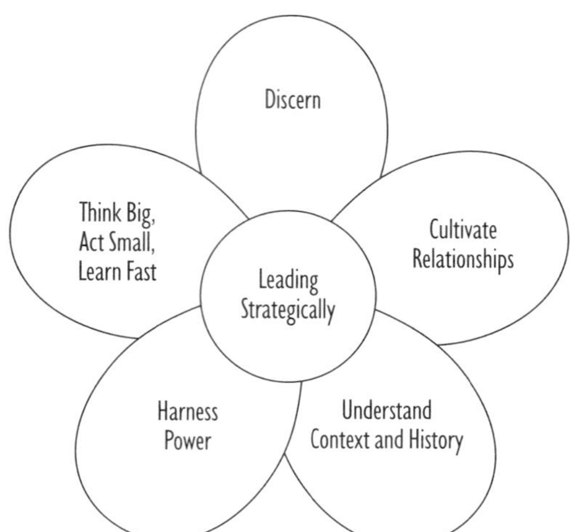

There are three dimensions of discerning: (1) to identify purpose, (2) to understand a problem, and (3) to choose right action. Discerning to identify purpose asks leaders to begin anything they do by articulating to themselves and others why they are doing it. Discerning to understand a problem invites leaders to be curious and gather data by counting, seeing, hearing, and feeling what's going on, and then sifting through this information to define the problem and its root causes before taking action. This requires slowing down, which can feel hard to justify, countercultural, or just plain uncomfortable. Slowing down at the stage of discerning is done in service of making smart choices, which is ultimately much more efficient than running hard to pursue a choice that is destined to be less effective. Once there is clarity about the problem, discerning to choose the right action asks leaders to consider what is most important to do to make progress in the context of vision, larger goals, and a deep understanding of the issue. Strategic leaders discern among different options for action, considering their hierarchy of needs and prioritization, organizational capacity, potential for impact, and pace and sequence.

CULTIVATE RELATIONSHIPS

Cultivating relationships is foundational to strategic leadership. It functions at multiple levels and is often overlooked. At its most basic, cultivating relationships is about acknowledging colleagues' humanity, inviting them into work, and honoring their contributions. When this is done well, it creates a hospitable environment for impactful work to happen and nurtures promising work in progress. Yet we have seen time and time again how people don't tend to interpersonal relationships with intentionality, often thinking that they don't have time to do so or that it's a "nice-to-do" rather than a "need-to-do." The reality is that meaningful work happens through people having productive relationships with one another. This truth acknowledges the importance of both interpersonal and organizational relationships. Focusing on relationships organizationally means identifying interdependencies across departments and organizing and collaborating in ways that leverage them to maximize impact.

UNDERSTAND CONTEXT AND HISTORY

In our own leadership practices as well as in our work with others, we have seen how frequently leaders pursue ambitious work without learning from relevant past efforts or building their understanding of historical and contextual dynamics. Strategic leaders gather information to understand the current context and culture and how they intersect and interact with their own roles and responsibilities in the organization. They also consider the implications of context when deciding what to focus on as well as why, how, when, and with whom to focus on those things in order to maximize the likelihood of success and impact. History is a crucial subset of context that strategic leaders pay attention to, with the understanding that the past informs the present and has important lessons to teach.

HARNESS POWER

"Power" is a word that often provokes strong reactions along a continuum ranging from an allergy to it to an ego-driven mindset focused on accumulating and wielding it. These stances can profoundly compromise leaders' effectiveness. Teaching leaders how to identify where power resides, what it looks like in action, and how to marshal it in service of their work can be game changing, both in terms of their sense of efficacy and their impact. To become skilled at harnessing power, strategic leaders must first understand the distinction between positional and personal power. And because power exists in a social context, strategic leaders pay attention to who makes what decisions, how power flows, and the politics, biases, and inequities reflected in those things. This awareness informs leaders' calculus of when to assert, share, or cede power, and the opportunities and costs associated with each.

THINK BIG, ACT SMALL, LEARN FAST

The combination of thinking big, acting small, and learning fast is essential in work that is complex and does not have clear, technical solutions (which constitutes so much of the work of educational organizations!). In that work, leaders don't know, with certainty, the right thing to do, so they need to make well-informed bets, learn quickly, and adapt as they go. These are hallmarks of strategic leadership. They are an antidote to some of the most common challenges that we see in educational organizations: thinking big in ways that are abstract and do not lead to action; doing lots of things without enough intention and a clear, commonly held vision toward which the action is aimed; and taking action without harvesting learning to apply to future actions. To think big, act small, and learn fast, leaders must hold the big picture in mind while constantly thinking about the parts of the whole and the relationships and interactions among them. Doing all of this well requires learning in action and continuous improvement.

Throughout the first five chapters devoted to the elements of strategic leadership, we include question boxes and tools. Question boxes offer a set of questions that you can ask yourself any time to better understand how an individual element is showing up in your work and how you can use it to greatest effect. Tools are specific processes that you can engage in to both deepen your understanding and inform the action you take as a leader. You can use both the questions and the tools by yourself or with colleagues, depending on your situation and what you're trying to accomplish.

Part II of the book explores how the five elements of strategic leadership show up individually and in relationship with one another in leaders' authentic work, as well as how that ratchets up the complexity of leading strategically. We begin this part of the book by introducing the idea of dualities that strategic leaders encounter in their work. These are a big part of the complexity of leading strategically. By naming and explicating multiple sets of dualities, we try to normalize their presence and to orient you to them so you can recognize them in the subsequent cases and when they arise in your own leadership. We hope that this will help you make strategic decisions about whether, when, and how to address them. Examples of these dualities include how strategic leaders both simplify and hold complexity, act and reflect, emphasize process and product, be humble and confident, play the short game and the long game, and be flexible and consistent.

The rest of this part of the book is devoted to real mini-cases and composites from our work with leaders. The cases explore leadership successes, failures, and dilemmas. We present them in ways that both invite and offer analysis aimed at deepening your understanding of what's going on, where the hazards and/or opportunities lie, and what strategic leadership looks like in this context. You have the chance to apply your learning about the elements of strategic leadership and to reflect on your own leadership as you engage with other leaders' work and dilemmas. In each case, you will be invited to try to figure out what's going on, generate different options for action, choose the approach that you would take, and understand why. We support you in this effort by providing our own analysis and imagining what a do-over might look like in certain instances.

In the conclusion, we synthesize all the ideas introduced in the book into the Essential Eight—a set of questions you can ask in any situation or context to help you lead strategically. This is our effort to hold the duality of simplicity and complexity.

There are a variety of ways you can read this book, and we wrote it with this variety in mind. You could read it on your own, applying the content to your practice using the tools and resources provided. You could read and discuss it with peers—a group of teacher leaders, principals, or department heads whose work will be most impactful if they collaborate. You can also read it with your organization's leadership team to build shared understanding and practices. Embedded in each of the collaborative, team-based approaches to reading the book is the opportunity to build both individual and team capacity, share your success, and problem-solve the obstacles you encounter. Whether the group is a superintendent and her senior leadership team, directors who work on a team or cross-functionally, a community of principals, or aspiring teacher leaders, the simple act of engaging in conversation and learning supports the curiosity and openness that form the bedrock of strategic leadership. This has the potential to be transformative. We intentionally wrote each chapter so it can stand alone, hoping to give you the option to read the book in any order or chapter by chapter, individually or in community.

Finally, we want to share that as we wrote this book, we were very aware of our identities as white women who grew up middle class in the 1970s and 1980s, in homes that our families owned and paid mortgages on, with parents who were educators and had advanced degrees. Throughout the process of writing, we were reminded that our experience is not universal. We worked to make ourselves conscious of the unconscious ways that we framed ideas and chose examples and stories to include. Then we revised the manuscript with the goals of making every reader feel welcomed and seen and of making visible the ways that systems and structures reinforce existing power dynamics and the status quo. Along the way, we reached out to colleagues of different backgrounds who have led successfully in a variety of contexts for feedback and guidance. We have incorporated their feedback to the best of our ability. Nonetheless, we expect that we didn't always get this right. Our missteps are our own and reflect where we are in our own development as strategic leaders.

A small note on our use of honorifics: As you will see in the text, we refer to other people by their first and last name only, as is a convention in many publications. We have made the choice not to include titles (e.g., Dr., Reverend) with intention. While we want to recognize people in their accomplishments, we also don't want to implicitly privilege some forms of knowledge over others, use incorrect titles, or use titles other than ones people would choose for themselves.

We hope that this book supports you in developing your own and others' capacity to lead strategically; to sustain yourself in important, hard, joyful work; and to make progress toward your audacious vision.

PART ONE THE FIVE ELEMENTS OF STRATEGIC LEADERSHIP

1

DISCERN

WE LIVE IN A WORLD WHERE WE ARE bombarded with things trying to get our attention. All the boxes in the cereal aisle. News outlets that run 24/7. Email. Social media and ever-present pop-up ads. The incessant stimulation simultaneously amps us up and dulls our senses. Our attention span shortens. We feel pressure to respond. It's all too much, too fast.

There are two opposing ways that this dynamic of too much, too fast affects leaders. For many, the hopped-up feeling of being constantly engaged and taking action is almost addictive. If we see a problem, we think we should address it immediately. Reacting becomes reflexive; it makes us feel like we are helpful and important. Conversely, we can become overwhelmed and immobilized by everything coming at us. We disengage and retreat. We struggle to hold steady long enough to understand and help our adolescent child figure out how to navigate tricky waters with friends or honor the wishes of our family elders as their health declines.

While overengaging and disengaging are different reactions, they both encourage a superficial treatment of the topic at hand. The results of each are strikingly similar: we give up our ability to think, to make sense, to decide and then act with intention. These strategic behaviors are not easy. They take time and require us to tolerate the discomfort of taking action with no guarantees of the hoped-for impact and—even more challenging—sitting with a question or dilemma without immediately taking action. Discerning is aimed at addressing this problem.

DISCERNING IN OUR DAILY LIVES

We are constantly offered opportunities to *discern*. Some examples in our everyday lives follow:

- Do I get up early to have thirty minutes to myself before the household's hectic morning begins, or is the additional sleep more important?
- What do I do when a peer or direct report comes to me with a problem that they want me to solve?
- What do I eat for lunch?
- Do I ask the questions I have about the plan that my peers have developed to address a crucial organizational issue when no one else in the meeting is voicing any concerns?
- Is there time both to give my child a bath and read her a story before bedtime, or do I need to choose between the two?
- Do I relax in front of the TV with my partner/friends/children, or is there something more engaging to do with them that will foster a deeper connection?

These questions don't have clear, right answers. The right answer for each of us depends on many factors, including the day, the status of our relationships, our goals, the level of trust we have with others, and how full our personal fuel tank is. Yet asking the questions helps us discern the right thing (for us) to do. Of course, knowing the right thing to do doesn't always ensure that we will do it. We have competing commitments: we want to relax before bed, so we scroll on our phone, realizing in a blink of an eye that we've lost an hour and cut into the sleep we hoped to get. Knowing doesn't always lead to doing, but it usually leads to a deeper awareness of trade-offs and the ability to live and work consciously from intention rather than reaction.

WHAT DISCERNING IS AND WHY IT MATTERS

Life, school systems, and organizations more generally can be a bit like Instagram or a cereal aisle. There are many things going on, vying for our attention. The immediacy of children—twenty-five in our classroom, six hundred in our school, or fifty thousand in the system—is very compelling. They are counting on us. We want to do right by them. And there's no time to waste. We do something quickly to solve a problem. Often, we choose something to do that has limited enduring impact, but we don't know that at the time. We're in too much of a hurry to think it through. As a result, we end up in a cycle that resembles the game of Whack-a-Mole. A problem pops up, and we hit it with our problem-solving hammer. Then another one pops up, and on and on. We're so busy hitting the next problem that pops up that we may not even realize that the same problems are popping up again and again. They may look a little different, but at their core they're the same. They keep reappearing because we didn't address them thoroughly the first time. Examples of issues that we play Whack-a-Mole with in education include the following: monitoring and addressing student behavior, preventing absenteeism, improving instruction, building teacher capacity, engaging with families, and meeting the needs of our most vulnerable students. The cost of these quick, problem-solving behaviors is that we find ourselves in constant motion but never making progress—hamsters on a wheel. Ultimately, this is maddening and exhausting, both of which run the risk of leaving us demoralized by our lack of success. This loss of self-efficacy often negatively affects our engagement and performance.

Whack-a-Mole isn't the only way that our lack of discernment shows up. Other ways include the following missteps: doing too much of one thing or too many things at the same time; making a long, impossible to-do list that is so overwhelming that we never choose something and get started; choosing something and pressing on with blinders, unwilling to look around to see what's happening and reassess the situation; and losing focus and becoming easily swayed.

The *Oxford English Dictionary* definition of "discern" is "to distinguish (someone or something) with difficulty by sight or other senses."[1] When we discern, we cut through the constant noise of everything coming at us in order to focus. As we focus, we make sense of several things: what's going on around us, data and evidence, how we are feeling, what we can anticipate or predict may be important in the future, and how the thing in front of us relates to a bigger goal or vision. We ask questions, listen, and hold multiple things simultaneously. Our understanding deepens and becomes more nuanced. That more sophisticated understanding helps us make sense of the various things we can do and their relative merits. It is from this place of discernment that we then can make conscious, strategic decisions about where to focus and how to achieve maximal results.

We are much more effective and impactful leading our lives generally, and leading strategically in our classroom, school, department, or organization, if we discern *what* is important, *why* it's important, and what these things mean for *how* we spend our time. Clarity about these things keeps us as individuals, teams, and organizations from being perpetually buffeted about by the constant noise. It reduces organizational distractibility by letting us focus, be thoughtful, understand before we act, and then take strategic action. And while our decisions are not sure things, they are well considered, which increases the odds that they will have a positive impact.

Our attention and time are among our most valuable resources. The way that we direct them defines us, our effectiveness, and our happiness in our lives and work. *Discerning* comes first in this book because it is essential and foundational to the other dimensions of leading strategically. We also lead off with discerning because it's often countercultural and requires persistent effort to avoid the whirling vortex of busyness; addressing this vortex is crucial to being a strategic leader. Discernment is an ongoing process of prioritizing amid competing demands. Strategic leaders discern in and across three domains: to identify purpose, to understand problems, and to choose right action. Strategic leaders focus and prioritize among many possibilities or competing demands, use an array of inputs to inform decisions, and tend to the process they use to do these things.

DISCERN TO IDENTIFY PURPOSE

In *Alice's Adventures in Wonderland*, Alice and the Cheshire Cat have an exchange that highlights the importance of discerning to identify purpose:

> Alice: "Would you tell me, please, which way I ought to go from here?"
>
> Cheshire Cat: "That depends a good deal on where you want to get to."
>
> Alice: "I don't much care where—"
>
> Cheshire Cat: "Then it doesn't matter which way you go."[2]

The Cheshire Cat, who understands something about strategic leadership, explains the importance of discerning to identify purpose and then linking what you do and how you do it to that purpose. Alice is not a strategic leader; she wants to be told what to do and doesn't understand the importance of having an ambitious purpose to guide her actions, help her measure her progress, and adjust along the way. Articulating a purpose requires you to think ambitiously about *why* you're doing what you're doing and to identify the bigger thing that you're trying to accomplish through your actions. People call this *why* by different names: *purpose*, *vision*, *goal*, *objective*, or *outcome*. What you call it is less important than ensuring that you have it and that it guides you.

Purpose exists at three levels in organizations. At the macro level, it is the vision toward which the organization's strategy is aimed. At the middle level, it's the clarity teams have about why they are doing the things they are doing. At the micro level, it's the clarity of purpose each person in the organization who is leading work has. For an organization to be successful in pursuing its macro, organizational purpose, the purposes identified at the team and micro levels must align with it. This is what ensures organizational alignment and coherence and maximizes the likelihood of realizing the purpose.

The reason why an ambitious purpose is important is that without it, it's easy to get myopic, focusing on things right in front of your nose (which are often problems that need to be solved) rather than assessing whether and how they connect to a longer-term outcome. Without a vision to guide your treatment of the immediate issues, your treatment of them will likely lack ambition.

An example of a strategic leader pursuing ambitious work is a nonprofit leader excited about the idea of starting a brown-bag lunch series in her organization. In this series, colleagues would share promising developments in their work, as well as dilemmas with which they need support and thought partnership. That is *what* she wants to do. If she's strategic, she has a purpose—the reason or reasons *why* she is doing it. Her purpose might be some or all of the following: to build relationships and a culture of collegiality that will sustain staff and strengthen the organization; to highlight promising practices in the organization that may be transferable and supportive of overall organizational effectiveness; to recognize colleagues for their great work and tap their expertise to support the organization more broadly; and to provide staff with more learning opportunities.

If her purpose includes all these things, it is indeed ambitious. She's not going to achieve all these things at once. So she needs to map backward from them to think about what is required to realize each element of the purpose, if some elements provide the foundation on which to build toward other ones, and if some can be pursued simultaneously and in combination. She might ask herself some questions: *Do relationships need to be built before expecting people to take lessons from colleagues' work and apply them to their own work? Is people sharing what they learn from their sessions with other colleagues a way to build relationships? What would it take to bring together the different presenters from across the organization and have them focus on an organizational priority and work collaboratively to address it?* This is the discerning to identify purpose that strategic leaders do.

Alternatively, it's possible that when she begins, her purpose focuses on one of these things. She might have started the lunches with the purpose of building relationships. Over time, she may have observed how engaged people were in the learning and realized that the potential for learning and transferring good ideas across the organization was important. So her purpose for the work grew to include these things. Through doing things in pursuit of her purpose, she developed a deeper sense of the problem. Originally, she identified the problem as an unfriendly culture where people didn't know one another, seldom interacted, and worked in isolation. Over time, she gained a clearer sense of how these dynamics were negatively affecting the organization's work, and when strong collaboration and innovation were needed for specific projects. Her deeper understanding informed an evolution in the purpose of the work. As this example illustrates, there is an interactive and iterative relationship between purpose and problem definition.

Defining purpose also exists on a continuum of time. Regardless of whether you start with something big and ambitious or with something smaller and build on it to make it more ambitious, what is consistent is that the purpose evolves over time based on what's done and the learning that is achieved by doing it. In this example, the leader sees how bringing people together to learn about one another's work can support bigger ambitions about identification of talent to nurture and tap to lead the organization's work, as well as the development of cross-functional teams to tackle that work. As the purpose grows and evolves, so do the actions. Maybe the nonprofit leader builds time into the session for colleagues to talk in small groups about their learning and how they might apply it in their jobs. Maybe a workgroup grows out of the series, focused on how to apply the learning from the series to a problem that the organization is facing. Suddenly, she is accomplishing multiple things—realizing twofers and threefers—as the series recognizes colleagues for great work, taps their expertise and experience to support the organization more broadly, and fosters cross-functional collaboration. You can see how the purpose is growing increasingly ambitious.

Questions to Guide Discerning to Identify Purpose

- Why is this endeavor important?
- What will success look like?
- What does success make possible?
- Where might there be an opportunity for a twofer or threefer here?

DISCERN TO UNDERSTAND THE PROBLEM

You are likely already familiar with many tools and processes for identifying problems. While these can be very useful in your leadership practice, in Liz's twenty-plus years of experience with Data Wise, instructional rounds, and other similar processes, these tools are often used as events rather than as ongoing ways of discerning.[3] If you are fluent in problem identification, those skills and ways of thinking will be useful to you more broadly as you discern. This section highlights what strategic leaders do (and don't do) when they discern to understand the problem they're going to focus on.

Dig Below Symptoms to Find the Problem

Problems generally present as symptoms. For example, high school students are not coming to school. If you try to tackle that issue knowing only that students aren't coming, you are jumping into a game of Whack-a-Mole. You don't know enough to choose an effective response. You can't yet answer the *why* question: Why aren't students coming to school? *Why* is an essential question for digging beyond the symptoms to get to the underlying causes. Think of it as getting past the dandelion to get to the roots. If you take care of the part that you can see most easily—by cutting the dandelion—it may appear in the short term to be gone, but then it grows back. When you ask *why*, you expose the roots. Why is this board member so worried? Why are the buses late? Why are people starting but not completing our new program? Why is the baby crying? Why do I have a cough? Until you understand the *why* beneath the symptoms, you don't have enough clarity on the problem to choose the right action.

When you're trying to understand a problem, questions and inquiry are your friends. Root cause analysis tools like the 5 Whys protocol and fishbone diagrams can help with the inquiry process. But you don't necessarily need formal tools. The W-questions—*who, what, when, where,* and *why* (+ *how*)—that you may have learned in elementary school to help you research a topic are a simple, enduring technique that you can apply to understand a problem at home or at work. For example, if students aren't coming to school, you might ask questions like the following:

- Who isn't coming? What do we know about these students? Are there patterns?
- How often aren't they coming? Are there patterns about when they don't come?

- What do the students who aren't coming—and their families—tell us about why they aren't coming? How do they feel about school more generally?
- What is a day in the life of a high school student in our system like?
- What are the perspectives of community members and community-based organizations on this problem?
- For how long has this been a problem? What changes have happened in high schools, the community, and society more generally in the time in which this problem has developed?

These questions push beyond yes or no answers to build deeper understanding. They bring in a variety of sources of information, which you can triangulate. They slow you down. They also offer some protection against reflexively taking on someone else's urgency to solve a problem, whether that person has particular authority (e.g., your boss or elder) or is someone you really want to help. Questions are a way of going slow to go fast. They home in on the root causes of problems; when you address root causes, you are more efficient and effective.

Asking good questions is central to discerning and a hallmark of a strategic leader. We will return to asking questions many times throughout this book.

Questions to Guide Discerning to Understand a Problem

- What is the problem that you're trying to solve?
- How do you know it's a problem? What signals do you see that identify that there is a problem?
  - What data, evidence, and artifacts can you collect to provide greater insight into the roots of the problem?
- Who is most in need of a solution to this problem? Consider which groups of students/staff/community are affected by this problem.
- Who has important perspectives on the problem? Who might be key to unlocking a solution that will help them and others?
- What are the next steps you will take to better understand the problem?

Curiosity is the most important thing you can bring to this process. It requires you to be open and willing to learn as you probe the information you have collected to see what it can teach you, and as you identify additional information you may need.

Be Promiscuous with Data Sources

Strategic leaders draw on multiple types of information to inform their understanding:

- **Count:** Anything with numbers (e.g., collect and disaggregate student attendance data to better understand the scale of the problem, the students most affected, and patterns)
- **See:** Observations (e.g., look at what happens in classrooms/in the halls/the cafeteria, student tasks and the work they produce)
- **Hear:** In person, through surveys (e.g., listen to the people you're trying to help)
- **Feel:** Your own emotional responses and intuition, try to understand the lived experiences of the people you're trying to help (e.g., follow a student's schedule for a day)

The *altitude* of the information matters too. Are you zoomed out on the problem, looking at trends and broad categories and outlines, zoomed in close enough to see individual details, or somewhere in between? Picture using Google Earth to look first at the planet of your problem, then at the mountains and rivers, and then close enough to see the house where the problem resides. In their book *Street Data*, Shane Safir and Jamila Dugan talk about three levels of data:

- **Satellite data:** High altitude; illuminates high-level patterns (e.g., test scores)
- **Map data:** Medium altitude; identifies gaps (e.g., diagnostics, surveys)
- **Street data:** Low altitude; describes the experiences of individuals proximate to the problem you're trying to solve (e.g., via conversations, observations, empathy interviews, and student work)[4]

Safir and Dugan make the case for the essential (and often underutilized) role of street data, while acknowledging that different levels of data are helpful for different purposes. Street data are a way to hear the voices of people who are often overlooked and to increase the likelihood that the solutions developed are truly responsive.

Gathering information and artifacts across types and altitudes of data lets you dig beneath the presenting symptom to gain a rich understanding of the dynamics, textures, and complexities of the problem. Many leaders have a tendency to draw on only one or two kinds of data. While the particular data may vary by the problem itself, individuals tend to have personal preferences (e.g., numbers over stories or vice versa) and can also be influenced by what data are easily accessible or most valued by stakeholders. There is nothing wrong with starting with data that are easy to get or particularly valuable. But strategic leaders don't stop there. See the Data Tracker for support on collecting a rich and varied set of data.

Data Tracker

The Data Tracker provides a simple template to track what information you're collecting to ensure that it's rich and varied. Choose a problem that you want to understand more deeply. List your sources of information in the appropriate boxes. Make sure that you're not overrelying on one or more of the categories of information at the expense of the others. Rebalance your information-gathering approach as needed to get a good variety of types of information. You don't necessarily need something in every box. For lower-stakes or less complex issues, you may have a smaller array of data sources. For higher-stakes or more complex issues, you may want to collect a richer array.

Data Tracker				
	Count	See	Hear	Feel
Satellite data (high altitude; illuminates patterns)				
Map data (medium altitude; identifies gaps)				
Street data (low altitude; describes the experiences of individuals proximate to the problem you're trying to solve)				

Once you've filled out the template, step back and consider the chart holistically. Consider the following questions:

1. What are your observations?
2. Are a range of perspectives from stakeholders implicated in or affected by the problem reflected in the Data Tracker?
3. What gaps and/or overlaps in information collection do you see? How well do the data locate problems in systems versus reinforce a deficit mindset about people and communities?
4. What additional data sources are most essential to deepen your understanding of the problem and challenge common narratives and assumptions? Or, conversely, what data sources are least essential for understanding this problem?
5. How much time do you have for this inquiry, and which data sources are most essential?
6. With all the analysis in mind, the final question to ask is: *What do we need to do next?*

Strategic leaders go beyond the first pass at data with an awareness of what is informing their understanding and what hasn't yet been considered. They understand that problems are not monolithic. People are affected differently, and it's important to disaggregate data to understand who is affected and how. Otherwise, the experience that's most frequent or aligned with the default culture may be considered the norm. The purpose of discernment is to understand nuance and to question assumptions. This takes time and the ability to resist latching onto early data and interpretations that feel compelling but are likely incomplete. Things that take longer, such as deeply listening to a variety of people, can be particularly helpful in surfacing critical information that cannot be gathered any other way, as well as building relationships to support making progress together.

As strategic leaders develop a more nuanced understanding of the problem and start to question assumptions, they take an asset orientation with people and try to "see the system" around people.[5] They know that people (e.g., students, teachers, and families) act within the context of systems. Rather than using a deficit mentality and blaming people, they focus on the system conditions that limit people's ability to act in the ways that would be most helpful or that incentivize choices that don't support progress toward purpose. They look for where there are opportunities to focus efforts to achieve significant results. Table 1.1 shows the difference between framing focused on individual deficits and framing focused on the role of the system.

Table 1.1 Deficit Framing versus Framing Focused on the System

Deficit Framing	Framing Focused on the System
Third graders don't understand what they read.	• What time, materials, and supports are available to teachers to help them use more nonfiction texts in content areas to build students' knowledge in the early elementary grades? • How much practice with nonfiction texts do students have?
Teachers resist change, so they aren't administering formative assessments and/or recording students' performance.	• How do teachers experience the new formative assessment policy and tools? • How well do the formative assessments align with what we most value around student learning?
Families aren't participating in school activities because they aren't committed to their children's education.	• What does the system need to understand about the different things families care most about relative to their children's time in school? • How welcoming are we to families, and how well do we respond to their interests and concerns?

The left column of the table reflects judgments that extrapolate based on specific data and assumptions. Each statement may have some prompting evidence—for instance, third-grade reading comprehension test scores, an absence of formative data even though teachers are supposedly required to collect it, or low attendance by families at school events. While there is a data source, the judgment in the deficit framing comment reflects a singular interpretation.

Tend to Process

As you gather an array of data, evidence, and artifacts, varied perspectives enrich your understanding of the problem. Engaging stakeholders and ensuring that their voices and experiences are heard and visible are essential. The outreach deepens your understanding and builds trust and relationships that may be crucial to solving the problem effectively. Listening to understand is a key complement to asking good questions and a key ingredient in discerning. Questions are designed to help you gain information (and sometimes to demonstrate care). Listening ensures that you actually take in the information. To do that, you must be genuinely curious. You are not asking teachers or families or students or clients questions just so you can say that you've checked in with them. You are asking them because they know some things that you don't. You are asking them because you care about what they have to say. One superintendent we know sat down with parents in their homes, faith leaders in their places of worship, and community leaders in their workplaces and said to them, "Tell me something I don't know that I need to know." And then she listened—deeply. She left with a new understanding about priorities and problems from their perspectives, which she learned by doing what civil rights lawyer Bryan Stevenson calls "getting proximate"—going to the places people are—and by listening.[6]

How you discern matters as much as *what* you discern. *How* you discern affects *what* you learn, *who* feels included and excluded, how people *feel* about the problem and how motivated they are to address it, and how well you've built a shared understanding of *why* the problem exists. Process particularly matters when there is a history of people having things done *to* them or *for* them rather than *with* them. One of the best ways to motivate people to solve a problem is to engage them in diagnosing it. This is another dynamic that invites you to pay attention to when to slow down versus move to action.

Quick Questions to Inform the Process

1. Who is asking the questions?
2. Is the person asking the questions listening to understand or listening to confirm assumptions?
3. Are the people affected by the symptoms of the problem involved in diagnosing the problem?
4. Are the people implicated in the solution involved in diagnosing the problem?
5. Is the speed of inquiry appropriate for the complexity of the problem, the risks involved, the level of trust, and the history/context?
6. Who is excluded and why?
7. Is it clear who has decision rights and how others can offer their perspectives?

Often, people assume that gathering a rich array of data and including others in a process means going more slowly. And sometimes it does—but not always. Sometimes it means being choosier about which data to collect and why, or whom to involve and why. Sometimes it means being clearer about what questions to ask. Sometimes it's much faster to go straight to the people most proximate to the problem and engage them in diagnosing it than to have people farther from the problem hypothesize and perseverate with distant data sources. And sometimes going slower initially saves a lot of time down the road.

One challenge that strategic leaders can anticipate and hold themselves and others steady through is this: when you ask questions, listen to the responses, collect a variety of data, and include a variety of people, your thinking is inevitably complicated. *Complicating your thinking is a good thing.* It helps you see the complexity of the situation, which supports you to develop a robust response. Sticking with discerning to understand rather than rushing to action requires you to stay in the problem space longer to probe and deepen your understanding, which maximizes the likelihood that the action you take will be strategic and have a high impact.

One of the most frustrating (or for some people, fun) things about collecting data is that it leads to more questions and data. For example, in an inquiry about high school attendance, after an initial review of data, you may be curious about some of the following:

- What do classroom/course tasks and student work make you want to better understand about curriculum and teacher supports?
- What does your data analysis make you want to focus on in your survey and focus groups?
- Who are all the people in the central office who have a hand in high school student support, and what are their roles?
- What relationships or disconnections do you notice when you look at the student and teacher focus groups' data side by side?
- What additional data do you need? Are there potential partners outside the schools who either have these data or are particularly well positioned to gather them?

These questions dig into what may be critical interactions among some of the variables that contribute to student absenteeism and dropouts—students feeling bored and underchallenged in class; a curriculum that doesn't feel relevant; a sense that no one at the school sees them, cares about them, and knows them well; undiagnosed reading disabilities that they've covered up for years; mental health challenges; family or work responsibilities outside of school; and long commutes to school. Deeper probing helps you get smarter about the problem. With your thinking complicated, you realize that the response to the problem needs to be multifaceted and robust enough to address the various issues you're unearthing. In Table 1.2, we contrast nonstrategic and strategic approaches to discerning to understand problems.

Table 1.2 Nonstrategic versus Strategic Discerning to Understand Problems

Discerning to Understand Problems			
	Nonstrategic Approaches	**Strategic Approaches**	**Key Questions**
Identify problems, not solutions	• Leap into action immediately. • Take on someone else's urgency. • Address the most visible part of the problem without understanding the roots.	• Be curious about *why*. • Understand that behavior is always a symptom. • Dig for the roots.	• Why? • What problems are you trying to solve? • *W* questions: who, what, why, where, when (and how)
Be promiscuous with data sources	• Focus on one or two data sources. • Collect and analyze data endlessly. • Look for data that confirm your thinking.	• Use count, hear, see, and feel data sources. • Use satellite, map, and street data sources.	• What do you not know that you need to know? • Who are implicated in these data? Have you heard from them?
Tend to process	• Assume that urgency justifies ignoring process. • Listen primarily to the loudest voices. • Operate from anxiety rather than intention.	• Understand that process is important for outcomes. • Engage the people most implicated in the solution in the diagnosis of the problem. • Be open to data that surprise you and complicate your thinking.	• Who are you engaging and how? Who are you not engaging? Why not? How might you engage them? • How can the process support a good outcome? • Of the various additional lines of inquiry that you could pursue, which are most essential, and why? • How fast do you need to move? Why? • When/how will going slow pay off?

Strategic leaders pay attention to when problems are described as the absence of a particular solution. For example, "The problem is that principals are not holding teachers accountable for implementing the new formative assessment system" or "The problem is the staff's lack of urgency." When you hear a solution disguised as a problem, it's a signal that you haven't identified the root cause yet. Most problems have multiple solutions, so if your problem sounds like it has only one solution, then you may be caught in that trap. Fear and anxiety can prompt people to latch onto quick explanations and action.

Beware: Fear and Anxiety

Taking time to dig deeper into the problem when discerning to understand is hard for leaders who are used to moving to action quickly (and are, perhaps, attached to a sense of themselves as action-oriented doers). Asking questions, listening, and probing further all require openness and a willingness to take in a lot of information. Seeing the array of issues related to a problem increase and become more complex when you're in a hurry to solve it can provoke anxiety. Common responses to these anxieties include cherry-picking data to tell a "single story" or support a solution that feels feasible, which allows you to move along quickly, or the inverse, perseverating and ending up with a morass of data and evidence that leads to analysis paralysis.[7]

To avoid these unhelpful responses, strategic leaders anticipate this anxiety in themselves and others. You can observe yourself to understand what your initial reactions are about and then intentionally choose how to act rather than simply reacting. The power of self-awareness and choosing rather than reacting cannot be overstated. It is a hallmark of strategic leaders. It helps you manage your own emotional state productively, which then puts you in the right frame of mind to help others no matter what they are feeling. Strategies that you might employ to help yourself and others include:

- Chunk the work into manageable pieces. You don't need to ask all the questions about high school students' attendance at the same time. You can choose which questions to ask, as well as the pace and sequence in which you ask them.
- Remind yourself and others that you can't do everything for everyone. Ask two questions: What is within our control or sphere of influence? (Let's not waste time on things outside our control.) If we understand this problem correctly and solve it, will it have a high impact? These questions will help you focus on a meaningful problem.
- Remind yourself and others that you have time and space to discern. Share the secret that sometimes a little breathing room allows people to gain perspective or new insights, something that feels charged to lose some of its power, and problems to shrink or even resolve themselves.

DISCERN TO CHOOSE RIGHT ACTION

Once you've deepened your understanding of a problem well enough to see its roots and the interconnections of things that contribute to it, it's time to *discern the right action* to take. In this context, "right" does not mean the one right thing to do, for certain. There is no such thing. Instead, there is the best, right action that you can think to take, given your current understanding. At the end of the day, you are placing a bet. This does not mean that you are gambling with children or others whom you aim to serve. It means that there is uncertainty in any choice you make—and yet you need to make one. Because if you hedge your bets, you will try to do too many things, making it hard to do any of them well, and if something does work, it will be hard to understand what worked and why. That is why discerning to choose right action is the complement to discerning to understand the problem. It lets you be as strategic in choosing the action as you've been in building your understanding of the problem. This combination is what sets you up for success. Figure 1.1 shows the components that set you up for right action.

Figure 1.1 The Path to Choosing Right Action

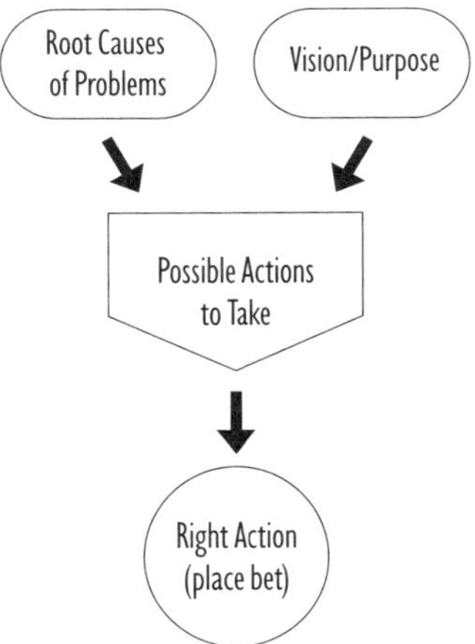

In the shift from *understanding the problem* to *choosing right action*, it's important to hold in your mind both the problems that you're trying to solve and the vision for what you hope to make possible. Just trying to solve problems tends to lead to solutions that are not very ambitious or forward-thinking. Solving the problems of the past doesn't prepare you well for the future.

Questions to Inform When to Move to Action

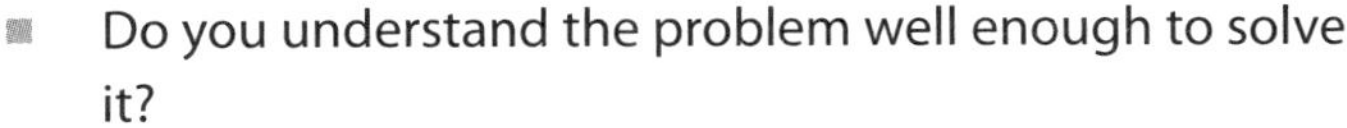

- Do you understand the problem well enough to solve it?
- Do you have some momentum (e.g., agreement, buy-in, resources) to solve the problem?
- What is the timeline for solving this problem?
- How consequential is the potential action?

Know When to Move to Action

One of the first acts of discernment related to *choosing right action* is deciding when to move to action. Facilitators in meetings face this dilemma when an unexpected topic arises or when an agenda item runs long—do you press on or do you slow down? Do you engage in more discussion or stop the discussion? Outside of work, when do you stop researching possible vacation options and just pick one? Stop flipping through Netflix for all the possible movies and watch one? Notice that moving to action often requires *stopping* some act of inquiry or exploration. You can ask questions to help you figure out whether it's time to move to action.

If you have only five more minutes to pick a movie in order to have enough time to watch one before you fall asleep, you might just pick one without deliberation. But if your decision is weightier, like deciding how to improve high school attendance or scale the work of a small nonprofit, you will take more time. That time can support both deeper inquiry of options and stakeholder engagement to build input and buy-in. When you move to action, you often balance imperfect information and contradictory opinions with some urgency or deadline for action. Sometimes you have to move quickly with limited information. Conversely, when there is no urgency or deadline for action, ensuring deep understanding of and commitment to solving the problem is the focus. Discerning leaders sometimes use the natural rhythms of the calendar year (school vacation breaks, upcoming board meetings, and budget cycles) to create some deadlines and urgency for decisions.

Figure Out Options for Action

As you move to action, you need to decide what action to take. When Liz was first working with schools on using data to inform learning, a principal said to her in frustration after many months of looking at data and defining a problem of practice, "Liz, if I understood what to do, I'd be doing it!" This was the principal's way of saying that deep inquiry doesn't always yield ideas about how to solve problems. Sometimes the knowledge about what to do and how to do it exists within the people and the organizations trying to solve the problem. Other times it doesn't, and you need to look for other knowledge sources. Similar to seeking a wide variety of data to inform your understanding of the problem, seek a variety of knowledge sources to inform your understanding of possible solutions.

Questions to Generate Ideas

- What research might be relevant?
- Who are other people and organizations in the field who have success around this problem? What can you learn from them? What did they do, and why? What would they do now, given what they know at this point?
- How might you need to adapt for your history and context?
- With whom might you collaborate to generate options?

Engaging other people to find and consider a wide array of options makes it easier to uncover more options in less time than if you try to do this by yourself. It also lets you tap into networks, experiences, and knowledge sources beyond your own. Not only does this hopefully yield a more diverse array of possibilities, it also increases engagement. If you are intentional about whom you engage, you can disrupt the organizational tendency to replicate existing power dynamics. And if the people you enlist are also implicated in the action, they are more likely to understand why and what the solution is, which will support implementation down the road.

Discerning leaders consider how their context is similar to and different from others, as well as what that means for their interpretation and application of the things that they have learned. They also seek critiques of ideas that they are considering. Strategic leaders hold the tension between their context being unique in some ways while not being so unique that they can't learn from other situations. Strategic leaders discern what is most and least relevant when applying possible solutions to their context.

While there is no single "right" action, there are sometimes "wrong" actions—illegal ones being the most obvious, immoral or irresponsible ones being more subjective and yet important to consider, and then harder-to-discern-as-wrong ones, which aren't supported by evidence, have high risk of causing harm, or bear little relationship to the problem or some audacious vision.

Ideas may also surface when discerning to understand. Looking at the high school attendance example, after a strong process of discerning to understand that identified root causes, ideas that surface for how to respond might include the following:

1. All-hands-on-deck outreach efforts to high school students and their families to invite and welcome them back to school alongside specific school- and community-based investments to ensure school-based support of student wellness and mental health
2. Provision of a high-quality virtual learning option
3. Development of a robust set of social-emotional supports and a culture of caring and community, including an advisory system
4. Alignment of students' work outside of school with their coursework to create a richer learning experience and prepare them for careers that pay a life-sustaining wage
5. Redesign of the high school program to be personalized to the needs of students, available in person and virtually, and anchored in the community through partnerships with higher education and growth industries that pay a life-sustaining wage

The list includes some fairly discrete ideas (item 2), as well as vast, complex ideas (item 5). The ideas are aimed at both problem-solving and pursuing an ambitious vision for different ways to meet the educational and life needs of high school students. The time frame, organizational and operational demands, stakeholder engagement, and potential impact of each are similarly varied. How do you decide what idea to pursue? How do you *discern to choose right action*?

Figuring out options for action is a key time to slow down. Even taking twenty minutes in a meeting to engage in a combination of brainstorming from the lived experience in the room, generating ideas with artificial intelligence (AI), and searching for high-quality research on possible solutions will broaden the scope of what you are considering and prompt avenues for deeper exploration.

Being clear about the problem (and its potential solutions) relative to the organization's vision and strategy is crucial as you discern to choose right action. If it's a top priority, you may be positioned to bite off a big chunk of work to pursue. Maybe you want to do everything on your brainstormed list, but you simultaneously know that is untenable for a whole host of reasons. How do you choose among many possibilities of what to do?

Prioritize Options

Thinking about the ease of doing something relative to the impact of doing it can both help you discern to choose right action and give you invaluable information that can inform how you approach implementation of whatever you choose.

There are a common set of things that affect the ease or difficulty of doing something:

- **Internal and external capacity to do the work required** (e.g., knowledge and skill, operational and managerial capacity, partnerships)
- **Stakeholder engagement** (e.g., who needs to be engaged in the decision-making, design, and implementation for substantive and/or political reasons)
- **Change management** (e.g., how many people need to make a change in the way they work, how big the change is, and how hard that will feel to them)
- **Resources** (e.g., time, people, money, and technology)
- **Opportunities** (e.g., grants, supportive policy that can support and accelerate the work)
- **Political will** (e.g., within the system and the larger community)

Continuing with the high school example, let's look at the five possible directions that surfaced in the "figuring out options for action" process. Thinking about them from the perspective of ease of implementation and the level of impact helps you discern to choose right action. Table 1.3 shows an example of discerning to choose right action in process.

Table 1.3 Assessing Ease and Impact

Idea	Ease	Impact
All-hands-on-deck outreach effort to high school students and their families to invite and welcome them back to school alongside specific school- and community-based investments to ensure school-based support of student wellness and mental health.	Prior success doing outreach to draw on. Community partners to help with outreach. Strong but insufficient supports for mental health. Early in work on student wellness with great potential partners and lots of enthusiasm. There is increased federal and philanthropic funding available for wellness.	Brings students back to school; prepares students for learning but does not touch instruction itself; not clear that it addresses all the underlying reasons why they stopped coming to school.
Provision of a high-quality virtual learning option.	Postpandemic, there are a lot of resources (internal and external) to use to build a virtual high school. The immediate change management demands are smaller; this is a discrete effort.	Reengages students who have left school; it's likely a fairly small number at the beginning. Could be a catalyst for rethinking the broader high school program delivery model.
Development of a robust set of social-emotional supports and a culture of caring and community, including an advisory system.	Requires review of current system capacity regarding social-emotional support programming, staffing, gaps, etc. Requires synthesis and integration of a variety of disparate supports, which may demand some reorganization. Creating a culture of caring and community and an advisory system has implications for a large number of educators (e.g., skill building, change management). Could skip the advisory system, but then what would be the impact?	Coherent system of social-emotional support and school cultures that are healthy and nurturing. The research is clear that this contributes to students' readiness for learning.
Connecting students' work outside of school with their school coursework to create a richer learning experience and prepare them for careers that pay a life-sustaining wage.	Requires more college and career pathways, with rigorous academic coursework aligned to out-of-school shadowing and work opportunities. Possible to partner with education and industry partners to build, and then develop, rigorous aligned coursework. Will be easier if the system has an infrastructure designed to manage this work. If not, resources will need to be allocated for that. There is a question of availability of quality higher education and industry partners with capacity. This is an area where both federal and philanthropic dollars are available.	Potential to make school more relevant and increase the readiness of students for college and careers.
Redesign of high school program to be personalized to the needs of students, available in person and virtually, and anchored in the community through partnerships with higher-education and growth industries that pay a life-sustaining wage.	Deep capacity building and change management required for whole-scale change in every high school. There might be resources, opportunities, and some potential partners to support work of this sort in a couple of schools, but there currently are not external partners who could support a systemwide effort. There is the question of a pilot to reduce demand.	Increased student engagement, quality of learning experiences, outcomes, identity development, and life trajectories.

This example illustrates getting at the nuances of what makes things easier or harder to do and how capacity, stakeholder engagement, change management, resources, opportunities, and politics interact with one another. Some things may emerge as likely contenders for priorities to pursue. Others may fall off the list. An idea as originally stated may evolve. You may begin to think about a multiyear approach that starts with one or two initiatives that lay the foundation for complementary initiatives that drive deeper change and higher impact in subsequent years. The complexity of it all may be overwhelming, and falling back on a familiar option could seem appealing. This is where other people can be helpful. Not only can other people help you be more strategic, but enlisting them also builds their capacity for strategic leadership.

As you do this discerning, you may need to iterate, moving back and forth between gathering information to understand and choosing right action. Strategic leaders do this, understanding that these processes are dynamic and not linear.

While you may work through ease-impact in the form of questions or a chart like table 1.3, one of our favorite strategic tools is a simple 2x2 Ease-Impact Matrix (figure 1.2). You put potential actions to take on separate sticky notes and have a conversation about the ease or difficulty of pursuing each one and each one's potential for impact. Based on the conversation, you agree on where to place each item on the 2x2 matrix. (See the appendix of this book for a detailed explanation of how to use 2x2s.)

Figure 1.2 Example of the Ease-Impact Matrix

High Impact, Hard	**High Impact, Easy**
High school redesign Social emotional supports; culture of caring Connect school and work Outreach and school-based support	
Low Impact, Hard	Virtual high school **Low Impact, Easy**

Strategic leaders are always on the lookout for easy, high-impact actions to take. In many contexts, the outreach effort (first on the list in the high school attendance example) would be easier than a number of the other possibilities. The impact could be high, though likely only short term. It could be worth doing if you complement it with something that's happening in school that will keep the students coming to school once you've reengaged them and their families. Linking several ideas and actions increases both the level of difficulty and the potential impact. Often, the highest-impact ideas are the hardest to implement. This means that you can't do a lot of them. Organizations generally don't have the capacity to pursue a bunch of hard, high-impact ideas. So, it's important to prioritize and sequence hard, high-impact ideas.

Prioritizing options includes deciding what *not* to do. Anything in the hard, low-impact box ideally will be put on the "don't do" list. If forces outside your control (e.g., mandates) make you do something that you know isn't high impact, then the question is: How might you make it either higher impact or take less capacity to do? Actions identified as "Low-impact, easy" require a close look. If they build buy-in or momentum for other high-priority work, or if not doing them has a high political cost, they're worth considering. Otherwise, they can also go on the "don't do" list. Discernment includes—in fact, requires—*not* doing some things, which increases the likelihood of success.

As you think about the ease and impact of potential actions, we encourage you to use john a. powell's frame of Targeted Universalism to guide your process.[8] Targeted Universalism asks you to define what everyone deserves relative to the topic under consideration as the standard to work toward, rather than aligning to what the dominant group has. This frame moves beyond the binaries of who wins and who loses by acknowledging that even the people at the top may not be getting what they need. Having set this standard, you then think about the targeted ways to provide support to ensure that everyone can reach the universal standard. Inevitably, this requires thinking about structures. American high schools provide a great example of this. There is a fair amount of evidence, based on student participation, satisfaction rates, and readiness for postsecondary opportunities, that high schools are not providing what every adolescent learner deserves. The first step is to define the universal experience you want for all high schoolers. Then, because all adolescents are not situated the same, you need to think in a targeted way about what they need. This is a form of differentiation.

Beware: Fear and Anxiety

When discerning right action, the messiness of the process and the desire to pick the "right" thing often provoke the most anxiety. You worry that you'll never get through the muck and messiness to clarity about what to do, or you'll pick the wrong thing. In an effort to banish the fear that sits beneath the anxiety, you may rush through the process, which produces less thoughtful decision-making, or you get stuck in the muck and messiness and don't make a decision at all.

To navigate fear and anxiety, you need to get comfortable with uncertainty and discomfort. Strategic leaders understand there are no sure things; there is risk in any action, as well as in doing nothing. These truths are hard for people to hold. It helps to be aware of your own tuning about this. (What parts do you find hardest? What tendencies and default behaviors do you fall back on when things feel hard? How can you support yourself to keep your wits and good humor about you?) You might share your own tendencies with your family or team in a way that both normalizes people having challenges and creates the opportunity to get support for yourself.

Tending to yourself helps you lead from a centered place, where you can observe and clearly see what's happening for you and your colleagues and create a safe environment for them to stay with the messiness.

Specific ways to support people include the following:

- Name this tension and normalize the feelings that people are having; make the uncertainty discussable.
- Anticipate rough patches and plan for them by pairing up people with complementary outlooks and providing additional support as needed.
- Discern what discomfort needs to be held and what discomfort is actually a flashing hazard sign to be heeded.
- Communicate clearly and frequently about the vision for the work, the state of the process and progress made, key considerations, decision-makers, and next steps.
- Figure out the best pace—when things need speed and when slowing down will yield new insights or opportunities.

Tips for Prioritizing

Context Matters

As you *discern to choose right action*, it's important to consider your particular context, which is inevitably unique. Something that worked in an organization like yours or a neighboring school system won't necessarily work for you. If your system is piloting an online high school program, expanding it to be an option for any high school student in the system may be a fairly easy thing to do. Or, if the community you serve associates online learning with a pandemic-era necessity or as something that only self-motivated students can do, expanding it to be an option for any high school student may be a hard thing to do.

Pay Attention to Energy

As you think about the possibilities and play them through in your mind, notice if parsing the ease and impact of one idea leaves you fired up while doing it with another idea leaves you feeling heavy and unmotivated. Ask yourself what that's about. How you are feeling is important information. If the action you're trying to choose is primarily for yourself, we recommend that you follow your energy.

If the action is for team and/or organizational efforts, once you understand your reaction, it may also be important data to share. Your reticence may reflect more broadly held concerns that need to be considered as part of assessing the viability of the idea. If it's hard to speak up due to organizational culture, power dynamics, or your own personal inclinations, try to find a time and method that works—maybe you can share concerns in a one-on-one setting where it's more comfortable or won't be perceived as a challenge to authority, maybe you can offer a question that invites further inquiry in the area of your concern, or maybe you can ask what assumptions are underlying the idea or what success would look like in order to test and potentially offer your own assumptions.

Conversely, if you're really energized and it's visible to people and you hold particular weight in the group, other people may be less willing to voice their questions and concerns. You may miss important information and perspectives from them. You may need to invite people to poke holes in an idea or, more formally, spend three minutes expressing all the ways that this idea may not work. When working with a team, you can also simply ask individuals how they're feeling as they go through the ease-impact activity. This may generate important data to consider, and it will also raise colleagues' awareness of paying attention to the important information that their bodies have to offer.

Questions to Ask Before Placing a Bet

Before placing a bet, check on these parts of you and your team:

- **Head:** What's the evidence that this is a wise bet (e.g., research, promising practices, etc.)?
- **Heart:** How do you feel about it? To what extent is anxiety driving you versus some confidence that this bet will move you toward a larger goal?
- **Hands:** What capacity is required to do this well? How does your current capacity measure up against what is needed? How will you get more capacity if needed?
- **Risks:** Who or what is at risk here? What's the risk to you, either professionally or personally? Who else is at risk here? Are there legal or financial risks? What is the risk (for whom) of not doing this action? How is the risk analysis affecting your decision-making? How do the risks compare to the potential gains, and for whom?

These questions can also be used when managing the uncertainty of adjusting something in progress or stopping it entirely.

Assess Risk

After thinking about ease and impact in all their dimensions, it is helpful to put the contenders for action through a final screening to assess risk. Political and financial risks are important to consider. In addition, burnout and loss of credibility and trust are risks that need to be assessed because of their impact on individuals' standing and effectiveness, and the sustainability of the work. Returning to the example of addressing high school attendance concerns, some of the options require a large financial investment that will raise expectations within the system and the larger community, and thus the stakes for success. Failure could negatively affect political and financial support for the school system more broadly. Building a virtual high school may challenge the system's credibility as people wonder if a bureaucracy can think far enough out of the box to pull off such an innovation. An outreach effort aimed at high schoolers and their families could damage trust if executed poorly. Trying to build and implement a robust set of social-emotional supports and a culture of caring and community using existing staff and relying heavily on teachers with no shifts in their other responsibilities could lead to burnout and loss of confidence.

The goal is not to avoid risk. That's not possible. The goal is to be clear-eyed about the risks and to factor that understanding into discerning to choose right action (see chapter 5 for an example of how to use a variation of the Ease-Impact Matrix to assess risk and capacity). The higher the risks, the more important it is to make sure that you are confident in the idea's potential to solve the problem and move closer to the vision *and* in your ability to execute the idea well. If you have fundamental concerns about organizational capacity to execute the idea and there is a high degree of financial and political risk in pursuing that idea, it might be smart to choose something else or give yourself time to build the needed capacity before starting to implement the full idea.

All this prioritizing can inform both the choice of the immediate right action and the pace and sequence of longer-term, multidimensional improvement efforts with different pieces of work that are paced and sequenced to eventually add up to something greater than the sum of the individual parts—something that offers a more ambitious pursuit of the vision. For example, if the high school outreach and engagement efforts with a focus on student wellness and mental health are pursued with a longer-term commitment to pursue the related priority of developing a culture of caring and community, you have an opportunity to intentionally build the former in a way that lays the foundation for and supports the latter.

When *discerning to choose right action* effectively, strategic leaders balance looking forward and responding to existing problems and needs. Think about the actions that are likely *both* to be effectively implemented and have the highest impact. Consider the relationship between specific bodies of work that you might pursue and the larger aspirations to which they contribute. All of this helps you choose right action. It helps you think about building a strong foundation for future work, and it also reminds you of the power of pursuing a series of initiatives that are interconnected building blocks to maximize coherence, alignment, and impact.

Building Others' Capacity to Discern

- Model and explicitly teach the skills and use the various processes described in this chapter in one-on-one meetings and your team's work.
- Ask questions of peers and direct reports in a way that invites them to discern, like "What's the problem you're trying to solve here?" or "What feels most important to focus on today and why?"
- Invite others to tune into what their bodies and intuition are telling them in combination with a variety of other data sources.
- Build the expectation among your team through what you say and do that discerning to understand problems and take right action are part of the way of doing business.
- Normalize and give people permission to slow down before taking action.

TAKEAWAYS

- Discerning happens at multiple levels—individual, team, and organizational—as well as on different timelines.
- There are three kinds of discerning that strategic leaders do: (1) discerning to identify purpose; (2) discerning to understand the problem to address; and (3) discerning to choose the right action to take to address the problem and pursue the purpose.
- The importance of discerning to identify purpose is to ensure there is a clear, ambitious why to be achieved that is more expansive, forward-thinking, and impactful than simply solving a problem.
- The goal of discerning to understand is to complicate thinking by seeing the complexity of the problem that you're exploring. This helps you build robust responses.
- When discerning to choose right action, the goal is not to come to a conclusion of certainty. There are no sure-fire right answers, just well-researched and well-considered bets. Discerning what *not* to do is as important as discerning what *to* do.
- Digging into problems and trying to find effective ways to respond can cause people stress and anxiety. They can respond by wanting to hurry through the process or getting bogged down in it. You need to tune into and manage your own emotional responses to this messiness and uncertainty and to help your colleagues do the same.

REFLECTIONS

What are your strengths, areas for development, and lingering questions about discerning?

2

CULTIVATE RELATIONSHIPS

THE LONGER THE TWO OF US LIVE, the more sure we are that nobody does anything meaningful all by themselves. When we scratch beneath the surface of any significant accomplishment, we usually find people, great ideas, and promising work in relationship with one another. Nature knows this truth about relationships and interdependence. Trees are connected through an extensive network of roots, through which they communicate and share nutrients. The healthiest trees nourish the more vulnerable ones, contributing to the overall health of the forest.

In the absence of relationships, people, their efforts, and the organizations they're a part of grow isolated; their sense of perspective and possibility narrows, reducing their capacity. We've all seen it: the elderly person who declines quickly after their partner dies; the toxic school culture in which adults are alienated and cannot serve students effectively; and the siloed organization with weak communication that struggles to build momentum toward its goals. And then there is the inverse: the person who blossoms in a relationship; the team whose members work well together, engaging in conflict when necessary and performing brilliantly; and the organization that focuses on the relationships among people, departments, and bodies of work and realizes promising results.

We all come to the idea of relationships with our own individual contexts about the power and importance of relationships. Do we love to be connected with lots of people, or do we find that exhausting? Were we raised to believe that we need to be able to do everything on our own and asking others for help is a sign of weakness? Did we play a team sport as a kid where we learned the power of teamwork? Are we an only child, or are we part of a larger family where we constantly navigate relationships? Do we like figuring out how things work or relate to one another, or do we like to put our head down, stay in our lane, and just do stuff? Our individual contexts interact with the cultures in which we're immersed. Are we in a culture where we share a cup of tea, acknowledge our ancestors, or otherwise connect as humans before talking business? Is the collective valued over the individual? Does the culture defer to people by positional authority or age? Depending on our answers to these questions, the idea of relationships as crucial may be intuitive, foreign, or somewhere in between those two. How we think about relationship preferences may be different from what is the norm in a team or organization.

This chapter addresses three dimensions of relationship building—connecting with people, connecting work, and communicating—in service of accomplishing impactful work. First, we make the case for why cultivating relationships matters, interpersonally and organizationally, and then we explore what that looks like and how to do it effectively.

WHAT RELATIONSHIPS ARE AND WHY THEY MATTER FOR STRATEGIC LEADERSHIP

Relationships are defined as "the ways in which two or more concepts, objects, or people are connected, or the state of being connected."[1] They are connections: between friends; between a principal and the staff at her school; between the teaching and learning division and the school supervision division of a school system; and between the human resources and programmatic departments of a nonprofit. The relationships that matter most in strategic leadership are those that exist among individuals, bodies of work, and divisions or organizations.

Given the role strong relationships often play in high-impact work, it's amazing how many work cultures reinforce silos rather than nurture connections. We can get busy, feel harried, and forget or think that we don't have time to ask after a colleague's sick mother, check in when a colleague sits through a meeting in silence, or wonder about the connections between our project and the one our colleague is leading. Maybe we're great at personal relationship-building but don't parlay it into a resource to tap into to do meaningful work. Or we're astute about how bodies of work interact with one another, but inattentive to the people doing this work.

In work cultures that focus on product over process, relationships can seem like a nice-to-have rather than a need-to-have, or something that will simply develop on its own, spontaneously. Yet the health and well-being of individuals and collectives suffer when we aren't intentional about building relationships. Our effectiveness and impact suffer. Inattentiveness to relationships puts us and our work at risk. Think of a brilliant principal who figures out how to get every student sixty minutes a week of small-group instruction focused on their growth areas in math, but the effort becomes divisive because she neither considers the implications for specialists teaching noncore classes nor engages those teachers in a conversation, much less in the design of the effort. Or the central office leader who is a relational wizard, able to make everyone in the room feel comfortable and valued, and yet she doesn't know how to use that to get everyone collaborating to address the ongoing challenge of student absences.

Collaborative problem-solving, creative thinking, experimentation, and learning are essential to success in complex environments where there aren't clear solutions to problems. Each of these things is most impactful when it is done in relationship with others and with awareness of other bodies of work. These things can either be built on a foundation of strong interpersonal relationships or pursued in a way that builds relationships through doing work—or both.

Relationships between people are complemented by those that can be built and activated among different functions, initiatives, or departments in an organization. When these relationships are identified and nourished, they make work coherent and more impactful. Understanding this reality and how it shows up in organizations contributes to leaders' effectiveness. We see this in a variety of examples: drawing a tight connection between the reading and writing efforts in elementary schools leads to leaps in student learning; revamping a nonprofit's accountability process ensures that it relates to the organization's new strategic plan; or focusing on interdisciplinary literacy at the secondary level builds teachers' sense of themselves as teachers of subject area literacy.

In organizations, we often focus on structures, systems, and rules. This tendency is understandable, as they are more discrete and less messy than the interactions between people and the culture of the organization. Structures, systems, and rules can guide and support people and their work, but they sit in the shadows of relationships and culture as key drivers of people doing great work individually, as part of a team, and as part of the larger organization.

There is a powerful refracting quality about interpersonal and organizational relationships. By nurturing them, leaders offer a model for others and increase the likelihood that others will do the same. We know a superintendent for whom relationships are a superpower. In every interaction she has with people, she is kind, attentive, and curious. Organizationally, when she talks with the board, community, or direct reports, she explores the relationships among different lines of work and emphasizes how strengthening them will maximize the likelihood that they aggregate up to a whole that is greater than the sum of the individual parts. Her team tries to replicate this in its work. Leaders have a powerful role to play in highlighting the centrality of relationships. People watch them, make meaning from their behavior, and follow their lead.

CONNECT WITH PEOPLE

Since leading strategically is a collective act, you need to be in relationship with other people to lead well. Fundamentally, just as healthy ecosystems in nature require nourishing conditions and a variety of organisms in relationship with each other, so do healthy people need a web of connections and conditions to thrive. Connecting with people can range anywhere from warmly greeting people once to cultivating close and trusting connections over time.

Connecting with people across differences both visible (e.g., race/ethnicity, gender, age, physical disability, language, organizational role) and potentially less visible (e.g., neurodiversity, politics, religion, class, expertise, race/ethnicity, gender) is one of the keys to strategic leadership. It allows varied experiences and perspectives to inform complex work in meaningful ways that often lead to better results and creates an inclusive culture in which people can thrive. Weaving a web of connection with people who are different from yourself along multiple dimensions often requires intention, energy, and care. And it can lead to relationships that foster deep connection, healthy challenge, and mutual growth. Strategic leaders can build this web for themselves and create the conditions for others to do the same.

Strategic leaders do a number of things well in connecting with people:

- **Recognize people in their full humanity:** See people; appreciate that each person brings their own stories, sorrows, passions, and complexity; honor each person's dignity.[2]
- **Make time:** Leave enough space in your schedule to connect with others and for unexpected human needs to arise and receive attention.
- **Anchor in shared purpose and values:** Understand what's important to people and why, and focus on finding shared purpose and making connections that bring people together.

- **Be vulnerable:** Share something about yourself that feels uncomfortable or perhaps even risky (e.g., a time when you did not know an answer, a mistake that you made, or something personal about you); vulnerability reveals your humanity and makes space for others to share their own, particularly when you are in a situation where you have more power.
- **Give grace and credit:** Give grace to yourself and others for "mis"-es (e.g., mistakes, miscommunication, missed deadlines) and give credit to people for their ideas and actions; grace does not mean absence of accountability for harm, errors, or procrastination, but it does invite opportunities for growth and improvement.
- **Find delight:** Smile, laugh, have fun, and find joy in the work together.[3]

In each of these domains, strategic leaders can take specific actions themselves and can also support teams and organizational cultures in which these domains and the related behaviors are both expected and practiced.

Ways to Connect with People

- **Recognize people in their full humanity.**
    - *Smile and say hello.* This is a basic acknowledgment of other people's presence as you pass them on your way to your desk or sit beside them at a meeting.
    - *Remember names and details.* This is a way to show people that you hear, respect, and value them. Remember their names, use them, and be sure that you pronounce them properly. This is particularly important when the pronunciation doesn't come easily to you. Remember some details of people's lives that they've shared with you. Maybe they're a mad baker, a hip hop aficionado, or part of a multigenerational household.
    - *Express interest.* You can do this relative to people's lives both within and outside of work as a way to show care and curiosity. In response to a picture on a colleague's desk, you can ask, "You look so happy in that picture. What was the occasion?" When working with people on a project, you can ask, "What about this new project is most exciting to you?"

- **Make time.**
  - *Understand that connections deepen with time and attention.* Ongoing cultivation of connections builds strong, resilient relationships that endure through challenges.
  - *Leave open space in your schedule.* This could be five or ten minutes before or after meetings, which leaves time for a quick connection with people who are in the meeting, or some unscheduled space in the day in case someone or something needs more of your attention.
  - *Schedule time with the people you want to connect with.* Putting coffee, lunch, or a walk on your calendar is a way to ensure that you actually take the time (these can be done virtually with people in different locations).
- **Anchor in shared purpose and values.**
  - *Ask about someone's "why" and share your own.* Ask what's most important to someone about a particular effort, what part of their work they enjoy most, or why they became an educator; and share your own answers to these questions. This is particularly valuable with people you disagree with or across people who disagree, to learn what they care about and what you all care about in common.
  - *Anchor in the "why" of the specific work that you're engaging in with others.* State the purpose of this particular collaborative work frequently and invite people to share what's most resonant and personally motivating about it for them. This is another way to learn about the individual whys that drive people.
- **Be vulnerable.**
  - *Ask for help.* Helping another person is one of the fastest ways to improve your mood and sense of well-being, both of which support interpersonal connection. Conversely, asking for help is a way of expressing vulnerability, which is hard for some people. It acknowledges your interdependence and

contributes to relationship building. Remember that when you ask for help, you offer people the chance to boost their mood by helping. The request can run the gamut: "Can you hold the door for me?" or "Can you help me figure out how to make a chart of these data that will illustrate the storyline most effectively?" or "I can't go to that meeting. I know you're going. Can I check in with you after it to get the highlights?"

  - *Ask for feedback*. Asking for feedback says, "I know I'm not perfect and I think you have something valuable to offer me in my own growth," which can feel risky for the asker. And it feels validating to the people who are asked, particularly if they feel that it will be heard and used toward shared purposes or values. When asking for feedback, make your ask specific, leave room for feedback on something you didn't ask, and at some point reflect back what you heard and what you did and didn't do with it.
  - *Share something personal*. What feels personal, safe, and appropriate to share will vary by person and context. It could range from small descriptive things, like what you did this weekend, to facts about your interests or background, to more private things like a challenge, sorrow, or joy.
- **Give grace and credit.**
  - *Give second chances*. When someone (including yourself) makes a mistake or disappoints someone else, normalize it and move on when appropriate (e.g., someone forgets a meeting with you, and you say, "I'm glad I'm not the only one who messes up my calendar sometimes!") or make a clear statement about the impact and leave room for learning (e.g., "Your being late with your piece of the work meant everyone else had to scramble, and I didn't feel prepared for the presentation. What could we do differently next time?").
  - *Appreciate people*. Recognizing people builds connection and positivity. This can range from something as superficial as commenting on the sharp tie a colleague is wearing to giving

people credit for something they said or did. These things are easy to do, but they require attention and intention. You can appreciate people one-on-one: "Thank you for reminding me about the survey results I should take a look at as I'm developing my plan." And you can do it in a bigger setting, such as in a meeting: "Luis, your question really pushed my thinking about what we most want to accomplish with this event." Building on someone's idea with attribution by saying something like, "As Cynthia said . . ." is another form of public appreciation. The added value of giving people credit in public is that you're modeling the behavior, signaling that recognizing others is something you do in your organization. This contributes to a healthy culture.

- **Find and share delight.**
  - *Enjoy small moments*. Notice the small things that make you smile and share them with others; if you're setting a meeting agenda, invite people to share a highlight from their week; welcome laughter, smiling, and fun.
  - *Cultivate your joy*. What brings you joy? Playing music, cooking, or spending time with loved ones? Whatever it is, make time for it—it will nourish you and give you the fuel to be fully present with other people and nurture connections.
  - *Celebrate success*. When a person or group accomplishes something, celebrate it—including when you're part of it! Celebration reminds us of our shared purpose and that we honor each other's accomplishments and can be proud of our collective efforts and achievements.

You may do some or many of these things intuitively. The goal is not to be great at all manners of connection. Everyone has personal tuning and contexts that affect this. Maybe you're shy or introverted. Or you want a certain boundary between work and the rest of your life. Or you work in a place where people don't regularly ask others about their weekend or where you don't feel entirely safe or welcome to share important parts of yourself. What matters is to commit to a series of connection-building actions that build a sense of safety, trust, and community among people.

You need many kinds of relationships in both your life and your work, from respectful interactions to the people who have your back no matter what. A mix of them provides a web of connection that contributes to your well-being and success. It supports balance in your life, so you aren't relying too heavily on one aspect of your life for fulfillment. It also lets you apply the good feelings about and insights into relationships in one domain of your life to support you in others. You see the power of this when you go back to work energized on Monday after a restorative weekend of connection or come home feeling calm and relaxed after talking through a messy work problem with a colleague. Part of the wonder of connecting with others is that relationships can evolve from something that is initially friendly and casual to something intimate and deeply supportive.

Remembering *why* nurturing interpersonal relationships is important can be a great motivator to help you commit to building your own and others' interpersonal skills. Doing things to cultivate relationships makes people feel seen, connected, and valued and contributes to their positive experience of you personally and the collaborative environment that you're creating together. This is a meaningful end unto itself and a contribution to humanity. It's also good for work. When people feel good at work, they're more likely to engage and do their best work. And when people get to know each other as people, their ability to hold differences, disagreements, and multiplicity increases, which in turn supports complex, purpose-driven work.

CONNECT ACROSS WORK

While strong interpersonal relationships create a sense of connection between people and the conditions for collaboration, there is a parallel set of equally important organizational relationships. The vast underground network that connects trees in the forest to one another illustrates that relationships exist between things as much as they exist between people. Trees have symbiotic relationships that support the health of both individual trees and the whole forest. In organizations, these relationships can exist between departments, bodies of work, or initiatives. Nurturing these relationships is essential to organizational health and effectiveness. Strategic leaders are always considering these relationships and how to foster them to realize their impact.

Imagine that a school system wants to develop teacher leadership roles to support teachers' collaborative planning time. The teaching and learning, human resources, and budget departments need to work in concert to define the roles, select teacher leaders, hire them, and get them on the payroll. This collaboration could be technical and discrete. However, the relationship between teams' work will deepen, with greater potential for impact, if the work becomes more connected. Imagine integrating the need for teachers who can lead common planning time with the desire to create a teacher career pathway that engages, recognizes, rewards, and retains great teachers. You're accomplishing two things at once. It becomes a threefer when the teaching and learning team decides that the focus of teacher leaders' work with their peers will be on preparing to teach a new curriculum, integrating strategies that encourage student engagement.

As different bodies of work are related to one another, the vision for the work grows richer, more ambitious, and potentially more impactful. It also becomes more coherent. Rather than having to manage three distinct initiatives focused on teacher leadership, career pathways, and engaging, curriculum-aligned instruction, there is a web of connection between these things that creates its own whole. Figure 2.1 demonstrates this web.

Figure 2.1 Web of Connected Work

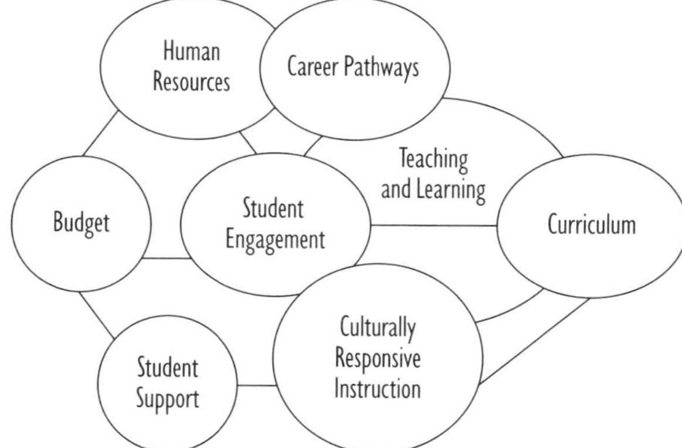

When people and organizations struggle to identify and nurture relationships among bodies of work, the challenge falls along a continuum. At one end, people focus on just one thing when they actually need to focus on two or three or four things. At the other end, they try to do many things but in a disconnected manner.

Of course, you have to start somewhere and break complex things down into manageable pieces. The trouble arises when you focus singularly on one thing at the exclusion of other key components, thinking that it will address the need, rather than thinking of all the things and the process of sequencing them. The common response in the early 2020s to the "science of reading" is an example—the first instinct in many schools and school systems was to dive deeply into phonics rather than tending to all the various components of the science of reading and how they lead to students' comprehension. While choosing phonics as a starting point can be helpful, if it doesn't quickly become part of a richer vision of literacy, there is a real risk of oversimplification and myopia. The other elements of the science of reading get short shrift, which means that students aren't getting what they need to become literate.

At the other end of the continuum are lots of initiatives focused on a common issue or goal, where the relationships between the disparate efforts are neither highlighted nor leveraged. High schools sometimes suffer from this challenge as they strive to graduate students who are college- and career-ready. They may be working hard to offer rigorous coursework through access to Advanced Placement (AP) classes, college courses, and career pathways including internships. Yet each of these opportunities is designed individually, often in isolation, by different departments, with limited attention to the relationships among them. Students may explore engineering careers in their pathway, but their math and science coursework is completely divorced from that. Or they may want to both take an AP course and pursue a career pathway, but the schedule makes that impossible, putting the offerings and their goals in competition with one another. The result of all the system's effort is a fractured, incoherent experience for students that limits their learning.

Whether you focus on one thing or pursue many things in a disconnected manner, the people on the ground are often the beleaguered recipients of directives that may seem anemic or in competition with one another. Front-line staff respond to this in one of a few ways: (1) pursue each thing discreetly, risking overwhelm and reinforcing incoherence; (2) pick and choose what they pay attention to based on their personal preferences or beliefs or the quality of their relationships with the people leading the different bodies of work; or (3) ignore it all and keep doing their own thing. None of these options leads to success at scale. But they are recipes for both the on-the-ground staff and the creators of initiatives to feel frustrated, unsupported, and ultimately distrustful of each other. Worse yet, the incoherence leads people to lose confidence in the work itself.

Nurture Organizational Relationships

Organizational relationships can be nurtured by simple actions: asking people in other departments their opinion about something; inviting members of your team not to simply report on their work but to problem-solve dilemmas together; or visiting several schools to see instruction in classrooms. These small efforts can lead to new insights, relationships, and collaborations.

When pursuing an initiative, understanding the relationships needed for success is a vital first step. What different people, departments, and/or organizations are implicated in the work? Relationship mapping is a simple way to identify these relationships.

Relationship Mapping

Use relationship mapping to make explicit the relationships currently at play in a body of work and where there may be critical gaps. Doing this with other people, particularly people with different roles and experiences, often brings more perspectives that add to the richness of the analysis.

Steps

1. Write the name of the issue/priority that you want to address in the center of a sheet of paper and circle it.
2. Write the names of the people, departments, and/or organizations that need to be part of responding to this issue/priority on sticky notes (one per sticky note). Place those most closely connected to the issue nearest to the center circle and those most peripherally involved farthest away.
3. Map the relationships between what's written on each sticky note by using lines and arrows.
4. Step back, reflect, and discuss with others what is most striking to you about the map. Some things to consider include the following:
    a. Where do expertise, capacity, resources, and political influence reside? How much of each is there, relative to how much may be needed? Are there different ways to think about these four things?
    b. Which current relationships can support your purpose and goals? Which relationships need to be built?
    c. Are traditional dynamics of power and privilege reflected? If yes, are there ways to shift those dynamics?
5. *So what?* Consider the implications of your analysis for how you address the issue/priority and any necessary groundwork that needs to be laid.

See the appendix of this book for more detail about how to use Relationship Mapping.

When the prioritized work has lots of tentacles or disparate efforts that need to be knit together, a robust mechanism to support cross-functional collaboration may be necessary. There are lots of ways to pursue this: formal work groups of cross-functional teams, protocols to learn about others' work and to think about ways to collaborate, and new initiatives designed to force integration. These are all reasonable approaches—but we encourage you to proceed with clear eyes and caution. Bureaucracies are notorious for lots of meetings and much less action; work groups can be no different, and they are often assembled with the assumption that if you get people with varied expertise together, they will somehow figure out how to overcome all the ways that the current organizational culture is working against collaboration and coherence. Without considerable attention and intention during the process of establishing and using a work group, the group is likely to function like a sapling planted without enough light and water—a promising start but unable to grow to its potential.

If you decide that a work group could be helpful in accomplishing the organization's ambitious goals, there are a set of things to consider before convening the group. Setting Up a Cross-Functional Work Group for Success offers some questions to help you think this through (see page 58).

You can take a similar approach when first convening any group or team, particularly if group members haven't had much opportunity to work together. It may feel difficult to take this time, especially if you are feeling a sense of urgency. Think of it as going slow to go fast. If you (or colleagues) feel anxious about going slowly, imagine building the foundation of a house in a hurry. When you go to put up the walls, you realize that the foundation isn't solid. Your walls aren't straight. Your windows and doors don't fit right. You are resigned to spending inordinate amounts of time, energy, and money trying to fix something that can never be properly fixed (without tearing down the house and beginning again) and living with the consequences. You can avoid this in your work by building a strong foundation for it.

COMMUNICATE TO BUILD RELATIONSHIPS

As every self-help book about relationships will tell you, communication is essential to relationship building. This is as true for organizational relationships as it for interpersonal ones. Strategic leaders are constantly communicating. And the people with whom they are communicating span a variety of roles: a peer or direct report, a grade-level team, principal colleagues, the leads of three different initiatives when they want the efforts to be coordinated and mutually reinforcing, or all the staff who are part of the school system's after-school enrichment programming. Effective communication shows people respect and nourishes reciprocity, which builds relationships

Setting Up a Cross-Functional Work Group for Success

Why

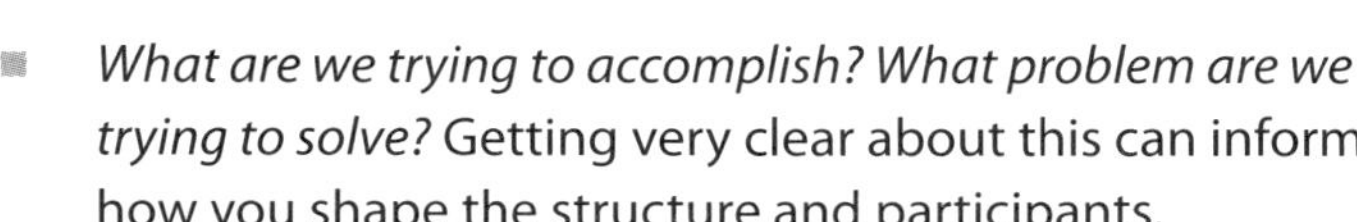

- *What are we trying to accomplish? What problem are we trying to solve?* Getting very clear about this can inform how you shape the structure and participants.

What

- *What is the charge to the group?* This should be related to the why question, but it may be more grounded in accomplishing specific things that will lead to the why.

When

- *How often will the group meet?* Does it require a consistent schedule of meetings over three, six, or twelve months, or could a lot be accomplished in just a couple of meetings?

Who

- *Who are the right people to get involved given the stated why and what?* As discussed in chapter 1, this includes thinking about who is or could be most affected, who is most proximate, and who brings experience, expertise, and relationships needed for success? In addition, *what group size will ensure that everyone's voice is heard and the group doesn't become unwieldy?*

How

- *How will the group function?* There are a number of dimensions to consider, including facilitation, norms, between-meeting work expectations, decision-making, and mechanisms for organizational learning.

See the appendix for more detail about how to use Setting up a Cross-Functional Work Group for Success.

and increases the likelihood that important ideas, emotions, and considerations that need to be heard will be voiced. Organizationally, effective communication can tell a compelling story that calls people to action, demonstrates the interconnectedness of individuals' and teams' work, and creates a sense of collective efficacy. All of this contributes to both individual and organizational effectiveness.

The importance of communication grows as your sphere of responsibility expands. With more senior roles or broader authority, it can be harder, if not impossible, to build one-on-one relationships with all the people you need to engage with to support the work for which you are responsible. As you assume more responsibility, your emphasis as a strategic leader shifts from primarily building one-on-one and team relationships to creating the conditions for relationship building among people, departments or grade levels, and bodies of work so others can take the lead in driving work together. For example, you may bring together (or ask others to do so) school and central office staff who spearheaded the successful rollout of the ninth-grade-on-track initiative to talk with the people interested in developing a similar effort for sixth graders as they enter middle school. This is akin to a teacher designing instruction such that students engage with one another to learn rather than all interactions having to go through her.

There are fundamental skills of communication required for strategic leadership at every level of the organization. These skills—listening, sharing information, and engaging conflict—support cultivating one-on-one relationships as well as broader communication up, down, and across the organization. Many books have been written about each of these topics, so we don't provide a primer on them here. Instead, we focus on the aspects of doing these things well that support strategic leadership.

Listen, Listen, Listen

There are lots of ways to listen. In *The Essentials of Theory U*, C. Otto Scharmer describes four ways of listening: "downloading—listen from habit; factual—listen from outside; empathic—listen from within; [and] generative—listen from the field."[4] In other words, you can listen from ego, looking for confirmation of your ideas or feelings. You can listen with your mind, focusing on facts that may provide new information or challenge what you think you already know. You can listen with your heart, trying to understand the experience of others, which by definition you don't know. And you can listen openly and expansively, holding everything you know loosely so you can imagine new possibilities. You often do several of these at one time. Your capacity to listen affects your ability to build relationships with individuals, create the space for others to build relationships, and see opportunities for and nurture relationships between teams and bodies of work in organizations. Effective listening is guided by a mix of care and curiosity, both of which are great relationship builders.

Listening also helps you learn new things and discern what's really going on, both of which are essential to leading strategically. To listen well, you must be willing to be changed by what you learn. Your willingness to be changed makes space for new ways of thinking and doing. This is where creativity and innovation thrive, both of which are invaluable when you are engaged in complex work. Table 2.1 shows some examples of nonstrategic listening compared to strategic listening.

Table 2.1 Nonstrategic versus Strategic Listening

Nonstrategic Listening	Strategic Listening
• Multitask (emailing, texting, reading) while in a meeting (which is particularly tempting in a virtual meeting). • Think about what you want to say to someone rather than listening to what the person is saying to you. • Talk to fill silence. • Assume that silence is proof of consent. • Get so excited, frustrated, bored, or angry in a meeting that you stop being curious and react or withdraw. • Proceed to action and assume that people will see the connection between what they said and what you said/did.	• Pay attention and remove distractions (set phone on desk, screen side down; turn off notifications). • Jot some notes before and during a conversation so you don't forget what you want to ask and say. • Ask yourself W.A.I.T. ("Why Am I Talking?"). • Watch and listen for dynamics related to power differentials, historical patterns of who gets listened to, and personal preferences around think time that affect who says what and how and who is heard. • Ask a question and then sit quietly and listen. • Seek out people you aren't hearing from and invite them to share their thoughts. • Seek out people who disagree with you and can push your thinking. Invite them to tell you what you're not seeing, name potential risks and hazards, and share what they're most worried about. • Notice what your body is telling you about how you're feeling. Take a few breaths if you need them. Then make a conscious decision about what you want to say or do (or not do). • Reflect back to people what you heard. Using some of their exact words demonstrates how carefully you listened and how their words stayed with you, which is affirming for them and helps you check your understanding.

Beware: What You Think You Heard May Not Be What They Think They Said

Strategic leaders need to recognize the limitations of their interpretations and the hazards of their myopia. Words spoken slowly and with precision can reflect anger, thoughtfulness, or tentativeness. Silence can tell a story of mistrust, confusion, or disinterest. Raised voices and animation can convey excitement, agitation, or anger. Each leader, depending on their background and life experiences, may be inclined to interpret certain behaviors in very specific ways. Maybe silence always implies mistrust. Maybe a raised voice is always anger. To guard against this and to be sure that you're accurately discerning what's going on, you need to check your interpretations.

In contexts where there is a high degree of trust, you can simply ask, saying something like, "I noticed the room got quiet when I mentioned the need to rethink the agenda for the upcoming meeting with principals. I'd like to better understand what that's about. Can someone help me?" Sometimes describing a shift in tone, behavior, or energy can be a powerful way to name something that others are also feeling but aren't yet able or willing to name. In less collegial environments where trust may be low or in contexts where there is a significant power differential, it may be hard to get people to tell you the truth in the moment. This is an instance when it is valuable to have someone you trust who you can check in with after the meeting and ask, "Did you see what happened after Justin made the comment about reduced student engagement in the after-school tutoring? What sense did you make of it?" This commitment to understanding rather than making assumptions is a building block of strong relationships.

Share Information

Sharing information is the complement to listening. It is one partner telling the other about how their middle school daughter cried when she talked about some hard stuff that happened at school; a teacher leader sharing information about an instructional strategy with which teachers are struggling; or a principal talking about potential budget cuts with his staff or talking to his supervisor about a groundswell of frustration growing among principals regarding an ongoing challenge. Regardless of the context, sharing information can help you do lots of things: deepen connections; bring someone up to speed; express support; help someone avoid surprises; make people feel like they are in the loop and respected; and tell someone with more power something that they may not want to hear.

Questions to Plan Communication

1. Why are you communicating at this moment, to this audience, and how does it link to a larger purpose or goal?
2. Whom are you communicating with, and how do your listening and message need to be personalized to this audience to address its interests, needs, and concerns?
3. What do you want people to understand? What do people need to know to:
   a. Do their jobs well?
   b. Feel respected and supported?
   c. Broaden their understanding?
4. How can you communicate in ways that will resonate? How can you check to see what people are taking away from the communication?

The *W* questions from chapter 1 can be applied with a sharing-information lens in mind. The most strategic and effective leaders we know think about the *who*, *what*, *when*, *where*, *how*, and *why* of their messaging and communication all the time. They understand that it is the glue that holds together interpersonal and organizational relationships.

Communicating with people grows in importance and complexity as you gain more responsibility and authority. As you assume bigger scopes of work, you can both overestimate and underestimate the power of the information that you share and how you share it. Each of these has the potential to degrade relationships, clarity, and trust.

Doing a few things well can go a long way to support productive communication and relationship building. Table 2.2 shows some examples of nonstrategic information sharing compared to strategic information sharing.

Table 2.2 Nonstrategic Information Sharing versus Strategic Information Sharing

Nonstrategic Information Sharing	Strategic Information Sharing
• Focus on *what* and *how*, without discussing the *why*. • Say things in the same way to different audiences. • Say something once or twice and assume that everyone will remember and understand it. • Assume that something that's clear to you is similarly clear to everyone. • Speak at a level of abstraction that leaves people confused about the topic and/or their responsibilities relative to it. • Think out loud and not be explicit that this is what you are doing, thereby leaving people with the impression that your inchoate thoughts should be taken seriously. • Assume that your urgency translates to collective urgency; offer urgency without hope. • Voice thoughts in writing or speech with others that you wouldn't want to see in the media. • Say things about people to others that you wouldn't say directly to them. • Avoid telling people something because you don't want to upset them. • Send an email when you're upset, frustrated, or feeling great urgency (a particularly dangerous thing to do late at night).	• Emphasize *why* and connect to *what*, *how*, and *who* in communications. • Keep the core message consistent while adapting its emphasis and form to respond to the roles, interests, and needs of the people with whom you are sharing. • Repeat things multiple times and ways (writing, speaking, images) and make communication multidirectional and sustained (up, down, across the organization, championed by more people than just you and your team). • Give concrete examples to make your point; check for understanding; invite clarifying questions; ask someone to restate what you said to confirm their understanding of it. • Signal when you are thinking out loud and invite others to share their thoughts in draft form, too. • Offer a compelling message, drawing on stories, data, visuals, and music to connect with shared values and convey both urgency and hope. • Assume that anything you write down or say out loud can and will be shared widely. • Save your venting for your partner, close friends (preferably outside your organization), or pet. • Figure out a time and manner to share information that may be upsetting in order to give others space to process and you whatever you need to feel safe. • Wait at least overnight, and possibly longer, to respond to any nonemergency that has provoked a strong reaction in you.

Anticipating and avoiding the things in the "Nonstrategic Information Sharing" column help keep people informed and motivated, support organizational coherence and trust, and reduce confusion, which slows progress.

It also can be very strategic to let the people around you know your communication tendencies so they don't make assumptions. This doesn't alleviate you of responsibility for communicating in a way that others can hear, and it doesn't alleviate them of responsibility for checking their own assumptions, particularly with people of different cultural backgrounds, but it can help avoid misunderstandings. For example, one leader we know tells people who work with her that she has "strong opinions lightly held" as a way of signaling that she can sound quite certain in the way she talks, but is very open to changing her mind. Another leader we know tells people who work with him that sometimes people think he's upset based on his facial expressions, but that's actually his thinking face, and he'll let them know if he's upset.

Beware: Avoiding Bad News

Strategic leaders are honest, transparent, and mindful of context. This is essential to building trust with others, which is foundational to strong relationships and to healthy organizations. This requires you to tell the truth appropriate to the context and circumstance from a centered place, grounded in purpose. Transparency can be tricky when a situation is dynamic and/or there are political or human resource considerations.

As an example, declining enrollment is forcing many school systems to consolidate schools, a move that often has few supporters and many opponents. People want to know what consolidations mean for their schools and community. Yet school systems have to work through a variety of painstaking processes to make these determinations, exploring many contingencies. In situations like this, transparency looks like communicating the needs and rationale for consolidations (*why*), and the process and criteria (*how*) that the organization will use to make consolidation decisions (*what*).

It is important to discern when sharing information is helpful and when it might actually be distracting and counterproductive, as when a situation is uncertain and changing rapidly. As you think about sharing information, remember that it can move through organizations as quickly as a thunderstorm (often the case with bad news or gossip) or as slow as molasses (often the case with information related to the steady, persistent work of improvement), and there is often distortion as it travels. Strategic leaders understand this and proactively take steps to communicate with intention.

Engage Conflict

The potential for conflict exists in every relationship and every effort to build relationships among bodies of work and departments. A principal puts off telling her teachers about the school system's new approach to collaborative planning time because she thinks that they're going to be upset about it. A friend hurts your feelings, and you debate whether to say something. You don't share your concerns with your boss about her approach to a new initiative. Nobody says anything when a colleague says something problematic in a meeting.

Many of us are scared of conflict and worry about the fallout—tension, damaged or ruptured relationships, or other problems—if it is not handled well. Our fear means that a difference or disagreement can seem potentially catastrophic. That is seldom the truth. Our fear of conflict often presents as avoidance, reluctance, or stalling. Regardless of how it presents itself, the effect is the same: we miss an opportunity to strengthen thinking, work, and relationships. By focusing on the downside of conflict, we limit ourselves, our relationships, and our effectiveness.

When conflict is normalized and navigated well, it can be a learning opportunity, a powerful relationship-builder, and an opportunity for a better outcome. Anyone who has had a successful but difficult conversation with a partner, a sibling, or a colleague knows how it deepens connection, trust, and resilience. You walk away with new understandings that challenge your assumptions and help you think more expansively about possibilities. You feel more confident in yourself, the relationship, and what you are capable of individually and collectively. You learn that your brother's anger at you not joining him and his family for Thanksgiving is tied to his worry about how you will stay connected after the recent death of your second parent. That understanding helps you imagine lots of ways to address that through and beyond Thanksgiving. And his willingness to share it with you deepens your connection. Maybe it makes it easier for you to share why Thanksgiving is a hard time for you and you don't feel like socializing.

To help you realize this potential, here are a few tips for engaging conflict:

1. **Focus on the why:** *Why is it important to have the hard conversation?* There are all kinds of possible answers, anchored in purpose: for example, the good health of your marriage and your love for one another; the best decision you can make about the care of your child/parent; and addressing the needs of students you are not currently serving well.

2. **Figure out what it's really about:** *What is underneath the conflict?* This is where the tools of discernment serve you well: getting curious, asking questions to improve your understanding, and listening openly can help you learn. Maybe the principal who doesn't want to share the common planning time initiative with her teachers is a new principal in a school where she used to be a teacher. She's uncomfortable directing her former peers. Maybe the person who said something problematic at the meeting has been trying to raise concerns for weeks but no one is listening; in his frustration at not being heard, he said things that he knew would get people's attention, even if he doesn't fully believe them.
3. **Decide how to move forward:** *What do you do now that you better understand the conflict?* Sometimes, when you get beneath the visible conflict to the heart of the matter, you're able to see a clear path forward. The brother and sister commit to ringing in the New Year together. The principal's supervisor coaches her on having the conversation with her teachers or finds her a mentor who followed the same path to the principalship. Sometimes the path isn't clear, so you need to continue exploring options and talking to figure it out. And sometimes there isn't agreement on a clear path forward. At that point, there are choices to consider: Is action immediately necessary or is a decision to do nothing viable? If a decision must be made, who will decide?

Much of what we've shared in this chapter, when done well, creates safe conditions for engaging conflict productively. By building relationships, you establish connection and trust, which are a kind of social capital you can draw on in a conflict. By listening, staying curious, and being willing to have your ideas or opinions change, you remain open, which maximizes your ability to find a path forward. By sharing information clearly and with purpose, you offer transparency, which lets you (and others) see the issue more clearly. Using all these skills to engage conflict productively makes it possible to turn conflict into an opportunity to gain new insights, deepen relationships, and find productive solutions.

One way that leaders can bring together the dimensions of communication—listen, share information, and engage conflict—is by linking what they have heard to a specific action, and then to a larger purpose (e.g., "We have heard X, so we're doing Y, which we think will help with Z [solve problem/make progress toward goal].”). Instead of just saying X or Y or Z, strategic leaders make the relationship between these things explicit.

This explicitness provides clarity, which can also encourage surfacing disagreement focused on the most important stuff. People can disagree with any point of the formula and add new information, while staying connected to purpose (e.g., “Well, I think we’re not paying enough attention to Q, which will make Y challenging” or “I don’t see how Y leads to Z; can you help me understand that better?”). This formula is also a way of communicating what you have discerned: we understand X, so we’re going to take right action Y, which we think will help with purpose Z. This transparent communication often helps people feel heard and helps link *what*, *how*, and *why*.

Building Others' Capacity to Cultivate Relationships

- Model ways of building connections between people; expect and make time for connecting as humans when you get together, both one-on-one and in teams and community.
- Encourage and support others to invest time in building a web of relationships.
- Expand whom you engage with beyond the people you're most comfortable with and invite others to do the same.
- Establish rituals in team settings that nurture relationships.
- Use the tools of this chapter, collaboratively, to map relationships and set work groups up for success.
- Devote time in teams to share how individuals'/team's work connects with others' work and the work of the larger organization.
- Encourage others to think about the *who*, *what*, *when*, *where*, *how*, and *why* of their messaging and communication.
- Model engaging with conflict productively and create spaces where this is both tolerated and encouraged.

TAKEAWAYS

- Work happens through people and their relationships with one another.
- Think about the relationships among things: no person, idea, or initiative in isolation.
- Strong relationships between departments and bodies of work support coherence.
- Listening, sharing information, and engaging in conflict are crucial communication skills that build relationships. Doing each of these things with awareness and openness—head, heart, and body—can lead to expansive thinking and creativity and better process and outcomes.
- As leaders assume more responsibility, they have to develop proxies for one-on-one relationship building, and communication becomes increasingly important.
- Talking about the *why*, *what*, *who*, and *how* of any topic supports clear, transparent, and compelling communication. The why, which explains the underlying rationale, is crucial and often overlooked; it is what orients people and moves them beyond compliance.

REFLECTIONS

What are your strengths, areas for development, and lingering questions about cultivating relationships?

3

UNDERSTAND CONTEXT AND HISTORY

CONTEXT AND HISTORY ABOUND. They are like the air we breathe, ever present and often invisible to the naked eye. We all have our own personal contexts and histories. Do you live in a city, a suburb, or a rural area? Are you financially secure or do you struggle to make ends meet, and how does that compare to how you grew up? Are you a parent? A single parent? A stepparent? Are you a devoted alumnus of a historically Black college with generations of excellence and pride? Are you the first person in your family to go to college? What are the core values that guide you, and where did they come from? Does faith play an important role in your life? What jobs have you had? Are you a founding member of a thirty-year-old book club that's still going strong? Are you an athlete? What have been your struggles and triumphs? Are you an introvert or extrovert?

All these things and many more make up the context of our identities and lives. They are the things that shape us, the way we see and walk through the world, how others perceive us, and how we experience others.

CONTEXT AND HISTORY IN OUR DAILY LIVES

In every interaction we have with another person, our personal contexts are in play. When colleagues learn that Rachel's mother was a high school English teacher who wielded her red pen with as heavy a hand with her children as she did with her students, they don't take it as personally when Rachel marks up a piece of writing that they asked her to review. When we approach our neighbors about sharing the cost of trimming a tree of theirs that is hanging over our house, we bring our personal context to the engagement. Maybe one of us grew up with neighbors who were like family while the other had a contentious relationship with a former neighbor. Maybe one of us can afford a tree trimmer, while the other cannot. Maybe one of us didn't grow up in our own house with trees around and aren't sure what the norm might be. Maybe one of us is shy, or conflict avoidant, or friendly, or assertive, or aggressive, or a believer that the glass is always half full or half empty. All these things have the potential to shape our interactions and the outcome of them.

We learn about and create context and history when we *cultivate relationships*, collaborate on a team, or build partnerships with other schools, departments, or organizations. Maybe we learn that the person with whom we most need to collaborate to achieve great results had a conflict-riddled relationship with our predecessor, or that the teachers serving students with disabilities have historically not been included in curriculum adoption efforts, or that the team we've just inherited has never been asked to work together. Context and history can both be something that we *discern to understand* and something that we consider as we *discern to take right action*. As we try to figure out the most impactful way to support teachers in instructional planning and improvement, maybe we learn that there hasn't been a coordinated effort in decades to ensure that teachers use the same curriculum. Or maybe we learn there are multiple people in every elementary school charged with supporting this work, but it's unclear what they're doing, their expertise, and if the roles are complementary or in competition.

In this chapter, we explore the *why*, *what*, and *how* of understanding context and history and using that understanding to inform action or the decision not to act.

WHY CONTEXT AND HISTORY MATTER

Nothing exists in a vacuum. Everything exists in context. Anyone who has ever tried to take a great idea from another school, team, or organization and replicate it, only to realize mixed results—or worse yet, failure—has experienced firsthand the importance of context. Think about the school system that adopts a math curriculum that is highly rated and that peer systems are excited about because of the learning results they're seeing with their students. Eighteen months into implementation in this particular school system, student results are underwhelming and teachers are frustrated and overwhelmed. This experience is likely due to context. There may be differences in: the curriculum-based training available to teachers, paraprofessionals, and principals; the infrastructure that supports ongoing teacher learning, practice, and collaboration; the teacher pay scale and how it affects the ability to recruit and retain top talent; the presence of teacher leaders with deep math expertise who can lead the work with their colleagues; the curriculum that preceded this one; or the culture around new ideas. Fully understanding the contextual factors that contributed to the peer district's success may have led this district to choose a different curriculum, to pace and sequence implementation differently, to be very intentional about strengthening teacher capacity building efforts, or all of these.

Individuals, teams, and organizations have new, exciting ideas to pursue, as well as work that simply needs to get done. Understanding current context and history relevant to what we're trying to accomplish helps us prioritize work and make smart decisions about how and when we pursue it. This is a bit like gardening. Weather and soil conditions are important contexts. There may be frequent rain or the conditions may be droughtlike. Soil can be full of clay or sand, or it may be acidic. As we plan and plant our garden, we need to have these things in mind. We may choose plants that match the current context, or we may try to improve the context to accommodate plants that have different needs. Maybe we add compost to the soil to make it healthier or decide to water regularly to create a hospitable environment. The time and resources that we're able to invest in the garden are key considerations. Can we water the garden daily? Do we prefer to put in a lot of effort at the beginning of the season and then have the garden be self-sufficient? We keep all this context and history in mind when deciding what to plant and how to keep the plants healthy.

When we understand context and history, we're able to pursue our work with our eyes wide open and make well-informed choices. We reduce the likelihood of unexpected surprises, roadblocks, and failures. Depending on the circumstances, we may use context to tap resources and opportunities, do specific things to change or lessen the impact of the existing context, or choose not to proceed because the context is not currently supportive. Depending on context, any of these decisions may make us more efficient and effective. This amounts to strategic leadership.

WHAT CONTEXT AND HISTORY ARE

Context is the milieu in which we operate individually, interpersonally, and organizationally. It is both what is currently happening or true and how things are done. Context includes a range of things: the community in which a school exists, 20 percent of principals in a system being in their first or second year of service, the level of engagement of parents and what they care about, a nonprofit's forty-year history of activism, the level of functioning of a senior leadership team, a nonprofit receiving its largest philanthropic gift ever, the presence of a strong union and the quality of the relationship between it and management, the expertise level of teachers, a liberal city in a conservative state . . . we could go on and on.

Through our decades of work with school systems and education nonprofits, we have identified four categories of context that are essential to understand for impact. These categories are not comprehensive but, in our experience, they matter regardless of what work you're trying to lead and where you sit in an organization.

Important Categories of Context

- **Politics:** What are the political hot-button issues in the organization/community? How do people navigate/ignore/address them? How long has the chief executive officer (CEO) been in that role, and what do this person's relationships with the board, other key political players, and the community look like? How is power distributed? What do people with more power care about? Are they inclined to share power or hold onto it and wield it forcefully? What are the key alliances?
- **Human capital:** How well do the skills of the workforce match the organization's needs? How long will it take to build the capacity of staff? How easy or hard is it to fill positions? Do the answers to these questions vary by role? Does the organization offer competitive salaries? How much does it invest in developing employees' skills, nurturing talent, and building career pathways? Is there a succession plan for key roles?

- **Resources:** Is the organization in a moment of constrained, steady-state, or expanding resources (which include money, people, time, and materials)? What are the sources of revenue and the related implications for spending? What does the five-year financial horizon look like? Are there enough people to do the work that the organization has prioritized? Does doing that work require reorganization and/or retraining of existing staff, an infusion of new staff, or a reduction in staff?
- **Culture:** What are the rules, spoken and unspoken, about how people engage with one another and how things are done? Who talks in meetings (and who doesn't)? How are decisions made? Are people friendly and collaborative, or do they keep to themselves? What are the important rituals in this organization, and what do they tell you about what is valued in the organization?

Context is dynamic. The answers to these questions may vary from one school/department to another in the same school system/organization, or they may change over time. Contextual considerations can change quickly (there is a sudden public health crisis) or it can take years for them to change (build broad community support for the schools). Strategic leaders pay attention to changes in context, consider the implications of these changes for their work, and think about what they can do to change or develop new context.

History is a subset of context, a particular slice that focuses on the story of the past that has led to the present. History is particularly important because it is often tightly woven into the fabric of an organization, its people, its culture, and its present. It refracts into the present in powerful ways. You see it in the different ways that teachers have been taught to teach reading over the last thirty years; debates about admission to selective enrollment high schools; the eight years that the team of third-grade teachers have spent collaborating; and how principals have been engaged—told what to do, partnered with, left on their own, or all of the above—by the central office over the decades. To fully understand the current context, you need to understand its history.

HOW TO LEARN ABOUT CONTEXT AND HISTORY

Bound Inquiry

The first step in learning about context and history relates to drawing the circumference of your inquiry. You need to draw a boundary to keep from getting overwhelmed and potentially paralyzed by too much information. A boundary helps you discriminate among many different things that you might look at and choose where to focus. To do this, you need to develop a hypothesis about the most fruitful lines of inquiry and where there may be rabbit holes that you want to avoid. This helps you manage your time and energy.

Questions to Set Boundaries for Inquiry

- What are the two or three most important things to understand about the current or historical context?
- Why do those things matter right now?

Imagine that you're trying to choose a new place to live. You might ask a range of questions about a community you're considering: Is it affordable? What is the quality of the schools; does that vary by neighborhood? Can you walk to key amenities—grocery store, pharmacy, library? If not, is there reliable public transportation, or do you need a car? What's the commute to work like? Who else lives in this community, and is that what you're looking for? What services does the community provide, and how well does it do this? What has happened in this community's history (e.g., efforts to expand public transportation were unsuccessful, the community voted for a tax levy to support building new schools), and what might these things tell you about the community's values and commitments?

This is all context and history. Trying to answer all these questions is overwhelming. You seldom have time to explore all of them. So you prioritize. If your biggest concerns are the quality of the schools and the length of your commute, then you may want to visit schools, talk to parents, look at travel times on traffic apps, or try a commute to get a firsthand sense of it. As you visit schools, you learn that different schools have different programs; this may be something about which you want to inquire further.

At work, the scope of your inquiry into context and history depends, in part, on your personal circumstances: Did you get promoted, or are you new to the organization? Are you trying to lead something yourself or work in the context of a team? What is the scope of your responsibilities? Table 3.1 illustrates different scopes of inquiry based on circumstances.

Table 3.1 Examples of Scopes of Inquiry

Principal Promoted to Principal Supervisor	New (to the school system) Director of New Teacher Support	Human Resources Team Considering New Technology Platform for Hiring
• History of schools that the new supervisor is responsible for—demographics, programming, and performance; leadership of each school and their standing; unique needs/concerns; who has influence (with whom, about what, why) • History of collaboration (or lack thereof) among these schools—on what, to what end • How principal supervisors work—expectations (from whom), variance in practice and why • Culture among principal supervisors—is there a history of collaboration/competition; focus on compliance/authority/building agency • Relationship principal supervisors have with other departments and senior leaders	• History of new teacher support in this system—what was done, by whom, how, when, and why • Demographics of new teachers—how many, where they come from, level of training and experience • How things get done in the system—policies, practices, norms; who has influence; role of supervisor and board • Organizational culture—quality of relationship between schools and the central office; siloed/collaborative central office; level of openness and honesty about how things work/don't work • Important stakeholders—proximal to the issue, influential, deep experience/expertise	• History of current (and prior) hiring tech platforms: what was chosen and how (and by whom), when, and why • Biggest pain points for candidates for positions, new hires, and their supervisors • Functionality that users would like to see • Experience and expertise of platform users (on both the front and back end) • Process and procedures for exploring, choosing, and implementing new platforms • Resources (e.g., time, money, people) available to support platform selection and implementation • Other platforms in place in the system that may need to inform/interact with this one • The characteristics of successful platforms and implementations generally

As you can see from the table, what you need to learn about context and history may vary depending on your role, your tenure in the organization, and the work in which you are engaged. Yet understanding the history related to what you're trying to do, the experiences of the people closest to the work that you're trying to influence, the current capacity available for the work, and potential partners and alliances is always helpful.

Bring Awareness to the Process

To understand context and history, you must be part anthropologist, part historian, and part sociologist. Your inquiry can reinforce or give depth or nuance to what you think you know. It can also uncover all that you don't know. To get the most out of bounded inquiry, you must become aware of and challenge your unconscious bias—lack of awareness about biases that affect decisions and judgments. We all have unconscious bias. It's part of being human. Examples of unconscious biases include hearing the word "teacher" and picturing a woman or hearing the word "leader" and picturing a man. Or making other assumptions about people, like: people living in poverty don't know what they need; people with the most power and authority are smarter and more skilled than those without; people with lighter skin tones are more capable than people with darker skin tones; people with physical disabilities are less mentally agile. Because these biases are unconscious, we need to be alert to the ways that they will continue to come up so we can actively challenge them.

One way to challenge your biases is to pay attention to the questions you're planning to ask and ensure that they don't suggest that you've already developed an opinion. Leading questions generally seek validation of our own thinking and beliefs, which immediately limits our ability to have our thinking expanded. Open-ended questions invite bigger responses, which help us learn more. There are examples of each type of question in table 3.2.

Table 3.2 Leading Questions versus Open-Ended Questions

Leading Questions	Open-Ended Questions
• Did anyone think about expanding the program?	• How were decisions made about the size and scale of the program?
• Do you think that we should look at student work as part of our common planning time?	• What do you think we should do during the common planning time?
• Is Rayna likely to be the next director?	• Who are likely candidates for the director position?

Your unconscious biases also may be reflected in the people with whom you talk. You may be inclined to reach out to talk to people of similar backgrounds, experiences, interests, and beliefs. This limits your access to a range of experiences and perspectives, which are essential to develop a full picture.

The process of bounded inquiry is dynamic. You make your best guess about what you need to understand and get started. As you inquire, you learn things that encourage you to expand your inquiry in a particular way. Maybe you realize that one of the things you identified at the beginning as important to understand isn't as important as you thought; maybe something else surfaces as crucial that wasn't on your screen originally. The boundaries of the inquiry may expand in some ways and contract in other ways. Being flexible while being intentional about not getting bogged down in nonessential information is key. As discussed in previous chapters, your understanding will expand if you check with others along the way for ideas about what you should learn about, how to make sense of what you're learning, and assumptions that you may be making as you gather information. The goal is to know enough to lead you in the right direction. You will continue to learn about context and history as you engage in the work.

Decide Which Data to Gather

The *count*, *see*, *hear*, *feel* approach to data collection introduced in chapter 1 can help you understand context and history. You can look at data and artifacts, observe meetings and people's behavior, and pay attention to the tone and vibe of interactions and documents.

As you do this, your job is to describe what you see, hear, and sense while not conflating your observations with judgment. Judgment is problematic because it assigns meaning and value to what you observe, which may or may not be true. Your judgments may reflect your willingness to generalize based on limited information or may be guided by unconscious biases. Checking for judgments is important because once you make and accept a judgment, it is human nature to look for confirming data. This then skews your data and impedes your ability to see what's actually going on. Table 3.3 demonstrates the difference between description and judgment based on observations.

Table 3.3 Description of Observation versus Judgment Made from Observation

Description of Observation	Judgment Made from Observation
• Teachers ask a lot of questions about the new grading policy. • Children move around the classroom, gathering books and materials and talking to their classmates. • The executive director spends forty-five minutes of a sixty-minute staff meeting providing updates.	• Teachers do not support the new grading policy. • The classroom is chaotic. • The executive director wastes staff's time and runs terrible meetings.

The Ladder of Inference is a helpful tool for grounding in description rather than judgment.[1]

The Ladder of Inference

The Ladder of Inference is built on the idea that when you observe something or have an experience, you can't see and absorb everything that is going on, but your brain is a meaning-making machine and wants to quickly process what is happening and decide what to do about it. So you focus your attention on something. Your choice of what data to collect is driven by your biases, experiences, and beliefs. Inevitably, you miss information that may be crucial to a clear understanding of what's actually going on. Unaware of this limitation, you assign meaning to and make assumptions about the situation based on the data you collected. This then leads you to draw conclusions and generalizations and to develop beliefs that drive the action you take. This means that your action is driven more by your biases, experiences, and beliefs than the complex reality of the situation and your clear understanding of it.

The Ladder of Inference offers us a way to slow down, become aware of and name what we're doing, and interrupt the behavior.

Rungs on the Ladder of Inference

7. You take *action* guided by your beliefs.
6. You adopt *beliefs*, based on your conclusions.
5. You draw *conclusions*.
4. You make *assumptions* based on the meaning that you've made.
3. You *add meaning* to the data that you collect based on your biases, experiences, and beliefs.
2. You *select specific data* from what you see, hear, and feel.
1. A wide array of data is available.

Steps

1. Notice and name that you have jumped to a conclusion and, perhaps, are ready to take action.
2. Move back down the ladder by making explicit what you saw, heard, or experienced that led you to your conclusion or belief (there is usually a mix of something observed and beliefs in play) and inviting others to

do the same. Ask, "What am I thinking? Why? What did I see or hear that made me think that? Is my thinking sound?"

3. If you identify faulty reasoning, revisit it.
4. Go back to the facts of the situation, gathering additional data if you identify that your original facts were incomplete.
5. Start your thinking process again, moving slowly and consciously up each rung of the ladder.

For more on the Ladder of Inference, see the appendix of this book.

Wondering is different from judging, and it is very helpful when inquiring about context and history. It is born from a place of curiosity and the desire to understand. You can wonder about both what you see and what might be underneath it. Your wondering can guide you as you probe to better understand the why behind things. For example, it is useful to notice and wonder about the following: How your new colleague introduces herself to her teams; the way that one of your teachers always asks, "How can we ensure that this initiative meets the needs of our multilingual learners?"; why your new boss saves five minutes at the end of every meeting to get feedback on what worked well about the meeting and what could be improved; how the central office of the school district feels disconnected from the schools; how the organization's values come up regularly in conversation; the alignment of the mayor's and superintendent's messaging to the community; or the strong, collegial, and collaborative culture among the youth-serving agencies in the community.

Talking with people is a crucial way to understand context and history. This is one of the reasons why relationship building is so important, particularly as you enter a new organization, take on new roles or responsibilities, or develop a new initiative. As you start to build a relationship, you can learn about the person's own context (e.g., What brought you to the organization/your role? Which of the services that the organization provides are most important to you? What are you most proud of/excited about regarding your work?). You learn things and build rapport, which supports asking deeper questions. It also helps you understand others' perspectives. Knowing that the person who is skeptical about building more robust tier 2 instruction led an elementary school from a "D" to an "A" rating through a deep focus on improving tier 1 instruction helps you understand the place from which they're coming.

You can ask about specific bodies of work (e.g., Have any career exploration activities been introduced in the middle school grades? How has collaborative planning time been used in this school? What are the after-school options for children in your community?). And you can ask about the organization (e.g., What are its greatest recent successes? How would you describe the level of trust that it has among parents? What have you learned about how the organization functions and how to be effective in it? Who are the people in the organization and outside of it who support you and push your thinking?). Note the value of the simple *who*, *what*, *when*, *where*, *how*, and *why* questions from chapter 1. Talking to the people whom the organization serves and the people who directly interact with them (think students, parents, and teachers) is essential. This proximity often surfaces truths and profoundly important information. It also demonstrates respect and a desire to hear a variety of voices.

Successes and strengths are often underutilized resources when it comes to understanding history and context. It's worth pausing to understand what has gone well in the past or what is going well right now, as well as what can be learned from that and applied to current work. The Success Analysis Protocol is a great way to harvest lessons learned from a group.[2] You can also simply ask questions (e.g., What was a recent success of the work? What do you think contributed to that success?).

Given all the things that you might ask people to better understand context and history, it's important to prioritize, sequence, and pace your questions, keeping in mind that the process of inquiry can support building relationships and understanding power dynamics. In other words, you are not just seeking answers. You are using the process intentionally to support the kinds of relationships that you want to be in and the power networks that you need to accomplish purposeful goals. For people you can talk to only once, what do you most want to ask? For people you have more access to, where do you want to start, and how will their answers direct you to the next questions? Where are your opportunities to ask multiple people the same question so you can triangulate their answers? How do you think about using inquiry as a way to build relationships (e.g., sharing what's important to you through the questions you ask, and communicating respect by the way you listen)? How are you mindful of power dynamics in the way you ask questions and listen?

The questions that follow offer a frame for clarifying what you're trying to learn in your inquiry and from whom you can learn it.

Questions to Clarify What and Who About Context and History

1. What needs to be true to make the work that you're pursuing impactful?
2. What are the current contextual conditions that can support or impede the work that you're trying to pursue?[3]
   - Related work underway—how it's going, lessons from it
   - Realities and happenings adjacent to your work that can affect it
   - Things happening in/around the system that are buoying or stressing your work
3. What do you need to know about the past to pursue this work productively?
   - Similar or related efforts pursued and their results, public opinion about them, and who was involved in them
   - Unresolved issues that may resurface or sit just beneath the surface as you try to do your work
4. From whom/what can you learn about the things you listed in response to questions 2 and 3?
5. What do you know or need to learn about the colleagues you're going to speak with in order to better understand their perspectives and actions?

Understanding context and history, like all *discerning*, takes time and requires curiosity. Time is a precious commodity, and it can seem as though there is not enough time to be curious. Strategic leaders resist the culture of constant action without pausing to *discern*. This is an instance where going slow ultimately supports going fast. Maybe you learn that principals have reservations about the usefulness of the current teacher evaluation tool and protocol, which makes you decide not to link your initiative to it. Or, while there is a lot of buzz about the success of dual enrollment in local colleges among high school students, you learn that only 8 percent of students are dual-enrolled and the demographics of those students do not reflect the overall student population. Investing time in learning things like these generally pays off, as it allows you to make strategic decisions, which reduces wasted time and increases the likelihood of success. Not taking time to be curious about context and history leaves you running the risk of repeating history, wasting time and energy, reinforcing existing challenges, and/or eroding relationships.

Considerations When Learning About Context and History

When learning about context and history from others, there are a few things to consider—subtleties, fresh eyes, historical perspective, and power—to ensure that you're developing as full and accurate a picture as possible.

Subtleties

Paying attention to subtleties can teach you a lot about how people are feeling and hint at things that may be going on beneath the surface. By definition, subtleties can be hard to identify or describe. Yet with curiosity and intentional attention, you can see them. Examples of subtleties might include the vague way teachers talk about the impact of the new student assessments on instruction or the way people seem to listen closely to one leader but not to another, even though both have equivalent formal authority. There are things to learn from each of these subtleties about understanding, buy-in, credibility, concerns, and organizational culture, which may be quite important to a strategic leader who is trying to understand the current state of affairs and/or considering taking a particular action.

Questions for Noticing Subtleties

- What pronouns do people use when talking about a topic: *we* (suggesting a collective); *you* (suggesting separation between the speaker and the person they're speaking to); or *they* (suggesting distance and an othering when used to describe a group of people)?
- What is the tone of the storytelling about the past? Is the description dispassionate or full of emotion? If it's full of emotion, which emotions are most present?
- Whom do people listen to?
- Do people answer your question? If not, assume that your question wasn't clear and try to clarify. If the person you're talking to still doesn't answer the question, wonder why.
- What does everyone talk about? What does nobody talk about?

Fresh Eyes

When friends come over to your house for the first time and comment on the beautiful photograph on your wall that you hardly even notice anymore, they are seeing things with fresh eyes. These same fresh eyes may observe the chipped paint, although they may not share that with you. People new to an organization and, perhaps to a lesser degree, new to a job within an organization they work in, often notice things and wonder why they are the way they are. People with fresh eyes are helpful to talk to when you are steeped in the organization and may struggle to see the forest for the trees.

While their perspective on your organization is fresh, like everyone else, these people bring their own lens and perspective born of their own personal context and history. Maybe they previously worked somewhere that served as a hub of partnership and collaboration among several organizations. As a result, they're predisposed to be bullish on these things and are always looking for signs of information sharing, collaboration, and joint problem-solving. Or maybe the culture was toxic where they last worked, leaving them with well-tuned antennae for people being unkind, disrespectful, or backbiting, and perhaps a tendency to work alone and not ask for help. Building rapport by asking about people's backgrounds and experiences helps you understand and take into consideration the perspective that they're bringing to the conversation.

Historical Perspective

While newcomers are often good at noticing what is done and how, organizational veterans often can offer insight into the why and when behind those things. They can tell us a number of things: how the superintendent, five back, led his cabinet or worked with the head of the teachers' union; the details of the failed near-merger eight years ago of two local nonprofits that are currently in conflict; why the approach to school improvement planning changed in the way that it did five years ago; how something similar or relevant to what you're trying to do has been done before and what you might learn from it; or their perspective on why particular colleagues behave the ways they do. People with historical perspective often provide nuance and depth to your understanding. Yet their lens is also not entirely clear. Their investment in their work and the organization may make it hard for them to see the organizational chipped paint or to ask hard questions. Or their disenchantment with the organization may make it hard for them to see anything beyond the chipped paint.

Power

As we explore more in chapter 4, dynamics of power are both something that you want to learn about and something that can limit your learning. People with positional power often simultaneously have more and less visibility into the work of their organization. They may have a strong understanding of the system-level priorities, strategy, and approach to implementation because they are engaged in developing these things and discuss them regularly. Yet this engagement and their other responsibilities often keep them further away from the on-the-ground work of the organization. So while they may be setting the direction for this work, they may have a less nuanced understanding of the details of its implementation.

This problem can be exacerbated by the tendency of others not to tell the truth to those with positional power, especially when the news isn't good. If you have positional power and are trying to learn context, you can try to address this by shaping your questions to invite feedback in a way that may feel less high-stakes, either by asking descriptive, informational questions or by asking questions that invite respondents to offer their opinions based on their expertise. Talking with multiple people with personal power (derived from expertise, informal influence, trust, and relationships) relative to the issue is a good counterpoint to talking with people with positional power. It can often surface nuances and details that can enrich your understanding.

All these considerations make clear why it is wise to gather multiple perspectives, drawing on people with different tenures, roles, identities, perspectives, and relationships to the work, organization, and community. You can then triangulate information that you gather to develop a rich, deep, and nuanced understanding.

Beware: Making Leaps

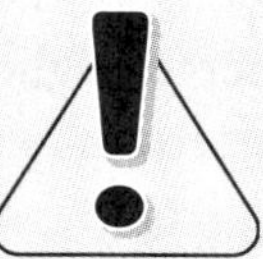

Building an understanding of context and history requires openness and mindfulness to ensure that leaders get a full, well-rounded picture of what is currently happening, what has happened before in this place, and how to interpret both. Part of being open and mindful is being aware of the pitfalls of skewing data and information collected in a way that provides a partial picture or biased perspective.

Strategic leaders manage this by checking themselves on a series of factors:

- **Data sources:** Collect a rich array of data sources that include count, see, and hear data and a variety of perspectives (by role, level of positional power, experience, proximity to the issue, understanding and analysis of the issue). The perspectives of people within and outside the organization who are involved in or affected by the issue can help you develop a more nuanced understanding. The goal of all this data collection is to build your understanding of the complexity of the issue; this limits the likelihood of a simplistic, insufficient response.

- **Bias:** When you're conscious of your biases, it is possible to step back and look at the data that you're collecting, the questions that you're asking, and whom you're asking, to see if you're cherry-picking them to reinforce your own biases. Unconscious biases are harder to identify because they are invisible to the naked eye. They often reflect stereotypes and lead to quick "judgments about character, abilities and potential."[4] Mahzarin R. Banaji, coauthor of *Blindspot: Hidden Biases of Good People*, discusses the following strategies to uncover unconscious bias: acknowledge potential for bias, learn about stereotypes, broaden your focus, and expose yourself to alien experiences.[5]
- **Ladder of Inference:** Tracking where you are on the Ladder of Inference as you gather information can help you catch yourself rushing to judgment based on limited data and information. Sometimes this is the result of biases; other times, it's the result of wanting to move quickly to analysis and clarity rather than sit with and work through the messy uncertainty. Reassuring the part of you that feels anxious about the uncertainty, and then slowing the pace and stepping down the ladder, lets you interrogate your actions, beliefs, judgments, and assumptions.
- **Intuition:** Sometimes you have an immediate understanding of a situation. Your instincts and intuition tell you something compelling that can be valuable in setting the course of data collection and can guide who you talk to and what you talk to them about. Yet because instincts and intuition function at an unconscious level, they must be interrogated to ensure that they do not reflect unconscious biases. Using a variety of data sources is a way to interrogate intuition and test if you can trust your gut instinct.

BRUTALLY HONEST TRUTHS

As you synthesize your data about history and context, it can be very helpful to explicitly articulate the understanding that you are developing. Brutally Honest Truths is a tool designed to help people see clearly the current context of a team, body of work, or organization and how it is generating its current results. We developed this tool because we were finding in our work with people and teams around strategy that often people said one thing and thought another. In particular, people often had a strong sense of why something wasn't working or wouldn't work, but they weren't saying so because they were nervous. We made this tool to help make it easier to say, "I don't think this is working." Once that statement is out in the open, it's easier to work toward a different outcome, acknowledging what you know about yourselves and your context and adjusting accordingly. When we work with leaders, this is often one of their favorite tools. This tool can be used at the individual or team level. Its influence tends to be powerful, so it can be a great way to help a team see the current state of affairs clearly.

Brutally Honest Truths

1. Identify the situation or body of work that you are trying to understand better.
2. Describe what (good, bad, and otherwise) is currently being done (or, if you're thinking prospectively about work to be done, name the things that you are planning to do) related to the things that you identified in step 1. Put an *IF* in front of the description of helpful things being done (or to be done).
3. Then add a *BUT* and include the things that are in place (or that you anticipate could happen if you're thinking prospectively) that compromise the effort.
4. Describe the results being achieved through the work described. Put a *THEN* in front of this description. This is the brutal reality (or the anticipated result, for prospective work) that you would not proudly proclaim.

5. Put the statements together and read them aloud. What do you notice? What does it tell you about what needs to be considered to ensure maximum impact of the effort? It should feel both "ouchy" and true—it should make you cringe and then exhale.
6. *So what*: What needs to be reconsidered to address impediments to success?

Example of Brutally Honest Truths

IF we build a strong home visit program to build relationships with families and improve student attendance, BUT students still experience instruction as boring and disconnected from their lives and don't feel a sense of belonging in school, THEN we won't be successful in keeping students in school and improving their learning.

For more examples and tips for using Brutally Honest Truths, see the appendix.

Brutally Honest Truths (BHTs) help you synthesize all that you've learned about context and history into a truth about how work is being pursued and the shortcomings that need to be addressed. While BHTs are inevitably sobering, people we work with really appreciate their honesty, clarity, and concreteness. The BHTs often put into words things that people have had misgivings about but haven't been able to name. Naming the challenges often brings a sense of relief and helps people identify the most important things on which to focus.

Building Others' Capacity to Understand Context and History

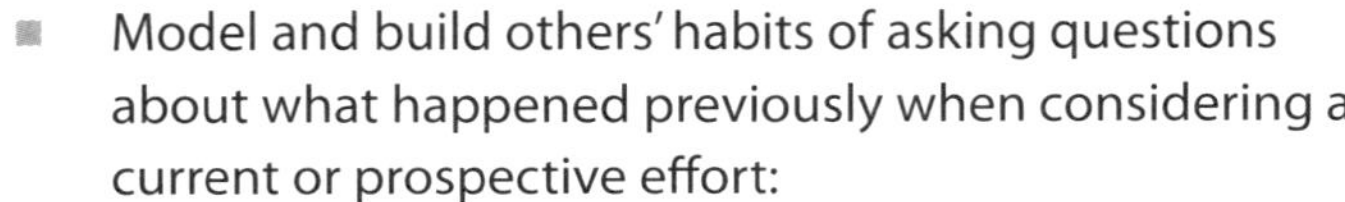

- Model and build others' habits of asking questions about what happened previously when considering a current or prospective effort:
  - What's been done? Why?
  - What were the results?
  - What did we (or could we) learn from past efforts?
  - What was the impact on relationships, trust, and engagement?
- Encourage them to think about the *who*, *what*, *when*, *where*, *how*, and *why* of the context and history relevant to the matter at hand.
- Model and build a collective practice of inviting people with different perspectives (e.g., fresh eyes and long histories in the organization) to share what they know, notice, and wonder.
- Discuss the concept of unconscious bias. Express vulnerability and make the issue discussable by naming how it commonly shows up for you and inviting others to do the same. Model how to identify when it's in play and how to combat it.
- Introduce the Ladder of Inference, model using it, and develop a habit, individually and collectively, of stating when you or others are running up the ladder (e.g., "Whoa, I think we may be running up the ladder. Let's slow down and check our reasoning.") Model walking back down the ladder, and ask others what evidence led them to a thought or conclusion.
- Collaboratively use Brutally Honest Truths for prospective work or current stuck places, or invite truth-naming in a more informal way, like "What one or two things do we predict are most likely to be obstacles to success based on what we know from past and current efforts?" Recognize people who speak hard truths as a way to build safety, trust, and a culture that values honesty and speaking up.

TAKEAWAYS

- People, teams, organizations, and communities all have context and history that deeply inform how they think, feel, and behave. Strategic leaders strive to understand these things and consider them before acting and as work unfolds.
- Understanding context and history requires curiosity, relationships, and inquiry.
- The goal is not to develop an exhaustive understanding of context and history, but instead to prioritize what you need to learn and then learn it from a range of sources.
- Be mindful of the biases that you and people you talk to may bring to conversations and develop ways to check your own bias.
- Understanding context and history is a dynamic process—something to do on an ongoing basis because context changes and history is always being made.

REFLECTIONS

What are your strengths, areas for development, and lingering questions about understanding context and history?

4

HARNESS POWER

"POWER" IS A WORD THAT PROVOKES STRONG EMOTIONS. Most people have a complicated relationship to power. What is your reaction to reading the word? Does your body tense up? Do you start to tap your foot, cross your arms, or sit a little taller? Do you lean in and think "Game on!" with delight?

How you think about power is integrally related to who you are, who you perceive yourself to be, and what you have experienced in your relationship to others and the systemic distribution of power. The complexities of your various identities and the families, communities, cultures, and society that you grow up in and into inform how you think about and experience power.

Understanding your own relationship to power is a prerequisite to harnessing power to lead strategically because there is an interplay between: our beliefs about power and our own power; how power dynamics play out in our interactions with others and with systems; and how we exercise our own power, leverage others' power, and share power to accomplish ambitious things.

In this chapter, we explore the *why* and *what* of power in hopes of complicating and broadening your understanding in ways that are expansive. Then we move to consider the *how*: noticing, assessing, exercising, and harnessing power. We include tools along the way to help you slow down and make strategic choices.

WHAT POWER IS

How would you define power? Jot down your definition.

____

____

Oxford Languages defines power as "the capacity or ability to direct or influence the behavior of others or the course of events" and "a right or authority that is given or delegated to a person or body."[1] Does your definition align with one of these? Does your definition further complicate things?

POWER IN OUR DAILY LIVES

We all engage with power all the time. We have things that we're trying to achieve, and we're always thinking about how to get them done. Here are just a few examples of how power shows up in our daily lives.

- How do you deal with an overtired toddler who refuses to get out of the tub?
- Whom do you sit next to at the staff meeting, and why?
- How do you support a new junior colleague who has just joined your team?
- Whom do you partner with to raise widely held concerns about how playground conflicts are handled at your child's school?
- How do you respond to a colleague who continually states the ideas of another leader without giving her credit?
- What do you do when new school system policies deny equal access to your child with a learning disability?

Your reactions or answers to these questions reveal something important about your beliefs about and relationship to power. These examples relate to power between individuals, between individuals and systems, and within organizations. Without careful attention to power, we end up with situations like the following, which reinforce the most destructive dynamics of power, when there are different options we could take that would respect people more, engage more talent, and make more progress toward purpose:

- Everyone in a meeting defers to the person with the most positional power; thus, no one speaks up about potential concerns. A proposed action moves forward and fails, wasting both resources and goodwill.
- A diligent employee works hard on something, putting in hours and energy above and beyond the workday, only to have her boss decide "to go in a different direction" or redo all the employee's work to better fit the boss's idea of what it should look like. The employee feels disheartened and is not too interested in putting her time and attention into the next thing her boss requests.
- After a long, collaborative process across multiple constituencies that results in a carefully constructed consensus, a person from the team most important to the next steps approaches the facilitator after the decision-making meeting and says, "This all sounds good, but my people aren't going to agree to this if you don't give us this [special interest of theirs]." The facilitator feels stuck, with the consensus in peril.
- An employee who has been brought into a project specifically for his expertise and perspective voices a concern. In response, he hears, "You need to get on board because this is the direction we are going. If you can't come along, we are going to pull you off the team." The employee feels coerced and unwelcome, and his insights and contributions are lost.

Power is something that both exists within ourselves and is conferred on us based on our position (social, economic, or professional), expertise, or affiliations. The power we possess within ourselves can be hard to see sometimes because society and circumstances may try to hide that truth from us. As you read this chapter, we invite you to imagine that positional and personal power are things we can build, create, and even share. Dolores Huerta, the longtime community organizer who coined the motto "¡Sí, se puede!" in 1972, describes how the motto resonates for her over fifty years later: "It means that people can have the power to change things in their lives, change things politically, and it means that every person should feel their own power and know that they can make a difference."[2] In her nineties, Huerta is still trying to help people feel and use their own power.

WHY POWER MATTERS FOR STRATEGIC LEADERSHIP

What's your answer to this question: *Why does power matter?*

When we ask leaders this question, we usually hear a range of answers that are about getting things done and about how power feels. Yes! Power is essential to accomplishing ambitious things. It is also a map of relationships and history that provides critical context to inform decision-making. Whether we're aware of it or not, power is always in play. So being intentional about seeing it, harnessing it, and trying to build more of it is a mainstay of strategic leadership. Strategic leaders understand the value of understanding where power lies, how it flows, and opportunities to influence it. They know how to tap into their own and other people's power. They know that power is always moving, it's always operating in particular contexts that shape it, and it can also be developed—within ourselves, within others, and across people.

Strategic leaders understand that there is an affective component to power. It matters how people *feel* in relationship to power because those feelings affect how willing people are to tap into their own power, how they respond in the presence of power outside themselves, and how comfortable they are with helping others see power and find and exercise their own power. That said, paying attention to the affective component of power is not enough. As one leader we know reminded us, "Feelings are critical; structures that genuinely enable the exercise of different forms of power are essential and much harder to create."

Changing the structures and norms of who gets to do what is often necessary to enable sharing power, to allow the exercise of different forms of power, and to disrupt entrenched power dynamics. This requires *understanding history* so you can explicitly try to counter it and avoid repeating it.

While power is something that each person has inside themselves, there is a developmental aspect to understanding and engaging with it. Our own trajectories as leaders and our work with other leaders have taught us that the skills of understanding and using power exist on a developmental continuum. Early in development, power is seen as hammers and nails, based on a limited understanding of what it is and how to use it. It is perceived as a tactic to employ, a move to make. This interpretation is limited and can lead to a feeling of powerlessness, which doesn't feel good and also compromises effectiveness. Many leaders' most nonstrategic moments have been when they felt least powerful or when they were least aware of their power. As understanding and sophistication grow, leaders realize that power is more like rivers and forests. It is something to watch as it flows, shape how it moves, and grow from a tiny seed. It is less about moments and moves and more about power as a dynamic force that is always in play and needs to be considered and, at times, harnessed to support progress toward purpose. As leaders we have a choice: learn about power through experience alone; or try to avert some of the hardest ways that life will teach us about power by accelerating our own development.

WHAT POWER IS: A DEEPER LOOK

Given the complexity of power, to build a nuanced understanding of it, let's look beyond the dictionary to several other definitions offered by people expert in the topic through practice and scholarship (see table 4.1). Each of these definitions captures important aspects of power.

Table 4.1 Definitions of Power

Martin Luther King Jr.	Srilatha Batliwala	Marshall Ganz	Julie Battilana and Tiziana Casciaro
"nothing but the ability to *achieve purpose* . . . the strength required to bring about social, political, and economic change."[1]	"the capacity of individuals or groups to decide or influence who *gets* what, who *does* what, who *decides* what, who *sets* the agenda."[2]	"the influence that's created by the relationship between *interests* and *resources* . . . [to] achieve the change you need or want."[3]	"the ability to *influence* another's behavior, be it through *persuasion* or *coercion*."[4]

1. Martin Luther King Jr., "Where Do We Go from Here?" (speech, Atlanta, GA, August 16, 1967), The Martin Luther King, Jr. Research and Education Institute, Stanford University, https://kinginstitute.stanford.edu/where-do-we-go-here. Italic added for emphasis.

2. Srilatha Batliwala, "All About POWER: Understanding Social Power & Power Structures," Creating Resources for Empowerment in Action (CREA), accessed August 4, 2024, 13, https://creaworld.org/wp-content/uploads/2020/07/All-About-Power.pdf. Italic added for emphasis.

3. Leading Change Network et al., "Organizing Guide: People, Power, Change" (2014), accessed August 9, 2024, https://commonslibrary.org/organizing-people-power-change/. Italic added for emphasis.

4. Julie Battilana and Tiziana Casciaro, *Power, for All* (New York: Simon and Schuster, 2021), x. Italic added for emphasis.

- Power is a means to the end of achieving purpose and vision. Civil rights leader Martin Luther King Jr. describes power as "the ability to achieve purpose," while community organizer Marshall Ganz defines the end goal of power as "achiev[ing] the change you need or want." Both signal that power can be used to drive profound change or to simply get stuff done; either way, the end goal must be clear.

- Power lies in the decisions about "who gets what, who decides what, who sets the agenda, and who does what"—social activist and women's rights advocate Srilatha Batliwala offers a concrete, practical definition that is grounding and action-oriented.
- Power is the interplay of interests and resources to achieve purpose and to influence others' behavior. Ganz highlights this asset orientation and describes engaging power as the act of trying to match shared or complementary interests with needed resources. While he has a community-organizing orientation, this idea is broadly applicable to building buy-in and ownership.
- Persuasion and coercion are ways of exerting power to influence behavior. Persuasion is about convincing people of the value of something, while coercion is persuasion with an underlying threat. Julie Battilana and Tiziana Casciaro, the organizational scholars that raise this point, acknowledge ways of exerting power that may be necessary and, when misused, can have negative effects.

Let's look at authentic examples of power in motion that show these definitions in action.

Imagine a new superintendent trying to build the capacity of the senior leadership team to champion the school system's strategy and drive its implementation. She is trying to achieve purpose. She can try to *persuade* the team to more fully assume its leadership responsibilities and build its skills by a variety of approaches: appealing to team members' individual and shared *interests*; building relationships and team norms and processes that support team members' assuming responsibility for the strategy, sharing work and updates, and supporting one another's work; and incentivizing the cross-functional collaboration needed for strategy implementation. She can also try to *coerce* the team with a variety of approaches: replacing members of the team; threatening team members who don't agree with her; and setting deadlines that require the team to work late nights or weekends.

Think of the parents who work to keep their kids' school open as it faces declining enrollment. They try to raise enrollment by talking to the families in their community about the school. They volunteer to provide extracurricular activities for students when the budget doesn't cover them. These are all acts of *persuasion* based on their *interests*. More *coercive* strategies might include pointing out to the system's leadership an inequity in the way that the system funds schools, showing up en masse at a school board meeting holding signs and dominating the public comment period of the meeting to talk about the inequities, or supporting their children walking out during the school day instead of attending classes.

Strategic leaders can move between persuasion and coercion or use a mix of them, being more coercive about nonnegotiables, as the superintendent might. Or start with persuasion and move toward coercion if persuasion is not leading to the shifts that need to happen, as the parents do. These are strategic decisions made with the context and long-term goals in mind.

A little coercion is sometimes required to encourage people to do something that they are reluctant to do, whether from fear of change, fear of failure, or something else. And it is also true that coercion often results in compliance rather than the buy-in and engagement needed for sustained improvement, which are easier to realize through persuasion.

POSITIONAL AND PERSONAL POWER

As you consider power, it's important to understand the distinction between positional and personal power (see table 4.2).[3] Parents and bosses provide great examples of people with positional power. Parents decide the rules in their households. Similarly, bosses set expectations for what their direct reports must do. In both cases, the role confers power. Parents and bosses have important information and control the flow of it. They can also offer positive consequences or remove negative

Table 4.2 Positional versus Personal Power

	Positional Power	Personal Power
Definition	Authority is conferred based on role, access to and control of information, and capacity to reward and coerce.	Authority is relational, grounded in trust gained through expertise, character, and reputation, as well as relationships with people who have more positional power.
Examples	• Principal tells teachers how they will use their collaborative planning time. • Nonprofit director makes the final decision on layoffs.	• Esteemed fourth-grade teacher shares instructional resources with her grade colleagues, who then use the resources in their teaching. • Well-connected staff person always knows about the senior team's decisions before everyone else.

ones and assign punishments. When Liz became chair of a nonprofit board, the position afforded her more power than when she was a board member. She could convene the group, sign the chief executive officer's (CEO's) contract, create a meeting agenda, and approve large contracts.

Anyone who has ever tried to do anything complex understands the limitations of positional power. You may have the most positional power in the whole family or organization—but that doesn't mean that everyone will do what you want. You may also need to rely on personal power.

A school system that Rachel works with was implementing a new elementary math curriculum. The superintendent used her positional power to say that everyone was going to do it and to provide the necessary materials and supports. Yet there is a long distance between saying and doing those things and having more than a thousand elementary teachers feel invested in and committed to this work. One day, Rachel watched the superintendent walk through the school district's headquarters, chatting with everyone she saw while barely breaking her stride. "Hi there. How is your son doing?" she said to a parent advocate. As she passed a central office staff person, she said, "Great job with the training the other day. People seemed really engaged and invested." As she passed the custodian, she said, "The floors are sparkling, Mr. Jackson." As Rachel watched faces light up, she realized the enormous personal power that the superintendent was building through her relationships. Remembering one of the superintendent's staff members telling her, "She [the superintendent] is so great. I would do anything for her," Rachel wondered how the superintendent would build on her strong foundation of personal power to support her curriculum implementation goal.

People who don't have power over things that matter to them—their schedule, their working conditions, what they do with their time—may think that if they had more positional power, life would be better. This can be a particularly common belief among people earlier in their career. But the teacher who didn't like the curriculum imposed on her becomes a principal who realizes how the district, parents, or the board constrain her power. And the principal who becomes a superintendent soon realizes that perhaps she can decree that the system will focus on instructional practices that respect and engage all learners, but that doesn't mean that the principals or the teachers will do it, or will do it in the way that she hoped. The limitations of positional power exist at every level of an organization. This is one of the reasons why having expertise and *building relationships* are so important. These can translate into personal power. Leaders with positional power often need to use personal power to drive significant changes in behaviors when people are resistant.

Questions to Identify Levels of Power

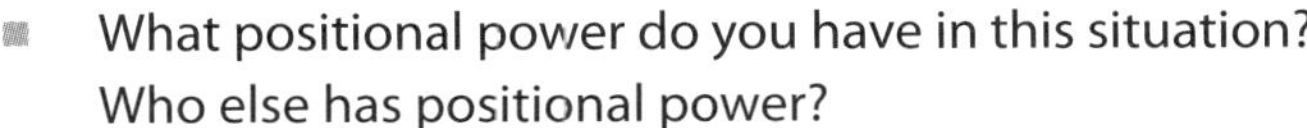

- What positional power do you have in this situation? Who else has positional power?
- What personal power do you have? Who else has personal power that is key here?
- Where do you see the limits of positional power?
- How might you tap into yours and others' positional and personal power to accomplish your purpose or vision?

NOTICE AND ASSESS POWER

A first step in harnessing power is noticing how power shows up and moves. This makes you smarter about the dynamics of power and how you might harness it.

Pay Attention

To notice power, you must pay attention. Batliwala's questions can guide your attention as you try to answer them: "Who *gets* what, who *does* what, who *decides* what, and who *sets* the agenda."[4]

The more you pay attention, the more you notice and the more nuanced your understanding becomes. This can be done on the micro level of dynamics in a meeting or the macro level of dynamics in an organization or community.

The tools of noticing are all descriptive. They are *who*, *what*, *when*, and *where* questions. When you are noticing power, the longer you can stay in the descriptive, the more you will notice. Resist moving too quickly to *why* questions. This is the tendency that the Ladder of Inference, introduced in chapter 2, is designed to address. Because your brain is a meaning-making machine, once you move to *why*—inference and judgment—you start looking for data that reinforce your hypotheses rather than staying open to a range of information that gives you a fuller picture. This is an aspect of *discerning*—you are taking in a lot of information and trying to figure out what's most important to understand power in a particular context.

Noticing is further complicated by the fact that power is always moving. Power is a dynamic organism that is continually shifting and evolving, moving between and among people. One person shares an idea that animates people and creates lots

Questions to Notice Power

These questions can be used to pay attention to how interactions, information, and ideas flow among people, particularly when they are in the same room (virtual or physical). It can also be used, in a slightly revised form (see asterisks in this list), to make sense of dynamics in a larger context (e.g., organization, cross-organizational collaboration, or the community more broadly):

- Who seems to be in charge? Sets the agenda? Drives the meeting?
- Who is talking? Do they speak for a long time or a short time? Who is silent?
- What happens when people speak?
  - Are they able to finish their thought, or does someone interrupt them? Who interrupts them?
  - When different people speak, are they responded to in different ways? If so, how? (*When observing community dynamics, look for what happens after someone/some organization speaks publicly, in media, etc.)
  - Are some people's points repeated by other people as if they were new ideas?
  - Do people build on each other's points, either explicitly by naming the person whose idea they're building on, or implicitly by adding to the content? Who shares information that is important to the topic at hand?
- What do you notice about how ideas gain momentum? (*Does this happen behind closed doors, through community channels, or in some other way?)
- Is disagreement expressed in the room? If so, who disagrees with whom, and about what? How is disagreement expressed? (*Are there signs of factions or alliances?)

of momentum. Then a colleague asks a question that makes everybody stop and reflect. Suddenly, attention shifts to the question and the questioner. As the conversation ebbs and flows in this way, the boss reminds everyone of the deadline for making a decision. Your job as a strategic leader is to track the movement and shifts of a variety of forms of power. Later, you can ask *why* and consider how to harness power to accomplish what you are working toward.

You can apply the same noticing to yourself. This helps you see *when* and *how* you engage with and assert your power, when you shy away from it, when you don't think you have any, and when you ally with others to either share power or create some collective power. Meetings, gatherings, and moments of decision-making often create opportunities to notice yourself in relationship to power.

Questions to Notice Self in Relationship to Power

- Are you in charge (of the agenda, of a decision, of resource allocation, of communication)?
- When do you speak? Do you speak for a long time or a short time? Why?
- When are you silent? Why?
- What happens when you speak? Are you able to finish your thought, or does someone interrupt you? Who interrupts you? When different people speak, are they responded to differently? If so, how?
- Do you build on others' comments with proper acknowledgment?
- If you have relevant information to the topic under discussion, do you share it?
- Do you express disagreement? If so, when do you disagree, with whom, and about what? Why? How do you express disagreement?
- How do you feel? What signals is your body sending you about how you are experiencing power in this space?

Noticing may provoke strong feelings about how power is showing up. You may be frustrated by your own challenges in taking up your power or your tendency to overexercise it. Or you may be upset to see how power flows and how that diminishes or reinforces your own power. The combination of your observations and your feelings about them provides the fuel to make changes in your own expressions of power and your efforts to catalyze the flow of power in different ways. The trick is to acknowledge your feelings without letting them impede your ability to notice, so you can deeply understand that which you want to change.

Becoming really good at noticing power is like wearing infrared glasses and being able to see in the dark. You can suddenly see light rays that were always there, but were invisible to you before. Suddenly, you have a bit of a superpower because you have access to information that is invaluable and invisible to many. People who have been denied power through traditional means are often the ones most able to see it and how it flows. Conversely, those to whom power is often given may have a harder time seeing it. Yet everyone can develop their infrared vision for power, which is particularly important when considering the experiences of people with different social identities from their own.

Slow Down

Strategic leaders don't just notice power. They manage it. Having explicit ways of managing power dynamics allows for better processes and communication, which can contribute to better outcomes. Yet it can be hard to be aware of and manage power because when you pay attention to it, you are often both an observer of and a participant in what's happening. It is hard to do both of these things simultaneously. When you really want something, feel coerced, or watch someone you care about be coerced, it is harder to stay in the noticing space. Slowing down makes this more manageable, as it gives you space to make sense of what's happening, what you think about it, and how to act strategically.

Slow Yourself Down

Slowing yourself down can help you see that the situation is not as dire as you might think when in a heightened state of emotion. When slowing down, the airplane oxygen mask directions hold true—help yourself, and then you'll be able to help others. Slowing yourself down first is crucial, particularly if you feel like you're being provoked or attacked. You cannot help slow down a group that's struggling with power if the voices in your head are shouting at you or you want to run from the room. Sometimes the way to slow yourself down is to physically slow your body, starting with your breathing. Deep breaths activate the parasympathetic nervous system, which then signals to the brain that you are safe. This calms anxiety. Intentional breathing can go a long way toward settling the fight, flight, freeze response of the amygdala, which then lets you access your thinking brain.

Using Your Breath to Slow Yourself Down

When you feel your anxiety rising, take a few deep breaths through your nose.

Even better: count 1, 2, 3, 4 on the inhale, hold breath for a count of four, and exhale through your mouth for a count of eight. Repeat as needed.

Even if something potentially risky and dangerous is unfolding, it's more about power than about you, and you need your wits about you and a calm body in order to lead from your own stores of power. You are not being attacked by a wild boar, even if it feels like it, so you don't need to defend yourself with every available tool just yet.

Help Everyone Slow Down

When people are in a group and feel under attack or it seems like others are being attacked or a decision train is hurtling down the tracks with only a few people on it, creating space and slowing down can bring down the temperature of a room or situation. That in turn may open up more possibilities or let people learn something that will help the group move forward together. Silence, reflection, writing, and physical movement can all help slow things down.

When strategic leaders slow things down, they're clear about why they're doing it. Is it about their own personal aversion to conflict? Or about bringing the temperature down in the room? Or gathering more information? Or learning something, or buying time? Or bringing people together? That awareness lets leaders match their tactic for slowing things down to their goal. Table 4.3 outlines some techniques for slowing things down in a group.

All of these can be suggested by anyone in the moment. You have to be willing to use your own power (whether personal or positional) to ask a question or make a suggestion in service of creating space (e.g., "I wonder if people might benefit from a few minutes to collect their thoughts on this topic and then share them with a colleague"). While it's possible for anyone to do these things, it is often less risky

Table 4.3 Techniques to Slow Things Down in a Group

Goal	Techniques to Slow Things Down in a Group
• Give people time to regain equilibrium. • Regulate emotions.	• Take a 5- to 10-minute break. • Take a few minutes for individual reflection. • Suggest returning to this conversation at another time. • Name what's happening. • Name what's happening and suggest an action. A lot of us seem to feel strongly about this! Let's take a quick break to breathe or move our bodies for a few minutes.
• Gather more information to better understand interests, resources, boundaries, and history. • Hear more voices.	• Invite people to share information/expertise they have. • Make space for more voices by inviting people to share who have been silent and/or who disagree. • Ask open-ended, reflective questions. What do you see as the advantages and disadvantages of starting the school day earlier? Who has a different perspective? *Or* What are some counter-ideas? Disagreement helps push our thinking and make better decisions. I'm curious what people we haven't heard from yet are thinking. *Or* Arike has been trying to get in for a while. What are you thinking, Arike?

for people with relatively more positional power or with social identities that are conferred more power in that context to use it in these ways. Those who have less risk have more responsibility to step up, open the space, and slow things down.

Everything we've described about slowing things down in a group can also be applied to a one-on-one situation—peer-to-peer, boss-to-direct reports—to good effect. When you slow things down, you are trying to create space for complexity, for differences in perspective, and for struggles to become bearable and, hopefully, productive. This space can feel scary, but it is also where important, consequential things can happen. Leading strategically requires decision-making, of course—but it also requires slowing down and resisting making decisions as a means of rescue, avoidance, or bailing yourself or others out of a situation in which power is flowing in powerful—positive, negative, or neutral—ways. Slowing down to notice what is happening is an act of power.

IDENTIFY PEOPLE'S VALUES, INTERESTS, AND RESOURCES

Once you've keenly observed how power is showing up among people, the next layer of understanding is about why people are behaving the way they are in the moment and what might be motivating this behavior. Marshall Ganz defines power as the "influence created by the relationships between interests and resources . . . [to] achieve the change you need or want."[5] If you want to build power, you need to start by understanding the interests and resources at your disposal.

Asking a couple of potent questions can help you *discern* the values, interests, and resources that you, the people you're interacting with, and the organizations represented bring to an interaction. Ganz, Battilana, and Casciaro offer guidance on this.

Tracking Power	
Battilana and Casciaro Questions	**Ganz Questions to "Track Down the Power"**
• "What do the people involved value? • Who controls access to what they value?"[1]	• "What are the interests of your constituency? • Who holds the resources needed to address these interests? • What are the interests of the individuals or organizations who hold these resources? • What resources does your constituency hold that the other individuals or organizations need to address their interests?"[2]

1. Julie Battilana and Tiziana Casciaro, *Power, for All* (New York: Simon and Schuster, 2021), 40.

2. Marshall Ganz, "Marshall Ganz' Framework: People, Power, Change," modified by Jacob Waxman, accessed August 9, 2024, 3, https://wcl.nwf.org/wp-content/uploads/2018/09/Marshall-Ganz-People-Power-and-Change.pdf.

All these questions center on the values, interests, and resources that people possess, each of which informs and/or contributes to their power. It's hard to think about values, interests, and resources all at the same time. If time is tight or tension is high, it may be hard to think about any of them. But if you can think about even one of them in the moment, it will help you think more expansively. When you have more time and space, you can elaborate on the values, interests, and resources and look at the relationships among them in order to decide what you want to do or not do.

Map Power

Mapping power, whether you're trying to anticipate how to build enough support to pursue a major initiative or how to word a delicate email, is an invaluable way to help you think about the power that is in play and how to use it to achieve your goals. Identifying Values, Interests, and Resources can help you map power among the people involved in a situation.

Identifying Values, Interests, and Resources

Fill out the table below to identify the values, interests, and resources of each of the key players in a situation that you're curious to explore. Be sure to include yourself. Add rows as needed.

What are you trying to accomplish?			
Names of Key Players	Their Interests/Values	Resources They Have	Resources They Need and Who Controls the Resources

Once you've completed the table:

1. Step back from it and see what you notice about the following points:
   - The values and interests that are shared *or* in conflict
   - The resources that people bring to this situation (Where do you see resources that could support people's interests and build power?)
   - The places where persuasion or coercion may be necessary to move forward
2. What new understandings do you have about the situation?
3. *So what?* What do your new insights suggest about how to address the issue?

Another way to map power is to think about it more holistically and in the context of support and influence. Macro power mapping is done at the level of a body of work that you're trying to move forward that requires or implicates other people and/or resources beyond your own. It is a valuable way to identify where power lies by considering the degrees and types of power your supporters and opposers possess, as well as what relationships exist between supporters, between opposers, and between supporters and opposers. This process clarifies if specific individuals/organizations have a lot of power by dint of their relationships, if a supporter might be able to influence an opposer, or if some people are creating a lot of noise but aren't actually all that influential.

Many power maps, used widely across sectors including nonprofit, organizing, and business, are variations of a simple 2x2 matrix with Opposition/Support on the x-axis and Power on the y-axis. The Power axis includes all the kinds of power discussed in this chapter.

Power Mapping

1. Identify the key stakeholders for whatever you're trying to accomplish.
2. Place each of them on the map based on your sense of the power that they can exercise and their level of support or opposition for the thing that you're trying to accomplish.
3. Use arrows to map the relationships between stakeholders to reflect where there are shared values and/or interests, people or organizations that can bridge the divide between supporters and detractors, and other interesting dynamics at play.

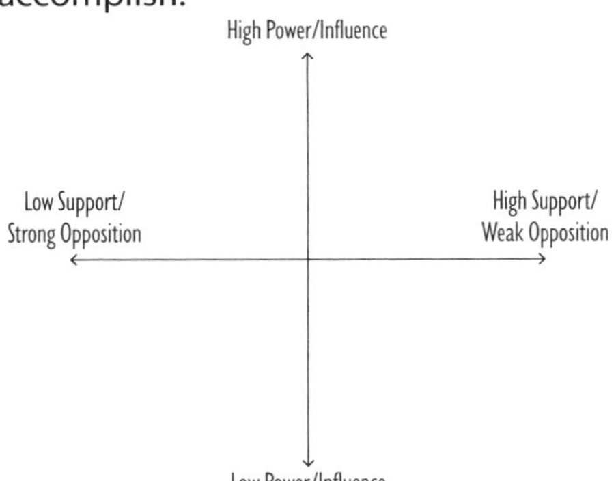

4. Reflect on the map to see what it can teach you about the following:
   a. where the opportunities lie for using power in service of your goal
   b. where stakeholders can persuade or coerce in service of your goal
   c. the extent to which the distribution of power is aligned with historically dominant groups and/or groups to which you are aligned, how that might help and/or hurt you, and where you may need to build alliances to accomplish your goals
5. *So what?* Identify next steps to take based on your analysis.

See the appendix of this book for the complete instructions for power mapping.

Some leaders prefer one power-mapping tool to the other. Some find that one fits a particular situation better than another, or one works better for an individual and the other with a group. Try them both and choose the one that's right for you in any given moment.

Questions for Mapping Power in Everyday Situations

- What motivates this person?
- Where does this person see their place in this work that we want to engage them in?
- What's the right-sized ask?
- What's a threat to this person?

Power mapping can also be done at the micro level, where the focus of analysis is something seemingly small and ordinary: how meetings are run; how an email is worded, when it is sent, and who is copied on it; and who is informed about work in progress and how. While the moments may appear small, they sometimes offer big opportunities to think about interests, resources, and influence, as well as how to build alliances. One leader we know uses these everyday opportunities to coach her team about power.

These are conversations that anyone can have, regardless of how much power or formal authority they possess. Questions are particularly helpful for more junior staff in an organization who want to do something bigger than their current position allows and need to employ someone else's power to achieve their goal. In the same way that it can be helpful to ask someone to react to your analysis in power mapping, it can also be helpful to run the results of micro mapping by someone with more experience in your current context or a different perspective from your own who can serve as a thought partner.

HARNESS POWER

If you want to accomplish complex, ambitious things, you need to move beyond assessing power to actually harnessing it, using what you've learned from your assessment. You often don't have enough power to get things done by yourself, so you need to engage others. Even if you could accomplish your goals on your own, there may be value in engaging others who hold power in order to make the work more fun, rewarding, and sustainable, as well as less dependent on you. To do this, you have to be able to use your existing power, combine and share power, and perhaps cede some of your power to create the opportunity for others to develop their power. That variety of ways to harness power is what it usually takes to get things done, ensure that progress is lasting, support healthy organizations, and address longstanding systemic challenges.

Discerning *which* of these things to do *with whom*, *when*, and *how* is the work of strategic leadership. Figure 4.1 shows the options for harnessing power on a continuum. At one end of the continuum is solo acts of power; at the other end is ceding power in service of a greater goal. As a continuum, the boundaries between each of the things are porous and you may find yourself doing more than one of them in any given situation. Strategic leaders move fluidly along this continuum, able to evaluate situations and determine which approaches will lead to the greatest impact.

Figure 4.1 Continuum of Harnessing Power

Sometimes this work is easy, and sometimes it requires deep consideration, which may include challenging your assumptions, facing your limitations and fears, and assessing risk along with your potential capacity to do harm. There are four key possibilities to explore to determine how to harness power when trying to accomplish ambitious things: understand your own purpose, power, and limitations; ally to increase power; share power; and cede power. Many situations require a combination of these approaches.

Understand Your Own Purpose, Power, and Limitations

In any situation, to lead strategically, you need to start by being clear about your purpose, your interests, and the sources and limitations of your power.

Questions for Planning to Harness Power

Strategic leaders draw on multiple sources of power. Because of the complexity of context and history, a source may be particularly powerful in one situation and less powerful in another. In addition, leaders may draw great strength internally from a power source that might be invisible to or not valued by others. Discerning leaders know what fuels them and which power to harness in different conditions. Here are examples of types of personal and positional power that you may want to consider as you plan.

Positional Power	Personal Power
• Role/position • Access to resources (money, time, people) • Ability to hire, evaluate, and fire people • Ability to persuade or coerce	• Expertise • Knowledge • Control of information • Relationships/associations • Ability to persuade or coerce • Race/ethnicity • Gender • Class • Language • Culture • Faith/spirituality • Ancestors

When planning to harness power, consider these questions:

- What are you trying to accomplish?
- What sources of power (positional and/or personal) do you *already have* that could be valuable in this situation? Do you have power sources that are not common in the situation or among the people involved, which may make them particularly valuable?
- What sources of power do you *need* to accomplish your goals but do not currently have?
- To what extent are you going to accept and use the power dynamics and structures of the organization, and to what extent are you going to push against them and try to create something different? If you're trying to create something different, what alliances do you need to build?

- What are the risks (potential bad results for you and others) of exercising your power in this context? How might you mitigate these risks?
- What's the cost (something that you or others give up or lose) of using your power? Can you afford this potential cost? Once you expend it, can you replenish it?

Strategic leaders consider these questions for both big and small things and understand that the answers are dynamic and change from one situation to the next and within the same situation over time.

Regardless of the context, asking these questions helps you *discern* several things: if you have enough power to simply move forward on your own, if you are lacking power and need to access some, or if you have power and want to share or cede it. Getting in the habit of asking such questions in daily life builds muscles for harnessing power effectively at work and beyond.

Ally to Gain More Power

Most ambitious, complex things—in other words, the things that require strategic leadership—need more than one person's power in motion. Mapping power helps you figure out who may be important partners in your pursuit of a specific purpose. When the math director and the supervisor of schools decide to partner up to prepare principals to lead the math work in their schools, they are combining their resources based on shared interests and increasing their collective power and the potential for impact. Imagine power as a pie that grows bigger through alliances.

Strategic leaders are intentional about whom they ally with and how. Whether you are the person or organization courting a potential ally or the one being courted, there are questions that you can ask to *discern* the value add of the alliance and to be intentional and strategic about developing it.

There are questions for when you are considering courting a potential ally and need to think through the *why*, *who*, *how*, and *what* in more detail.

Questions to Consider Before Engaging Allies

When you're in a situation in which you can't accomplish everything on your own and/or where alliances will make the process and the outcome more successful, the following are questions to consider:

Why

- Why do you need/want to ally? What exactly is the purpose that you hope they will join you in?

Who

- Who could be key allies in this situation? Who has essential sources of power that you need to accomplish your goal? Who has crucial contextual and/or historical understanding and/or life experience (e.g., elder in a community, longtime employee)?
- What are their interests and resources, and how do those relate to your own?
- Who is best positioned to make the ask of which ally? (Do you need an ally to invite another ally?) Why?

How

- Is there an easier place to start building a relationship with a potential ally because you share something with the ally that will facilitate building trust?
- What do you know about how specific potential allies like to engage and communicate, and how can you be in relationship with them in a way that works for them?
- If you have more positional power, resources, or perceived influence than the potential ally, how might you persuade rather than coerce? (How do you show them that you value what they uniquely bring and their role is important for accomplishing this meaningful thing that you are trying to do?)

What

- Are you clear about what you're asking the potential ally for and what's in it for them? How might you mitigate any potential risks to them?
- What are the potential risks to you if the ally says yes (e.g., large time investment required for the partnership, perceptions that people inside or outside the organization may have, expectations that the allies will have of you)?
- What's your backup plan if this ally doesn't want to partner with you?

And there are also questions to ask when being courted. These questions focus primarily on *why* you might want to or not want to ally with the *who* courting you, with a little bit of *how* and *what* in the mix as you consider risks and consequences.

Questions to Consider When Being Pursued as an Ally

- What do you gain from this alliance (e.g., positional or personal power, influence, access, prestige, relationships, new experiences)? How might this alliance benefit your organization and community?
- Would this alliance position you/your organization well for work that you anticipate taking up in the future?
- What are the potential risks of this partnership (e.g., what might you lose or how might you be damaged by it)? How might choosing not to ally carry a cost for your organization and/or community? For whom would the cost be greatest?

Allying isn't always easy. By definition, you are joining in a partnership in which each party brings clear, discernable power to the table with the goal of combining that power to build a greater collective power that is mutually beneficial. Allying can be a delicate and sometimes uncomfortable dance. One party may be more enthusiastic about the partnership than the others. One party may have something that the other one really needs, while the benefit of allying is less clear to the one who has it. The level of shared values may not be as high as the level of shared interests. And all that is before you layer in complexities of history and identity. People tend to trust more easily people with whom they share identities and interests. Thus, power tends to beget power. To disrupt these entrenched power dynamics, you have to be thoughtful about with whom you engage and how.

Sometimes strategic leaders ally with people with whom they fundamentally disagree on important things. Maybe you hold your nose to get the endorsement of a colleague, the vote of a board member, or money from a funder with whom you don't see eye to eye. Allying with people with whom you disagree requires a willingness to hold complexity (*I don't really want to partner with her, but she gets me access to power that's essential to achieving my goal, so I will*), and clarity about where the lines are that you won't cross and where they are dotted (e.g., when you will say, "This is a bridge too far and I can't continue," and when you will say to yourself, "I'm going to take his money and work for children"). Early in Rachel's career, a mentor told her, "You need to decide if you want to be right or effective." The distinction was a revelation—one that she still thinks about all the time, particularly when she is holding the complexity of imperfect choices for building alliances to harness power. At the most basic level, allies need to do a few things: understand and agree on what they are allying on, commit to their part in the alliance, and trust one another relative to their points of collaboration.

Share Power

Sharing power is about making your power available to others and/or you having access to others' power. While allying helps enlarge the pie, sharing power is about sharing a piece of the pie with someone (or some organization) to achieve greater impact.

Sharing power is a way to maximize resources, interests, and impact. You share power when you bring your unique expertise to a colleague's problem and when you stop holding all the resources and decision-making rights. Opportunities to share power range from small to monumental. Who sets the agenda (Batliwala's question)? Who has access to and discretion over resources? Does the person with the most positional power in a meeting talk first or last in a discussion of an important topic? Who decides who is included and excluded? Who makes the final decision? Sharing power is a liberatory act. And, like the continuum on which it sits, sharing power can be pursued to different degrees.

When thinking about sharing power, strategic leaders analyze the risk of sharing power or not sharing it. Setting guardrails can mitigate risk and help clarify what power is being shared and what isn't. For example, a school district decides to tackle high school redesign by deeply engaging school staff and community members in the redesign work to build greater ownership and investment in hopes of increasing the likelihood of success. The goal is sustained, substantive engagement rather than hosting a focus group or two. Because the district is committed to ensuring that the redesign work reflects the research on effective high schools and strong planning practices, it establishes guardrails for the community-based planning process that address the district's non-negotiables and provides every school with a facilitator to guide them through the planning process. The district holds tight the planning process and a few non-negotiables, while leaving the decision-making that comes out of the planning up to the school teams.

Cede Power

Ceding is about actually giving up some power. Using Batliwala's framing, ceding power is about changing who *gets* what, who *does* what, who *decides* what, and who *sets* the agenda.[6] Sometimes you cede power in very specific ways because the risk is low and the rewards can be high. An example is school-based instructional leadership teams with decision-making authority, which are comprised of teacher leaders and school administrators. The principal cedes some power to the team in order to bring more expertise into decision-making about the school. Other times, you cede power and the risk is higher, but you do it in the service of a greater ideal. The more power you have, the more likely you'll be perceived positively for ceding some of it. Conversely, the less power you have, the more your decision to cede it may be questioned and negatively interpreted as a commentary on your skills. Strategic leaders navigate these dynamics and do their best to name and disrupt them.

Questions for Ceding Power

In any situation where power is in play, there are often opportunities to cede it. Doing so can build relationships and trust, tap previously unnoticed or undervalued sources of personal power, and create space for others to empower themselves and exercise power. This is essential to disrupt longstanding dynamics that aren't serving people, processes, and outcomes well. However, it is not a neutral act. It can be both amazing and risky for all involved. Here are some questions to consider in order to make your assumptions explicit, analyze benefits and risks, think through trade-offs, and be clear about what else might be needed for success:

- What are the good things that could happen if you cede power?
- What are you most worried about? What are the worst things that can happen if you cede power (e.g., lose access to/discretion over resources and decision-making, become less able to prevent unintended harm to the very people whom you are trying to help)?
- When you weigh the downsides versus the upsides, what do you notice? What might you put in place to encourage the good things and catch/curtail any bad things?
- What are your non-negotiables?
- Is there something you can cede that really matters to someone else and isn't that important to you?
- If you are unable or unwilling to cede the thing that someone (or some organization) most wants, do you want to offer anything else as consolation or communicate why you can't/won't cede?

Note: All these questions can also be asked regarding sharing power.

When you cede power, by intentionally giving your power to people who don't have that particular power in the particular context, you help create the conditions for them to empower themselves. Ceding power means that the power is now theirs and they get to choose how to harness it. There are a common set of things that keep people from ceding power and empowering others: fear that power is a zero-sum game—that is, if I give you some of my power, I won't have enough left for myself; fear of what others will do with that power; and assumptions about what other people are and aren't capable of. These are further examples of how fear and anxiety can impede strategic leadership. This can be particularly fraught when power is in play. And power is *always* in play.

Much like other ways of harnessing power on our continuum, sharing and ceding power can happen in the same context, at the same time. In a household, maybe one partner cooks while the other buys the groceries and does the dishes. The grocery shopper cedes power to cook, while also bringing their resource of time to get the food and clean up. Conversely, the cook cedes the power of shopping while bringing the resource of cooking. In a school, a principal may share power by planning the professional development day with the instructional coach and two teacher leaders and then cede the facilitation to the teacher leaders. Sharing and ceding power are often about creating space for other voices to be heard and other ways of doing things to be considered.

When we and other leaders we know look back on what our younger leader selves would have done—or actually did—and how that compares to what we would do now, we see an evolution in our relationship to positional and personal power over time. Often, the more recent stories involve seeing power as dynamic rather than static, nuanced rather than binary, and shifting from a scarcity to an abundance mindset. We continue to develop a deeper awareness of how systemic power is more accessible to and less risky for those of us who have dominant social identities and/or positional power, the importance of allying with people for whom the risks of exercising power are higher to reduce those risks, and specific strategies to do so. We are less likely to see power as a fixed commodity, but, instead, something inside everyone—something that can be created, something to embrace rather than fear, and something to achieve purpose and realize oneself with the full depth and breadth of possibility.

Building Others' Capacity to Harness Power

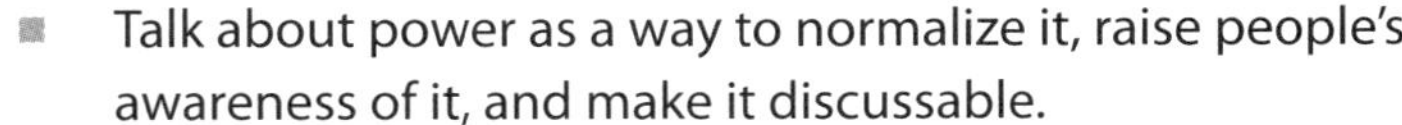

- Talk about power as a way to normalize it, raise people's awareness of it, and make it discussable.
- Invite people to think about the different kinds of power they possess and to think about the interplay between identities and power.
- Use power-mapping tools with colleagues or a team both to build awareness of power and to plan work strategically with power in mind. Invite people to share power maps to get feedback and support everyone's learning.
- Coach individuals or teams to think strategically about power when there is work that they can't do on their own that requires them to engage other people by asking questions like the following: "Tell me how you're going to approach that. Who needs to be at the table? What motivates these people? Where do they see their place in this work that we want to engage them in? What's the right-sized ask? What's a threat to them?"

TAKEAWAYS

- Power is about who gets what, who decides what, who sets the agenda, and who does what; how those things can be aligned to interests and resources to achieve purpose; and the role of persuasion and coercion in the process.
- Power is always flowing. There are opportunities to engage power on a daily basis.
- There is both positional and personal power: positional power is often anchored in a role, while personal power is tied to personal expertise or is conferred based on relationships with people who have power.
- Strategic leaders notice, assess, and track power continually in both micro and macro contexts; they understand their own power and are intentional about when and how to use it.
- Strategic leaders look for opportunities to ally to build increased power, share power, and cede power—sometimes when it's required for the work, and sometimes when it's less essential for near-term goals but important for sustainability or shifting general power dynamics.
- Becoming more powerful and more aware of and comfortable with power is a developmental process.
- At times, we all need others to help us find and use our power well, or to be that person for someone else.

REFLECTIONS

What are your strengths, areas for development, and lingering questions about harnessing power?

5

THINK BIG, ACT SMALL, LEARN FAST

IN ANY AMBITIOUS THING WE DO, whether planning a trip, hosting a family reunion, helping every child learn to read, or supporting first-generation college students to succeed, there are a lot of small steps to take. We make a plan, organize resources, adjust to small curveballs, communicate the essentials, make decisions about how to react when the conditions change, and learn from prior experience. And, there is always some big idea (adventure! family connections! literacy and freedom! access and opportunity!) that anchors, and hopefully motivates, the people responsible for the small steps. If we're clear on the big idea, it's easier to adjust the small things, especially if we are figuring them out as we go. If the big idea of the family reunion is to bring together as many family members as possible, there may be flexibility about the location based on what will make it possible for the greatest number of people to join. And the activities to happen as part of the reunion will be determined along the way, based on who says they're attending and what they're interested in.

In the last twenty-five years of education reform, an enormous amount of time, money, and energy has been invested in changing schools and schooling. Yet there has been very little improvement. Why? Improving schooling is complex, and of course, the answer to this question is multifaceted. But in its simplest form, the answer is *too much and not enough*.

Too much of doing too many things. Not enough purpose. Not enough learning.

The antidote to this "too much-not enough" syndrome is to focus on what's most important, move to purposeful action, and get better as we go. In other words: *think big, act small, learn fast*.

WHY THINKING BIG, ACTING SMALL, AND LEARNING FAST MATTERS

Thinking big helps leaders hold the big picture and stay anchored in purpose. There is a *why*, either implicit or explicit, in the big picture: because we want to develop readers who can learn on their own, because we want to prepare young people for the future, because our community is stronger when we all thrive.

Thinking big also helps us be more flexible about the *how* and the *what* and the *who*. If we're executing small things without holding the big picture, it's easy to be overly focused on what's right in front of us, forgetting that it is part of a larger equation. Instead, we can ask, "What's the bigger thing this is connected to, and how might we move toward that?" A stance of flexibility helps us respond nimbly to different contexts, conditions, and needs, as well as unanticipated challenges. It also lets us take advantage of positive twists and turns. Are we willing to adapt when conditions or feedback suggest that's necessary? Are we open to a compliment about something we did that helps us see what to build from toward the big thing we're trying to do?

Acting small helps us to actually make things happen, to not get overwhelmed by the complexity of the big thing, and to use our resources with intention. Acting small offers an alternative to the common challenge of spending lots of energy planning and less energy trying things.

One of the main advantages to acting small is that it sets us up, both tactically and emotionally, to learn. On the tactical side, acting small makes it easier to track what we tried, what it took to try it, and how it went. This helps us see if our small acts are moving us toward the North Star of our big thinking and where refinements and adaptation are needed.

Emotionally, when we act small, it feels less risky if things go awry because the impact is smaller and it's easier to adapt in response. When the stakes are lower, human nature is to be less worried about things going wrong. The amygdala (aka the "lizard brain") stays dormant rather than swamping the analytic part of the brain with fight-or-flight signals (aka panic). The combination of clarity and calm supports learning, both along the way and after action.

Learning is key to improvement. Learning fast helps us be more responsive and make adjustments that move us more quickly toward the North Star. It also contributes to a culture where it's okay not to be perfect and learning is the expectation—this is both helpful for improvement and important in education, where the core work is, in fact, learning. When the adults are learning, the children are more likely to be learning, too.

The combination of holding the big picture, focusing on small efforts that are aligned to the big picture, learning from our work, and feeding the learning back into our efforts ensures that work is substantive, meaningful, manageable, continually improving, and moving us toward our broader goals.

THE WHAT AND HOW OF THINKING BIG, ACTING SMALL, AND LEARNING FAST

Think Big

"Think big" means to keep the big picture in mind. Are you becoming the most literate community in the South, engaging youth who haven't been coming to school, reimagining core programs, helping formerly incarcerated young people develop skills, connecting agencies across a community to serve the most vulnerable people, or some other ambitious and meaningful effort?

What is the big thing you are working on? "Big" means something that is ambitious, worthwhile, and requires lots of smaller actions to make it happen. Whether the big thing is articulated as a measurable goal or as a more abstract concept (running a marathon versus being healthy), it's big when it's both within your sphere of influence and requires a deep investment of time, energy, or resources to accomplish. It's often something that you don't entirely know how to do yet. This is the "purpose" discussed in chapter 1. There are usually many ways to accomplish it, some of which may not be clear at the outset.

Thinking big can show up in words like *vision*, *mission*, and *goal*. Without getting bogged down in semantics and the variety of ways that those different words are used in practice, try anchoring on *big* as the North Star—the audacious something that you're trying to accomplish. It is the thing that you are both working toward and guided by.

Thinking big clarifies your ambition and helps inspire you and others to work toward it. Maybe you're not that interested in unlearning how you taught kids to read for years or in doing something that you just don't like to do, but when it's framed within a bigger purpose that resonates—ensuring all third graders can read and comprehend content-rich texts that build knowledge—that's enough to help you try. Instead of strength training being a "should" do, what if it were a pathway to having a choice-filled, active life as you age? Instead of avoiding a conversation with elders who are resisting help, what if it were an opportunity to partner with people you love to support their independence *and* get the care they need to ensure that independence? What if a disagreement with a friend, partner, or colleague were an opportunity to deepen a relationship and learn rather than a threat to that relationship? Without thinking big, it can be easy to get lost in the stuff immediately in front of you, which may be hard, distasteful, emotional, or all-consuming. But thinking big reminds you *why* it's worth doing.

Sometimes the "big" thing is implied or lives in the heads of senior leaders without translating to other parts of an organization. Maybe a leader articulated it once or twice, but it's not spoken about explicitly over and over to remind people. Or maybe people assume that they share an idea of the big thing because they're engaged in the same small thing. But the two are not always connected! People often engage in the same small steps with different notions (or no notion) of the big thing. Are you having a big adventure, or are you trying to see all the popular tourist sites on your vacation? Are you engaging families as meaningful partners in their children's development, or are you having a bunch of events and hoping people show up? Are you wanting to challenge each child to reach their full potential or are you restructuring the high school? Naming the big thing creates room for possibilities and can motivate ourselves and others.

Act Small

"Act small" means trying things on a small scale of time, effort, and/or people. The small things are related to the big thing and are significant in their potential for impact. They are not just random things you are doing—they are things that, when added together, are going to move you closer to your big goals. Often, the synergy of pursuing a series of small things creates a whole that is greater than the sum of its parts. Small is an activity, and big is the purpose behind that activity. "Small" can look many different ways:

- Doing things at a small scale to learn and then refine and scale up what seems most promising.

    - You are not just trying something with three volunteers or ten students (*small*). You are testing a new approach that can be applied more widely (*big*).
- Taking small steps that help you move toward a bigger goal.
    - You are not just having faculty meetings (*small*) because you have times booked on the calendar. You are building your community and helping adults learn what they need to develop students as mathematicians (*big*).
    - This week, you are going to the gym or a run with a friend three times and getting seven hours of sleep each night (*small*) because you want to take care of yourself physically and emotionally (*big*).
- Breaking a big thing into many small parts so it is less overwhelming and more manageable.
    - You are planning a trip by figuring out the transportation, lodging, and any advanced tickets you need for things you want to do (*small*) so you have a relaxing and fun vacation and return rejuvenated (*big*).
    - You are trying to build students' vocabulary and reading comprehension by deploying paraprofessionals in different ways, supporting teachers to learn one new skill at a time and practice it, and integrating more nonfiction texts in science and social studies (*small*) so students will be fluent readers who know that reading is a gateway to learning (*big*).

Acting small is hard because it requires discipline and trust. The discipline to narrow, to sequence, to pace, to not do everything simultaneously, and to pursue things with intention. Sometimes the small actions you choose are the only ones you can take within your sphere of control. You don't have the positional power and alliances required to sequence and pace a series of small actions that will lead to big impacts. So you act in a disciplined manner by narrowing your focus and homing in on a small action you can take that you know will make a positive contribution all by itself. You may do this hoping that your efforts will get a flywheel spinning and create the conditions for others with authority to pursue related small acts that maximize the likelihood that collectively, you'll get closer to achieving the big thing.

When you do have the *positional and personal power* to pursue lots of things, your discipline keeps you from doing so. It helps you be intentional, starting with a small action that is a warm lead into the pursuit of the big thing. And, you anticipate the other small actions that will connect to and/or build on the first small action to create something bigger and more impactful. You support the people who can help lead the pursuit of the small acts. You think about the pace and sequence of pursuing these things rather than pursuing them all at once.

Trust relates to your belief in the things that you choose to focus on and the idea that a series of these small things will add up to a big impact. And it is also related to your trust in the power of action to make a difference. Trust supports you to act with intention. This is where *discerning* comes in. Once you've done your data and root cause analyses (*discerned to understand problems*), you may identify a number of different things that you could do to respond to those findings. Many of those are likely small things. Using the process of *discerning to choose right action*, you determine which of these things you want to bet on, connected to the purpose that you have discerned. This helps with narrowing and not doing too much and builds your confidence that focusing on these things will have the impact you are aiming for.

The Difference Between Acting Small and Acting Big

Acting big is the opposite of acting small and is another way to pursue our big thinking. Acting big is: changing an entire curriculum quickly, launching a new program for one hundred people, holding a communitywide event with twenty-five organizations, or exercising every day in a week. There is a place for acting big—it usually comes after an accumulation of acting small when you have a strong base from which to act. For example, a school system we know moved quickly to flexible groupings across grades for math, which was possible only because they already had flexible groupings across grades for reading and the systems and structures that supported that move. Another school system mapped out its curriculum adoption in phases—starting a pilot in a few classrooms in one school and then spreading across the district over three years, developing a corps of teachers who were effective and confident with the new curriculum and could support other teachers. A different school system asked teachers to try one unit of a new curriculum, while heavily supporting their professional learning, and otherwise had them continue what they had been teaching. The next year, they added two more units. And so on.

When trying to determine if something that you're considering pursuing is a big or small action, consider the size/scale of the action, the time that it will take, and the capacity required to do it. Big actions generally touch more people, take more time, and require more capacity. When an action is smaller, it usually makes small demands on at least two of these variables. There are no hard-and-fast rules about what differentiates a small act from a big one. Think about momentum. If you can pursue an action quickly, with relative ease, and achieve a good outcome, it is likely a small action. See table 5.1 for a comparison of thinking big, acting small, and acting big.

Table 5.1 Comparison of Think Big, Act Small, and Act Big

Think Big	Act Small	Act Big
Meet the needs of all learners through differentiated support.	• Introduce assessments that make it easy to identify who would benefit from differentiated support. • Implement small-group practices that support differentiation.	• Implement a multitiered system of support in every school.
Recruit high-quality teachers who reflect the communities the school serves.	• Provide principals guidance on interview questions and a school-based screening process. • Recruit from nontraditional preparation pathways.	• Select and implement a teacher screening, selection, and onboarding software platform. • Increase access to the teaching profession by opening up the pipeline beyond certification requirements.
Improve organizational culture.	• As part of staff meetings, institute staff sharing promising practices and problems of practice. • Share meeting facilitation.	• Revamp job descriptions, hiring, supervision, evaluation, and promotion practices to highlight contributions to organizational culture.

If, as you read table 5.1, you find yourself thinking, *It's in the "act small" column, but that would actually be a big action in my organization* (or vice versa), you're probably right. Context matters as you try to discern the size of an act. What is already in place in an organization can make something be a small act in one organization but a big act in a different organization where there is no foundation on which to build.

There is a difference between thinking big and acting big. Thinking big helps us think about possibilities, interconnections, and purpose. It doesn't focus at the level of action. It is the North Star in the night sky, guiding a traveler. While thinking big asks you to think expansively, acting big places a great demand on the organization that is often underestimated. You don't start training for a marathon with a twenty-mile run; that's something you build up to. You don't change learning by installing a new program and expecting results in days or weeks.

Yet there are big things that can't easily be broken down, especially at a system level (e.g., curriculum adoption). The specific elements of the implementation can be broken down into smaller things, but they need to be pursued simultaneously. Doing all the small things simultaneously is what makes it acting big and hard. You have to understand what all the small parts are that add up to the big, you have to align all your resources, and you can't do much else. You figure out all the pieces, and then ask, "Can we do it? Do we want to?" Big things are often beyond the organization's current capacity to do well, in part because the organization is doing a bunch of other things, too. The same holds true for individuals—you could act big if you cleared the decks on everything else, but that's not usually how life works, which is why acting small is more feasible. If you're going to act big, you can do it well with only one or two things. Moving from nothing to acting big may be briefly exhilarating, but it is usually unsustainable and sometimes causes injury that takes a while to recover from.

Questions to Ask to Discern Small Actions and Big Actions

- How long will it take to do?
- How radical of a shift is this for how many people?
- Does it feel like you can start immediately? If not, what (and how many) steps need to precede this one to set it up for success?

Sometimes, out of urgency, people try to do too many things or try to tackle too big a thing without taking small steps first. But that can backfire and lead to the "too much, not enough" problem that turns best intentions into predictable failures. This is particularly true for complex challenges with multiple contributing factors. For example, high principal turnover might be in part because they don't have all the training they need for their jobs, so an online professional development series might support them some. The high turnover might also be because they feel isolated or because they are trying to do too many things (which is reinforced by the school system's tendency to overextend), in which case professional development won't entirely solve the problem and may even exacerbate it in the short term. Acting small would mean *discerning to choose right action* by looking at all the contributing factors, picking one that is easy to pursue and high impact to start with, and then addressing other factors over time.

Acting small has many advantages over acting big and "too much"–ness:

- More manageable
- Less risky
- Fewer resources required
- Easier to start
- Builds efficacy
- Higher potential for learning and adjustment

Learn Fast

The act of doing things is not enough to achieve an ambitious, "think big" purpose. Many years ago, Liz was excited to study with Richard Elmore about instructional improvement. She kept talking about "change," and Richard kept asking, "Yes, but how do you know whether the change is an *improvement*?" This lesson has stuck with Liz ever since. While it is true that accomplishing an ambitious purpose often requires change, it is not always true that change leads to progress toward purpose. This is where learning fast comes in. The problem is not that well-meaning, mission-driven leaders aren't working hard enough. But are they learning enough?

Improvement work over the last twenty-five to fifty years across many sectors has been grounded in approaches that go by many names, including Plan-Do-Study-Act (PDSA), Six Sigma, and Total Quality Management (TQM). Current popular versions include design-based thinking, processes grounded in improvement science, agile processes, and various data-based improvement approaches. While these processes vary in the particulars, they share several fundamental characteristics: try something, learn, adjust based on learning, and try again.

There is no magic "right" process. And it doesn't really matter which one you choose or whether you choose an existing one or design your own. What matters is that you learn. To learn, you have to try something.

If you ask people where they get stuck in the process of improvement, the answer is not usually in the early stages of gathering evidence or planning what to do. People get stuck in doing, adjusting, and trying again.

Most improvement processes are pictured as circles or cycles, but in practice, most people and organizations act in straight lines. Try something, try something, and try something else, either all at the same time or in rapid succession, with no links between efforts. Learning is what is required to bend that line back on itself: try something, learn something, and try something else *based on that learning*. Learning is the key to getting better more efficiently. It helps focus people's time and energy in more promising ways, and it acts as an accelerant toward a bigger goal. Figure 5.1 juxtaposes the typical approach with a learning approach.

Figure 5.1 Improvement Process: Typical Approach (a) versus Learning Approach (b)

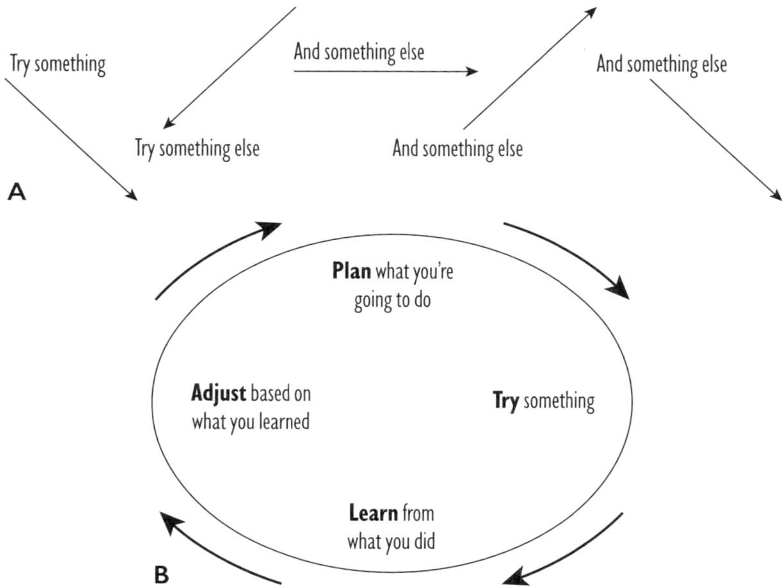

When you think big but act small, you can have more and faster learning cycles. You can have repetition with adjustment. If you're doing something only once a year, it takes a longer time to get better at it than if you do it multiple times in a day or week. When Liz and colleagues first started doing data-based inquiry work in what would become Data Wise over twenty years ago, they worked with schools and school systems to do one thoughtful inquiry cycle in a year. Some schools spent a year planning for the work and then did a cycle the next year. This usually meant that they completely ran out of gas by the time they got to the action part of the cycle—and they definitely didn't have the energy for learning from what they tried and adjusting accordingly! Once schools started doing much shorter cycles, across a few weeks or a month, they started seeing improvement because they could try more things and have those things build on one another, and then they got better at getting better—the process of improvement itself got easier as they practiced.

Often this learning mindset requires a reframing of a binary mindset of good/bad to a more expansive and nuanced focus on improvement. For example, one leader we know describes what happened when her team was making changes to the compensation structure for teachers: "The evaluators kept wanting to ask teachers about how good the system was at doing X and Y. We had to really reframe to pose the question of whether the new system was *better* at doing X and Y than what it had been before." This leader and her colleagues wanted to know if they were getting any better at it over time—if the shifts that they were making mattered for the improvement that they wanted.

Asking and answering the questions: "Are we getting better over time?" "Why are we improving/not improving?" "What are we learning?" and "How can we accelerate our improvement?" are crucial as part of acting small and learning fast. These questions address what are often the weakest parts of continuous improvement processes: gathering and analyzing data and evidence after you take action to see how it went and the impact of it; and then adjusting your action based on what you learn. This pausing to learn, fine tuning, and choose the next action is a form of *discernment* that drives improvement. Without it, you run the risk of getting stuck in a loop of constant action without *discerning* the value add of your actions and whatever else may be necessary to improve.

In the K–12 education sector, there is a tendency to rely on measuring inputs and lagging indicators, neither of which provides fine-grained information needed for real-time, mid-course corrections of small actions and for signaling what is the next small action to take. If you really want to know how things are going, the on-the-ground work of students, teachers, and school leaders often has the most to teach. This is the "street data" that Shane Safir and Jamila Dugan champion.[1]

A simple adaptation of the Data Tracker we introduced in chapter 1 can be used to support the critical steps of gathering and analyzing data and evidence from small acts, and then using that information to direct refinements or new actions. Often the hardest part is to decide what data and evidence to use. This chart is designed for you to list the data and evidence you will collect to assess both implementation and impact of the small acts you pursue.

	Implementation (Did we do what we said we would do? How well did we do it?)	**Impact (What happened as a result of what we implemented?)**
Street data (low altitude; describes the experiences of individuals proximate to our improvement efforts)		

Once you've filled out the template, step back and consider the chart holistically. Consider the following questions:

1. Do we have good representation from all of the key stakeholders?
2. Do we have a good mix of Count, See, Hear, and Feel data and evidence?
3. Do we need any additional information to deepen our understanding to support us to decide on the next action to take?
4. What do the data and evidence tell us about how well we implemented our actions and how impactful they were?
5. What are our biggest learnings as we review the chart?
6. With all the analysis in mind, the final question to ask is: *What do we need to do next?*

In addition to learning by doing, you can accelerate your learning curve by gathering what other people beyond your context have learned through research and lived experience (see *discerning to choose right action* in chapter 1). As you try things, you may find that you aren't making as much progress as quickly as you'd like. This is a good signal to look beyond what you're already trying to see how other knowledge sources could inform your next action. One advantage of acting small is being able to go deep, which includes tapping external resources to inform how you address complex problems.

Questions for Thinking Big, Acting Small, and Learning Fast

Wherever you sit, and however much power you think you have, you will be more strategic if you think in multiple directions at once. You can ask questions like the following:

- What is the big idea or larger goal to which this small project or activity is connected? Why do this small thing? How is this connected to the big ambitious idea or larger goal that you are trying to achieve?
- What are the smaller steps to get to the big idea or larger goal, or a smaller version of it?

- How audacious are you in terms of what's possible, and how audacious can you be?
- What small thing could you do to try something and learn?
- What lessons can you harvest from your own and others' experiences and fold back into your work?
- What knowledge sources beyond your experience can you tap into to help you answer questions to which you don't yet know the answer?

Lessons to Keep in Mind

As one principal we know said about thinking big, acting small, and learning fast, "This sounds so simple! But if it's so simple, why aren't we already doing it?" Great question! It's simple in theory, but in practice, the inertia of people and systems continually reinforces "too much doing, not enough purpose, not enough learning" approaches. Fortunately, we can learn from the last twenty-plus years of improvement efforts and try not to repeat the same mistakes.

Means versus Ends

One danger in being improvement-focused is confusing means and ends. It is easy to get so focused on the process of learning and improving, particularly if the habits, mindsets, and skills are new or unfamiliar, that the means becomes the end—in short, the *how* becomes the *why*. You might, for example, become so focused on how meetings are run and whether they have all the necessary components that you lose sight of whether the work of the meeting is meaningful and important. This can also take the guise of "becoming a learning organization" or "doing PLCs" (education shorthand for "professional learning communities") or using data or any other process that is supposed to help with improvement becoming *the thing* that you are trying to accomplish.

Those processes may be helpful for building relationships and culture, for learning, or for discerning—but they are not the same as *why* you are doing those processes. An intense focus on process can obscure purpose and runs the risk of making the process formulaic rather than dynamic. Process matters, of course. It is intricately tied up with outcomes and the way that people experience and feel about something, which is why strategic leaders pay attention to process and understand that process and purpose are related. Being clear about purpose makes it easier to hold process more lightly and flexibly to ensure that the process serves the purpose. For example, one leader we know stopped using all tools and protocols in her collaborative work because they had become formulaic and distracting from the substantive tasks at hand. Once she reconnected with *why* she was using them (which for her included both having a process that engages multiple voices and achieving the outcomes that she hoped to accomplish), she started using tools and protocols again with her colleagues in service of that *why*.

Tolerance for Failure and Uncertainty

People are often working really hard and are worried that they will fail to help people they serve and care about, fail to deliver on their own or someone else's aspirations, or fail to be as good as other people think they are. This four-letter "f" word is closely tied to another one: "fear." In combination, they hinder learning. Ironically, fear of failing often leads to the very mindsets and actions that increase the odds of failing—doing too much, with not enough intention and openness to learning.

Failing can be essential for learning, particularly when it is seen as expected and necessary rather than a commentary on people's value or worth. And yet, both individually and collectively, people and organizations tend not to have a high tolerance for it. Sometimes communities and organizations have a lower tolerance for failure from particular people (e.g., an outsider; someone of a different racial, ethnic, or gender identity; someone pushing hard on the status quo), which is palpable and constrains those people. And sometimes, the fear of failing can be more widely held and distributed.

Here's where acting small comes in. If you try something small, failing is less high stakes, and it's easier to figure out what went well and what didn't go quite right. If you act big beyond your capacity, many things can and likely will go awry. Sometimes the sheer number of things makes it hard to track them, much less learn from and address them.

Some leaders don't like to use the word "fail" at all, or they prefer to emphasize the learning part. They say things like, "Fail forward" or "Never a failure. Always a lesson." (Rihanna even has a tattoo with these words!) Strategic leaders celebrate failures for the lessons offered that can't be learned any other way.

Of course, heaps of failure are not healthy or good. As one leader we know said, "You can only fail so much—even if you are learning." As a leader, you have to know what sort of tolerance for failure you're operating in (or creating) and think about how much you can, want to, and need to push on that to create enough room to try and to learn. You can also deploy the approaches from earlier chapters to help learn early and mitigate failure—drawing on multiple kinds of evidence to discern how things are going, listening deeply to a variety of stakeholders to understand how things are unfolding rather than waiting for more lagging indicators, understanding context and history, and paying attention to power dynamics.

Closely connected to fear of failure is discomfort with uncertainty. Fear of failure is often rooted in uncertainty. Is this going to go well? Or will it be a disaster? A desire for clarity and certainty can lead you down wrong paths, or at least not the most strategic ones. A key challenge for strategic leaders is this: How do you build your own and other people's tolerance for uncertainty?

One way to start is by naming the uncertainty. One leader we know approaches naming it this way: "Here is what we know. Here is what we don't know. Here's what data we're going to collect along the way to help us figure things out." This is counterintuitive and may even seem risky in some contexts. *As a leader, aren't I supposed to project confidence and certainty?* Many leaders often pretend that there isn't uncertainty. But this doesn't make the uncertainty go away! There is always uncertainty. Name it. This will make some people nervous. That's okay. You just don't want them to be too nervous to do whatever their part is. Naming it does not make the uncertainty more likely to happen. It's just giving a name to the shadow lurking in the corner, inviting it to come into the light, and making it discussable.

Of course, what you name internally might be a bit different from what you name externally. Imagine that as part of big thinking about addressing pandemic-related learning loss, you have been pursuing a series of small actions that built readiness to adopt a new tutoring approach. The tutoring approach is the best you've been able to find for accelerating kids' math learning, but the evidence of its effectiveness is mixed. Telling teachers and principals this and asking them to be part of learning by sharing their experiences and suggestions for improvement along the way help everyone understand what they're embarking on and their role. At the same time, you might tell the school board and the community that while no intervention works for everyone, this is the best available option as you ask them to support a budget allocation for the tutoring approach.

The tutoring example shows building tolerance for uncertainty by engaging stakeholders at the point of implementation. It is also helpful to engage them earlier, in the process of assessing the level of risks when thinking about placing a bet on a small action tied to big thinking. One leader we know adapts the Ease-Impact

Figure 5.2 Risk-Impact 2x2 Matrix

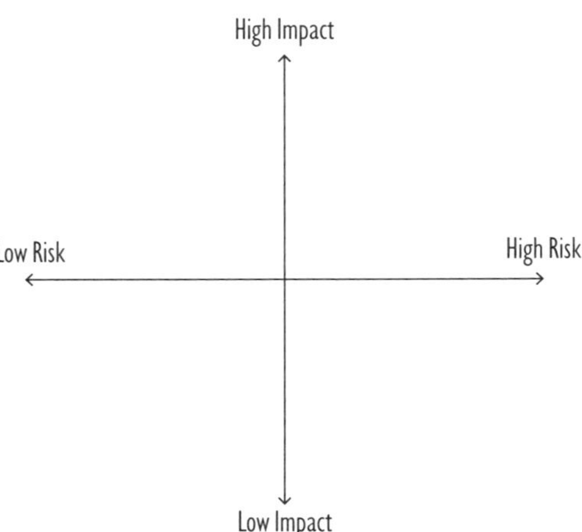

Matrix (see chapter 1 and the appendix of this book) to make a 2x2 that considers risks that are, by definition, uncertain alongside the impact (see figure 5.2). She and her colleagues think about and map impact and risk. *What are the risks? If it's risky, is it worth it? How might we mitigate the risk? What is the risk of doing nothing? To whom? What is the impact of doing nothing? On whom?*

Having the conversation about uncertainty can help people feel calmer about what might happen simply because they get to preview the possibilities, hear a range of perspectives, and have the opportunity to voice their own. In addition, the process may surface particular things that can be tended to that would reduce uncertainty and increase the opportunity for success.

Perspectives

How easy or hard it is to think big, act small, and learn fast can depend mightily on your own meaning-making preferences, as well as your position within a team or organization. For those who are big-picture thinkers—"N" on Myers-Briggs, "East" on Compass Points sorts of people—thinking big comes naturally.[2] You may not want to act until you understand the big picture, and you may not like getting bogged down in the details of what it would take to actually do something. For those who are concrete thinkers—"S" on Myers-Briggs, "West" on Compass Points sorts of people—thinking in actionable, specific steps is the way that you enter. You may not want to act until you understand what it would look like in practice, and you may not be too concerned about the *why*, so long as you understand the *what*.

And then layer in role, positional power, and context. Chief executive officers (CEOs) and senior managers are closer to the big picture in their daily work. The people on the ground (e.g., teachers, bus drivers, nurses, technicians, social workers) are closer to the small steps and the people they are trying to serve in their daily work. Middle managers are somewhere in between, where it is easy to lose sight of both the big picture and the necessary small steps because things are coming at them from all directions while they try to manage up and down and sideways. All these dynamics affect people's ability and inclination to think big, act small, and learn fast, and to trust and follow the lead of others in the organization as they do these things.

Efficacy

Thinking big and acting small help build efficacy by giving people multiple repetitions with lower stakes and faster feedback on what's working. If you try something small and it doesn't work, so long as you understand the big thing that you are working on, you can make adjustments and have not lost much momentum or confidence. It does not cost you much to try again. If you try something and see positive impact in a day or a week, or even a month, you are more likely to try again, to try something different, or to believe that improvement is possible and you can be part of it. Over time, this builds momentum and confidence, which then increases individual and collective capacity for acting amid uncertainty. It also creates more room to fail and to hold uncertainty.

For example, if you're trying to shift meetings from information-dumping sessions where you end up with all the action items (very safe, not much uncertainty) to a space that's more engaging and shared, you might start by inviting different people to play roles like note taker and timekeeper rather than doing all that yourself. Over time, you might rotate roles. You might invite feedback on meetings (higher risk, more uncertainty). You might also shift what you do in meetings by having people bring dilemmas or learn something together. As people get good at working together and learning, they feel more efficacious because they have confidence that even if something unpredictable or unexpected happens, they know how to adjust, respond, and make something of the experience.

Knowing whether what you're trying is effective and having the impact that you seek is an important part of efficacy. This requires measurement, which people and organizations are allergic to sometimes, given their history with externally imposed accountability systems and messages of failure, or the difficulty in measuring things that can't easily be counted. But measurement doesn't need to be scary or complex.

The key is being clear on how you would know whether something you're working on was successful, and how you would know whether you're making progress.

As a leader, one of the most important things you can do is build other people's sense of efficacy—their sense that what they do matters, and that if they try something, it might make a positive difference. Generally, the more efficacious a person, team, or organization feels, the more they can tolerate uncertainty. If you know that you're good at executing complex operational tasks, then you are less worried about implementing a new information management system.

Strategic Communications

Once you have some clarity and confidence about your thinking big, acting small, and learning fast (often built in conversation with many other people), then your task as a leader is to help a wider group of people get comfortable with the bet (*what*), the rationale behind it (*why* tied to thinking big), and the uncertainty related to it. For any important venture, one senior team we know thinks about and tries to articulate the *problem*, *solution*, *hope*, *urgency*, and *ask*. If they can't articulate all these things, first for themselves and ultimately in a way that is compelling for key stakeholders, then they don't think they're ready to move forward. Clarity on these things gives everyone involved some handholds and guideposts amid the uncertainty. The team calls this "strategic communications." Chapter 2, on *cultivating relationships*, talked about communicating to build relationships. Strategic communications help people see the relationships between the big and the small and get comfortable with uncertainty and learning.

"Strategic communications" could also be called "fear mitigation" or "hope kindling," both of which are important for action and learning. Part of strategic communication is creating a forum in which the risk-takers and believers can be heard and can help others get over or through their own worries and reluctance. If a board member speaks up at a public meeting in favor of an initiative, telling a story about how powerful it has been for her daughter, or a teacher speaks first in the room to say that he has found a new program so helpful and time-saving, or a youth on a student advisory board shares how this thing that you are proposing to do or expand has been life-changing for her, that sets a very different tone than elevating only the most scared voices.

This is not to say that you shouldn't listen to the worries. Strategic leaders seek out people who disagree and think something is a bad idea. These are the people most likely to point out blind spots or share information that's new to you.

Listening to these people often saves you trouble down the road by helping you anticipate obstacles and needs. It also signals that you respect others' perspectives even—and especially—when you disagree. You might just not want all the worries aired publicly. Strategic leaders are discerning about the volume and substance of both dissent and assent—it can be as dangerous to follow the siren song of those who most agree with you as to overcorrect for a lone dissenter.

In an attempt to address dissent, worries, and uncertainty about the doing, it is easy to get so hyperfocused on the *how* that you oversimplify and lose sight of the *why*. Reanchoring in *why* is important for both the integrity of the work and for people with different levels of risk tolerance and certainty to connect with purpose in a way that makes moving forward more comfortable.

Building Others' Capacity to Think Big, Act Small, Learn Fast

- Model and build others' habits of asking questions that distinguish between big and small things and the relationships among them, like, "Why is this important? What will it make possible for whom? What will success look like? What will you focus on to make progress? What are some small steps that would add up to something bigger? Where could you start?"
- Discuss the concept of think big, act small, learn fast with peers, direct reports, and teams; ask people which parts of it they think they excel at and what parts are harder for them; highlight complementary skills and encourage collaboration.
- Model learning fast.
    - Hold people accountable for learning, both individually and at the team level, and connect that learning to further action (e.g., while something is unfolding, ask "What are we learning? How does that inform our next steps?").
    - Pause, after doing something, to harvest and document learning before moving on to the next thing (e.g., ask "What did we learn from trying that? What might we want to do differently next time?").
    - Write the lessons down in a place where they can be found again by multiple people when ready for further action, then ask, "How are we building from or responding to what we learned?"
- Use tools (like the 2x2 Risk-Impact Matrix in this chapter) to explicitly name risks and weigh them in relationship to possible outcomes before choosing action.
- Model vulnerability and create a culture in which it's safe to take risks by pointing out when you make a mistake or don't know something, requesting feedback before and after action, and sharing your learning.
- Celebrate learning by appreciating people when they demonstrate learning even (and especially) when something doesn't go as well as they hoped.

TAKEAWAYS

- Think bigger, act smaller. Break the big into a lot of small parts and start. Keep asking how the small is connected to a big that matters.
- Go beyond your own scope. No matter where you sit, think beyond your position and direct control about the bigger thing that you're trying to accomplish. At the same time, try to think more granularly about what it would take to do this thing well. You need to understand both to help organize for doing it.
- Doing small things makes learning easier. Knowing the big thing anchors you in purpose, which both focuses the learning (*What is this learning in service of?*) and makes it easier to adjust action in response to learning and changing conditions.
- Place bets and acknowledge uncertainty. This combination creates the imperative for learning. Learning offers a pathway through the uncertainty.
- Learning includes learning by doing and learning by harvesting from a variety of knowledge sources.
- Build efficacy. By thinking big, acting small, and learning fast, you build the hope and belief that it's possible to change persistent patterns, whether that is generational outcomes or personal habits. Efficacy builds tolerance for uncertainty, resilience in the face of failure or setbacks, and confidence to keep striving for something ambitious.

REFLECTIONS

What are your strengths, areas for development, and lingering questions about thinking big, acting small, and learning fast?

PART TWO THE ELEMENTS OF STRATEGIC LEADERSHIP IN ACTION AND INTERACTION

WHILE WE HAVE INTRODUCED THE FIVE ELEMENTS of strategic leadership individually, in life and work they most commonly show up together and interact with one another. You're trying to build relationships with people or across departments in an organization, and power dynamics surface related to who has resources and what their interests are. Or you've been charged with leading a big, high-profile body of work, but the organization doesn't have the necessary capacity, so you're trying to figure out if you can start smaller and build to the big thing. Or you're trying to discern your next leadership move in a complex context and realize that there is a set of historical relationships that you need to understand to be effective.

Part II is devoted to showing the elements in action and interaction in a series of mini-cases in which leaders try to do ambitious, impactful work, leading strategically. We start this part of the book by naming common dualities (e.g., simplify and hold complexity, act and reflect, emphasize process and product) that inevitably surface in the authentic work of strategic leadership. These dualities are contradictory but inseparable, interconnected and counterbalancing, part of a whole. They arise organically and are dynamic. Leaders can influence the interplay between the two parts through their leadership moves. In the mini-cases, you will see dualities surface and have the opportunity to consciously choose how to manage them.

The mini-cases are composites of real situations that we've been part of as actors, observers, or supporters. Real situations are inherently rich and messy, providing great opportunities to see elements in action and interaction. You can practice applying your learning from Part I in authentic situations. The main actors in the mini-cases include a principal, central office department heads, a nonprofit director, teacher leaders, and senior system leaders. This array of actors and settings reflect our belief that the elements are ubiquitous, regardless of role, context, or experience. As you read them, you may identify strongly with some, and perhaps see your younger self or a glimpse of your future self in others.

There are two devices used repeatedly in Part II to orient and engage you. Figure Pt 2.1 shows an image of the five elements of leading strategically in relationship with one another and how a stance of strategic leadership is the glue that holds everything together. You will see it in each mini-case. Each time, it will look different as we adjust the size of the elements to reflect their prominence in the case. Sometimes *harness power* looms large and *discern* recedes, or *discern* and *think big, act small, learn fast* dominate, along with *cultivate relationships*, while *understanding context and history* is barely present.

Figure Pt 2.1 The Five Elements of Leading Strategically

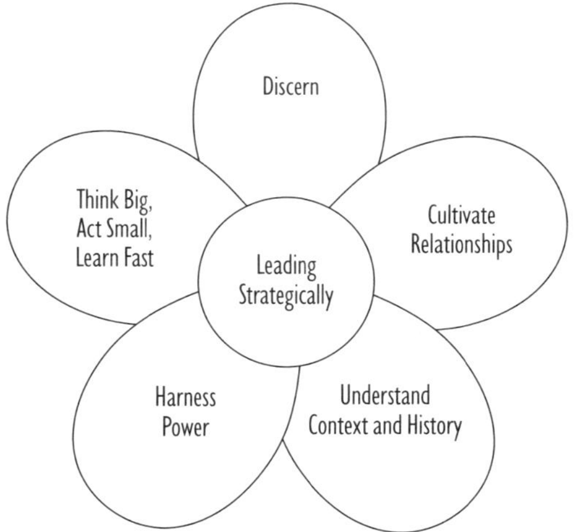

The second device, Stop–Opt–Go, is designed to engage you in the mini-cases. Stop–Opt–Go is a self-regulation strategy in the Zones of Regulation curriculum designed by Leah Kuypers.[1] We're using Stop–Opt–Go because it aligns with our approach to building leaders' awareness and supporting them to slow down, be conscious, and make intentional decisions. Stop–Opt–Go is a way of discerning in any situation. *Stop* is the pause where you analyze the situation to discern what's really going on. *Opt* is the point of identifying your options and thinking about how each will play out. *Go* is when you place a bet on what you've determined is your best option and move forward with action. We introduce this device here to help you practice applying your learning about the elements and building a leadership habit of stopping and assessing before acting, making a conscious choice among different possible responses, and then going forward with clarity and intention. In the mini-cases, we've created some extra visual space after Stop–Opt–Go moments to invite you to practice these strategic habits and apply your learning from Part I before continuing with your reading.

Both devices are resources to add to your leadership toolkit and use more broadly. In every chapter, we offer some of our own analysis for you to consider alongside your own analysis. Sometimes we also give the actors in the case a chance for a do-over, where we imagine different ways of responding anchored in an understanding of the elements of strategic leadership. We encourage you to take notes and capture your big takeaways, wonderings, and reflections on your own leadership and circumstances at the end of each case.

6

DUALITIES

EMBEDDED IN EACH OF THE MINI-CASES in this book are dualities: opposing ideas or forces that exist in relationship to one another within a larger whole. To understand dualities, just watch children on a seesaw. One child drops down toward the wood chips scattered under the seesaw, while the other sails upward, often gripping the handle a little tighter and bouncing in the seat when it hits the top. Then, something happens—the one on the bottom pushes off the ground or the one on top shifts from the front of the seat to the back—to put the seesaw back into motion. The two ends of the seesaw exist in opposition to one another within the larger system of the seesaw. The system is dynamic, influenced by small movements. The positioning of the two sides shifts in response to choices the children make. Playing in that space requires attention, intention, finesse, and learning.

Dualities exist everywhere you look. A duality is visible in parents who simultaneously want to protect their children *and* have them learn and develop independence, which will inevitably come with hurts and failures. Another duality is found in partners who want to be together while still valuing the pursuit of separate interests and alone time. They yearn for love, connection, partnership, *and* freedom. And then there is the reality that there are always at least two sides to an argument. When facing dualities, we are most effective when we consciously choose how we want the two aspects to be in relationship with one another. Do we want to emphasize one while the other recedes? Do we want to try to balance them, although that can often be maintained only briefly? What actions do we take to accomplish this? The dynamism of dualities means that the relationship between the parts shift and change, and we need to pay attention to that and respond.

Figure 6.1 Yin-Yang Symbol

Western culture tends to think in binary terms (either-or), rather than the both-and of dualities. The idea of dualities is a principle found in many Eastern cultures and religions. For example, the yin-yang symbol (figure 6.1), which originated in Chinese philosophy, captures the idea of opposing forces within a larger whole and the power and potential of the dynamic relationship between the two forces. Many indigenous cultures emphasize the deep interconnections of relationships among people, nature, and spirits. Engaging with dualities is a way to acknowledge and hold complexity, understanding that multiple things can be true at the same time.

Strategic leaders are aware of the existence of dualities, are able to notice them, and understand that their job is to hold and engage them. They see how the two parts of the whole exist in relationship to one another and how to influence the interplay between them to the greatest effect. Simply being able to see and describe what is happening helps us both name and understand a duality: *Oh, I want wide engagement, and I want to move quickly and focus. That's hard to achieve.* Naming the duality gives us the chance to make a conscious decision about if we're comfortable with how it is playing out, or if we want to make a move to shift the dynamic. Maybe we err on the side of broad engagement when we want to hear everyone's perspective at the beginning of a strategic planning process. Then, when it's time to identify the strategy, we consider all the input but choose a few foci, knowing both that they don't accommodate everyone's desires and that focus is necessary for success.

When we focus heavily on one part of a duality, the other part fades. Pursuing balance between the two parts is hard, and any balance achieved is fleeting. Balance is not the goal. This bears repeating. *Balance is not the goal.* The most productive way to engage with dualities is to pay attention to the movement of the seesaw and make conscious choices. The decision to shift things in one direction or the other, or to try to briefly hover in the middle place of relative balance, is made with awareness of the trade-offs.

As we wrote this book, we bumped up against dualities: we wanted to tackle big, complex issues and ideas *and* make the book easy to read and accessible; we needed to understand what we were trying to say before we started writing, *and* writing helped us understand what we most wanted to say; we wanted there to be some common ways that we engaged readers throughout the book *and* we didn't want to get stuck in a single way that might grow dull and/or less responsive to readers' needs and interests; we wanted the writing process to be expansive and collaborative *and* we wanted to finish writing the darn book already. As we encountered each of these dualities, we wrestled with how to let both things be true. And in the process, we got frustrated, laughed about the irony of it, and sometimes had to step back to get perspective.

To be able to identify and navigate dualities, leaders need to get comfortable with the whole idea of tension. Many of us don't like tension. Just hearing the word makes our bodies grip, as we associate it with conflict, discomfort, or someone winning while another loses. It can feel nearly intolerable—something to be banished as quickly as possible. When we feel that, we react from a place of fear, which deprives us of consciously choosing our response.

Understanding your own personal stance regarding tension is an important starting point. You may need to look for examples where tension has been productive to build your tolerance for it. Or realize that you can feel tension without having to react. Or think of times when things in tension breathed energy and dynamism into a situation or your life. Normalizing tension and things in tension is necessary to be able to see, hold, and navigate dualities effectively.

Understanding that dualities are a resource to employ in your leadership is a mindset you can cultivate. Identifying dualities, tolerating them, and understanding and modulating the interplay between their parts are all important skills that you can develop.

Through our leadership and our work with educators from the classroom to the boardroom, we have identified common dualities that we and leaders we work with encounter over and over again. We outline those next to provide a concrete introduction to the idea of dualities, build your understanding of the concept, and prepare you to identify additional dualities that surface in your leadership. These dualities show up in individuals' leadership, as part of the work of teams, and in the work of organizations.

Examples of Dualities

Embracing simplicity while holding complexity: Simplicity is the quality of being easy to understand and do: for example, I'm going to get out to see friends more often because it makes me happy. Complexity is about thinking holistically and considering interrelationships and intricacies: for example, I'm going to consider all the things that contribute to my health and well-being and how they relate to one another (e.g., diet, exercise, sleep, gratitude, friends, family, meaningful work). Too much simplicity tells an incomplete story, reduces dynamism, and can lead to actions that are not robust enough for whatever we're hoping to accomplish. Meanwhile, too much complexity becomes baffling and overwhelming. When complexity is reduced in the name of simplicity, the trick is to ensure that the bigger *why* isn't lost.

Acting as well as reflecting: Action is required for forward motion and progress. Reflection before action supports thoughtful action. Reflection after action invites learning. Some of us are prone to action, while others prefer reflection. Too much action without reflection leads to chaos and churn. But too much reflection encourages lethargy and the possibility of missed opportunities. In addition to our personal preferences, our emotional state affects how we manage these things in tension. When we are uncertain or scared, we can overdial in either direction: reflecting long past the point of usefulness because we're afraid to make a decision, or acting quickly in hopes of extricating ourselves from the discomfort of uncertainty.

Emphasize both the process and the product: Some people have an "ends justify the means" approach that prioritizes product over process. Yet we know that a strong process often introduces varied perspectives, experiences, and expertise, which respects people, contributes to a better product, and builds ownership. Too much process can make it hard to get things done. Too much focus on the product can lead to a weak process that negatively affects the product and/or people's experience of it and commitment to it.

Staying humble while projecting confidence: Humility is about having a modest or low sense of our own importance, while confidence is about feeling self-assured. Humility helps when we want to engage with others and learn. Confidence is valuable when we want to set direction, lead and influence others, and take risks. Too much humility can result in missed opportunities to lead and influence, and deprive people and the organization of our talents and perspective. Too much confidence can lead to missing critical information that should inform our thinking, decision-making, and actions, or overestimating our talents and capacities in ways that lead to diminished results.

Playing the short game and the long game: The short game is about attending to what's right in front of us and the immediate future. The long game is about setting our sights on where we're ultimately trying to get and what actions will best support us in that pursuit. Playing too much of a short game leads to lots of disconnected actions that are not seated in a longer-term goal or strategy. But playing too much of a long game can make us unresponsive to immediate issues that need attention. This duality requires us to consider how the short game affects the long game and vice versa.

Being flexible and consistent: Flexibility is about freedom, responsiveness, and the ability to adjust, while consistency relates to common routines, standards, or practices. Flexibility gives us leeway, while consistency creates predictability. Too much flexibility creates chaos and confusion. Too much consistency stifles innovation and learning. This duality is at the center of every debate about what autonomies schools can have and what things the school system must require. Similarly, consistency can be a vehicle to ensure equal access, while flexibility may be essential to differentiate in response to variable needs to achieve a shared goal.

There are other dualities that we frequently encounter: *work within existing capacity* and *expand capacity*; *focus* and *be open*; and *consider that things can be about you* and *not about you*. Our list is by no means exhaustive. We encourage you to add to it, drawing from your own experience.

Strategic leaders pay attention to these dualities in play. In real, complex, messy contexts, dualities seldom show up one at a time. They often interact with one another. You feel slighted by something that happens at work. You step back to reflect on what bigger issues are at play, and you have to decide if you want to do something about it or let it lie. Building your muscle of discerning dualities can help you see both individual dualities and the interplay between different dualities. This awareness helps you make strategic decisions about your leadership.

Dualities Check Tool

The Dualities Check Tool is a quick tool that you can use individually or in a team to identify dualities and respond with intention.

- **Stop**
  - Are you thinking in either-or terms? Are you waffling? Or are you very sure of yourself, unable to see other perspectives or options?
  - Is there one or more dualities at play?
- **Opt**
  - Try to name the duality/dualities. Describe the interplay of the two parts of each duality.
  - Identify choices that you have about how to respond.
- **Go**
  - What do you want to do or not do? Why?

TAKEAWAYS

* Dualities have two opposite parts that coexist in dynamic relationship with one another. They are inevitable.
* The goal is not to eradicate the tension between the two parts of a duality using either-or thinking, but instead to view it through the lens of both-and thinking, focusing on the dynamic relationship of the two parts.
* The ability to identify dualities allows you to consciously choose how to influence the interplay between their opposing forces to the greatest effect.
* Getting comfortable with the tension inherent in dualities and learning how to use it are key skills of strategic leaders.

REFLECTIONS

What new insights do you have about your leadership after reading about dualities?

7

MY WAY OR THE HIGHWAY

"WHAT'S THIS I HEAR ABOUT A 'NO ZERO' policy in the seventh grade?" says Paul, the founding board chair. Paul is one of the community members who had the original vision for this single charter public middle school. Amy, one of the first teachers hired by the school, was recently hired by the board to be coprincipal based on her knowledge and skill leading learning both in the classroom and with her colleagues. This is her first administrative job.

The board meeting agenda says nothing about the No Zero policy, but the board chair has decided that it is important to discuss. Amy is caught off guard by the topic, the timing, and the vigor with which Paul pursues it. She usually appreciates the board's role—mostly it focuses on budget and operations, leaving learning and teaching to her.

Paul continues, "It's ridiculous—why would we give students 50 percent credit for homework they didn't do? We should be developing students with a good work ethic who do what they're supposed to do. We shouldn't be rewarding lack of effort. I think we need a 'Full Zero' policy for students who don't do their homework."

Amy's body has an immediate and overwhelming reaction to this declaration—heart rate soars, throat thickens, legs prepare to jump or run or move somewhere, anywhere. She sits there trying to figure out what to do, but her fight-or-flight lizard brain has shut down the rational, logical part of her brain. She says, "Well, for this year we are trying a variety of approaches to homework. The seventh-grade team decided on a No Zero approach. It seems to be working well."

"By 'working well,' do you mean lowering expectations? The parent who told me about it said that her son is doing less homework now that he knows it won't hurt his grade as much," says Paul.

Amy waits for anyone else in the room to say something. No one does.

The muzzled part of Amy's brain tries to find words through the flood of adrenaline in her body. *How dare the chair suggest that I support low expectations! Which parent said something? He's oversimplifying a complex issue. The faculty doesn't totally agree yet either, which is why grade levels have different practices—it was a win to get teachers in each grade level to have a consistent approach. And why is Paul in my business all of a sudden? The board hired me to lead learning and teaching, committing to leave educational decisions to the educators.*

Since she became coprincipal, Amy has spent a lot of time looking at a variety of data, including test results, student work, homework assignments, observing in classrooms, and—her favorite source—talking with kids and understanding what school is like from their perspective.

It's clear to Amy that they have a caring, safe school, but students are bored. At least 50 percent of the in-class assignments aren't at grade level because teachers want to make sure that all students are successful, and teachers need more support to challenge and engage students who are performing on a continuum, between third-grade and high school levels. Amy wants to focus her energy here and isn't as concerned right now about homework-grading policies. Her early inquiries suggest that the issues with quality tasks exist in homework, too. She can hardly fault the students for not doing it. *I need to respond*, she thinks to herself. *I don't love conflict. And Paul clearly doesn't get the complexity of learning and teaching.*

Amy loosens her grip on her chair's armrests and explains, "The seventh-grade team feels strongly that zeros on missed homework punish students unfairly—a student could be earning all As on in-class tests and assignments and then get zeros on missed homework and end up with a B or C in the class. The final grade becomes a reflection of their compliance, not their mastery of the material. The teachers also argue that students have different levels of support at home, so homework completion may say more about home help than student effort."

"The eighth-grade team, however, feels that they aren't setting up students for success in high school if homework isn't factored into the grades more significantly, so that team does give zeros for incomplete homework, while also giving students the opportunity to make up missed homework within three days. So we're trying different approaches and seeing what works best for our learning goals."

Tapping her foot under the table, Amy continues, "By 'working well,' I mean that students' grades more accurately reflect what they know and can do rather than how good they are about turning in homework. We are trying to develop thinkers and problem-solvers here. I'm sorry to hear that one of our students is doing less homework now. That is certainly not the intent. There may be something else going on there, which the team and I can look into."

Another board member says, "This sounds like an important issue for us to discuss. What does 'No Zero' mean, anyway? It sounds like in some classes, students get a zero if they don't do their homework within three days, and in others, they get 50 percent credit even if they never do it. Is that right?"

Amy nods, and before she or anyone else can say any more, the board chair says, "Well, I think this is pretty simple: we should require Full Zeros for missed homework. And I think we should decide today. I don't want to hear from any more parents about our low expectations, and we should have one approach for the whole school." After a few more comments, at the chair's insistence, they get ready to call a vote.

Amy pushes herself back from the board table, scraping the chair legs against the linoleum floor. She stands up and announces, "Well, if we require Full Zeros, then I'm resigning." Then she walks out of the room to avoid yelling in frustration and anger.

Stop–Opt–Go

- What is happening here?

ANALYSIS

While all the elements of strategic leadership are at play here (see figure 7.1), it is fundamentally a story about power. To understand the power dynamics, a little more context is helpful. Amy is twenty-eight and has been serving as coprincipal of the school for a few months, after being a teacher there for two years. The board chair, Paul, is in his forties and a lawyer in his day job. While he often has strong

Figure 7.1 The Five Elements in My Way or the Highway

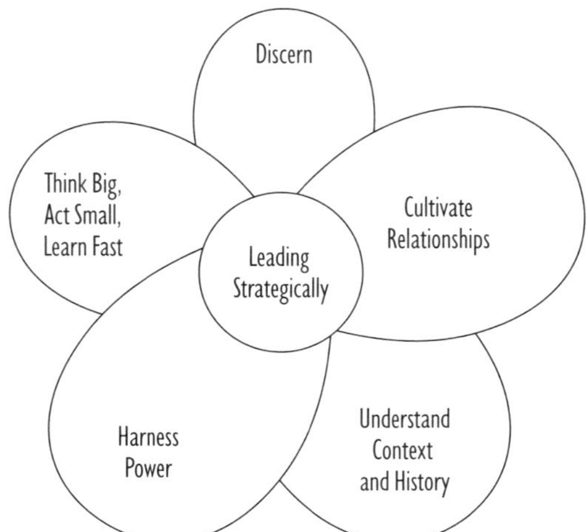

opinions, he does not usually assert them around the day-to-day business of the school, and before this particular meeting, Amy would have characterized their relationship as one of mutual respect. Amy's coprincipal is a veteran educator in his forties who wanted to be the sole principal. The board decided to make Amy coprincipal because she was effectively leading professional development in the building as a teacher leader and was well regarded by students, families, and colleagues for her teaching. Her coprincipal said nothing during this board meeting, watching the proceedings like a tennis match. All the board members are white, although the school reflects the racial and ethnic diversity of the community that they serve, which is almost evenly split between African American and white students, with less than 5 percent of students of other races and ethnicities. About 70 percent of the teachers are white, 25 percent are African American, and one is Arab American.

Amy is a second-generation Chinese American. On most days, she finds that being the only Asian American on the faculty makes it easy for her to bridge across groups. On all days, she is well aware that less than 2 percent of US principals have an Asian American background, and even fewer of those are women. Amy is determined to be successful as a principal for her students, for their families, and for the future women leaders who come behind her.

Power: Both the board chair and Amy are using a combination of positional and personal power—Paul to call for a vote of something that he has raised independently and Amy when she issues her ultimatum. There are other clues that power is at play:

- The board chair's urgency—urgency from someone with formal authority puts power in motion.
- Amy's strong visceral reaction and her need to leave the room to keep from yelling in response to comments from someone with formal authority suggest that she is reacting to power being asserted.

In the board meeting, the board chair is being unilateral, quite unlike the usual collective, collaborative spirit at the school. This does not sound like the same Paul who showed up to help paint walls two weeks before the school launched and tirelessly used his community connections to encourage families to enroll. Amy feels coerced by Paul. While she likes running things and making things happen, she prefers to lead collaboratively, facilitate others' learning, and minimize disagreements so she and others can stay focused on the most important work. She doesn't yet understand how and when to engage conflict, state her position clearly, or use her positional and personal power to center children when there are differences of opinion and perspective.

If Amy were able to notice and manage the signals that her body is sending her, she might be able to find enough mental space to consider the values and interests of the board (table 7.1). This would highlight points of shared purpose on which to focus.

Table 7.1 Values and Interests

Paul, Board Chair	Amy, Coprincipal	Other Board Members
Consistency and quality that ensure the school endures	Quality of learning at the school	Safe, calm school
Being in charge	Autonomy as a leader	Respect for teachers as professionals
Supporting students to be critical thinkers and reliable workers	Supporting students to be critical thinkers and high-agency people	Supporting students to be critical thinkers and good citizens

Because Amy is very clear about her own values and interests but less clear about those of the other board members, she makes a few errors in judgment:

- **Assuming** that everyone shares and prioritizes her values and interests, especially the most important one (which to her is having engaging, relevant, and rigorous learning),
- **Reacting** as if it were a personal attack on her or her teachers instead of a misalignment of values and interests, and
- **Issuing** an ultimatum.

However, at some intuitive level, she also understands her own power. Amy knows that the board respects her knowledge of learning, teaching, and professional development because they resisted pressure from her coprincipal to make him the lone principal. The board was clear with Amy that they wanted someone with learning and teaching expertise to complement her coprincipal's strengths in operations.

Discern: Amy is so flooded with emotion that she can't *discern to understand or to act*. If she were able to slow herself down, see the deluge of emotions as data, and engage her curiosity instead of her defense mechanisms, she could try to understand why the board chair seems to care so much about the No Zero policy and why he wants to vote on it that day. She also might be able to think through whether this is a situation in which *what* the chair is saying raises important considerations even if *how* he is saying it doesn't land well with her.

Understand Context and History: Amy isn't pausing to reflect on what might be relevant in terms of *context and history*. If she did, she might get curious about why Paul is acting out of character. Is No Zero a hot topic locally or nationally? Is the parent who said something particularly influential, or is the chair responding to some other force that Amy can't see? Is the chair having a bad day and wants to feel in control of something? Her analysis is less nuanced, more like this: *This is unusual and inconsistent with prior boundaries that we've drawn between the board and day-to-day operations of the school* and *Paul can be outspoken-bordering-on-aggressive sometimes, but that usually is directed at forces outside our school, not inside.*

Relationships: Amy and Paul have had a congenial relationship prior to this meeting. Paul is close with the other coprincipal of the school—they see each other socially, have many things in common, and are both part of the group that wrote the founding charter for the school. They see themselves as the wise veterans in a school where most educators are fifteen years younger. Amy had been a faculty representative to the board for two years, so she has amiable relationships with all the board members, but the people she sees socially outside of school are the other faculty in their twenties, like her. None of Amy's faculty friends are in the board meeting.

Think Big, Act Small, Learn Fast: Amy and Paul are approaching the issue differently: she is "thinking big" about what kind of overall learning the school aspires to foster; and Paul is "acting small" by wanting to make a Full Zero homework policy. Their stances perfectly reflect the *duality of simplicity* (Paul) and *complexity* (Amy) of the No Zero policy. The conversation quickly turns into a binary decision—have a No Zero or a Full Zero policy—when there are actually many options. Recentering on the purpose of homework and its relationship to mastery and a bigger vision for what they want learners to develop would help anchor the discussion and decision. If Amy and Paul could each hold a broader view of the issue, recognizing the interplay of *simplicity and complexity*, they might be able to agree to experiment and *learn fast* from the approaches that different grade levels are trying, which they could then use to create a consistent policy based on where they see the most success. This approach might help them also hold the *duality of flexibility and consistency*, starting with giving grade-level teams flexibility, learning from their work, and then agreeing on a consistent, schoolwide policy.

Stop–Opt–Go

- Given all that is happening, what other choices could Amy make, and at what points?

OPT

Here are three potential choices:

1. **Slow down (the moment)**
    a. *Cool down*: The first thing Amy needs to do is cool down so she can use all her senses. Since she isn't facilitating the meeting, she can't very easily propose some time to reflect or write. She could suggest

that they take a break, which would give her a chance to move her body and release some adrenaline. Otherwise, her best opportunity to slow down would be to take a few subtle, deep breaths to calm her fight/flight response. If she were in a virtual meeting, she could write a "Be right back" message in the chat box, turn her screen off for a minute, move her body, or holler (so long as she was on mute). This would help her release anxious energy and make space for the reflection part of the *act-reflect duality*.

b. *Delay*: A variation of "cool down" is to delay decision-making. Amy and another board member lightly tried to do this in the meeting, but the board chair pushed forward. Ideally, before he called for a vote, Amy could have said something like, "It sounds like you feel strongly about this. This is a complex issue. Could we come back to it at our next board meeting?" If the chair insisted on trying to move forward that night, Amy could ask for a break at that point, which she could use to calm her body and gather her thoughts.

c. *Inquire/be curious*: If Amy were not in lizard-brain mode, she might be able to inquire to better understand what is really happening. She might say something like, "This is something we haven't really talked about as a group before. I'm curious what the rest of you are thinking and whether you're also hearing from parents. What questions do you have?" Or she could try to directly inquire of Paul (e.g., "Paul, it sounds like this is really important to you. I'd love to better understand why."). Because of the power dynamics at play, Amy might find direct engagement with Paul harder than inviting other people into the conversation. She might find inquiring privately during a break or outside the meeting more comfortable (e.g., find a trusted ally on the board and check in about that person's take and ideas, or talk one on one with Paul to understand his position better and express her concerns more privately so it doesn't look like she is challenging his authority in front of the group).

2. **Push forward**

   a. *Count votes/allies*: Because this is mostly about power, Amy could quickly try to assess whether Paul has the votes to get what he wants.

This particular board has never had a split vote, usually deciding things by consensus. If Amy thinks that Paul would lose, she could let him proceed to a vote. Or if she isn't totally certain how the vote would go, this wouldn't be her best choice, unless she has some kind of break or delay in which she could talk with other board members and assess the situation.

b. *Cede*: Amy could decide that this is not the most important thing to fight for and let Paul have what he wants on this issue. The issue and his position on it aren't a deal-breaker for her because there are numerous ways to support students to success, even with zeros for missed homework. To cede would require Amy to take the long view and consider trade-offs, like how ceding her power on this issue might create goodwill that she could leverage for something else she cares about more. In the moment, Amy doesn't want to cede, and she worries about setting two precedents: (1) Paul gets what he wants if he asserts it strongly enough, and (2) Paul decides what happens in classrooms, not Amy and her teachers.

3. **Deliver an ultimatum:** This is what Amy does. It is more of a reaction than a choice. It's not a response that she would choose again, mostly because it isn't worth it. Outside the practical matter of her needing to have a job to pay the bills, the issue just isn't as big or pivotal as it seems to Amy in the moment. Homework is a very small part of what the school is focused on. While she feels very triggered by any suggestion that she supports low expectations, she knows that she is working on raising the level of challenge and support for all students every day, no matter what the homework policy is.

Stop–Opt–Go

- What would you choose to do if you were in Amy's shoes? Why?

REFLECTIONS

What new insights do you have about your leadership after reading this mini-case?

8

TEACHING A LEADER TO FISH

"WHAT WOULD YOU MOST LIKE TO FOCUS ON TODAY?" Eddie asks Kendra, the deputy superintendent of a school system, whom he is coaching.

Kendra says, "I'm thinking about how to frame the priorities for this year with the principals at our leadership institute this summer. I'm also trying to figure out the best way to help teachers double down on our focus on math, to deepen the work we began last year. But we don't yet have all the supports lined up that teachers need. Plus, we have three new school board members who may shift the balance of power on the board. I need to figure out how to orient them to our priorities and work with them productively. And the superintendent seems distracted, or maybe she's hesitant. I'm not sure if there are other things going on for her that I don't know about. I'm finding it hard to get a clear sense of her position on several things. We need to be on the same page, saying the same thing to principals, teachers, and central office staff."

Stop–Opt–Go

- What do you notice in Kendra's response?
- What do you think are the most helpful things that Eddie can do to support her?

STOP

Listening to the series of challenges Kendra is facing, Eddie senses that she is feeling pulled in lots of directions, and may even be overwhelmed. He knows from experience that the first ten minutes of a coaching session set the tone for the whole hour and the likelihood of it being productive and satisfying. They could spend the hour digging a little deeper into many or all of these topics. While that might feel satisfying in the moment, or maybe even cathartic for Kendra, Eddie knows that the relief will be short-lived. Instead, Eddie wants to help her *discern* where to focus the conversation for greatest effect, which will leave her feeling clearer, energized, and able to move forward after their conversation with a strategic mindset. He thinks about "greatest effect" in two ways:

1. What will relieve any distress Kendra is feeling that may affect her well-being and/or impede her ability to work effectively?
2. What will help her do high-impact work well?

These two questions acknowledge the duality of *the short game and the long game* of Kendra's work and her leadership development. Both are important. Before Eddie can help Kendra *discern* where they should focus, he needs to get curious and do some discerning of his own to better understand the situation. He watches Kendra on the Zoom screen and listens, drawing on the data immediately in front of him. Does her voice rise, or does she talk more quickly when she speaks of specific topics? When does she hesitate, suggesting her own uncertainty or real-time internal processing? When does she smile? Are her shoulders rolled forward or up around her ears, suggesting that she's carrying a heavy load or is stressed? Does she avoid making eye contact with him as she raises certain issues, suggesting discomfort or distance? These questions help Eddie assess Kendra's emotional state and any pressure points that need immediate attention. His assessment is that while she has a lot on her mind and plate, she does not appear to be in a state of distress that requires immediate attention.

With this understanding, Eddie shifts his efforts to *discern* the issues that Kendra has shared. He brings in data from previous coaching sessions. He's looking for patterns and themes regarding her work and leadership. This sifting and sorting help him discern the importance of each issue that Kendra has raised and her capacity to address each one. Here are some of the questions that run through Eddie's head as Kendra is talking:

- How would I prioritize these different topics based on previous conversations that we've had?
- What do I know about Kendra's work in the areas she's mentioned so far?
    - Where has she had good success?
    - Where has she run into challenges?
- What comes easily to her, and what skills and actions does she have to pursue with more conscious attention and could use support in developing?

Having done his best to answer these questions, Eddie now steps back a level, thinking about what he knows about the state of the school system and the larger context. Here, he's thinking about organizational capacity and readiness, opportunity for impact, and internal agreement. See figure 8.1 for the elements at play in this interaction. These are all things that have the potential to affect Kendra's

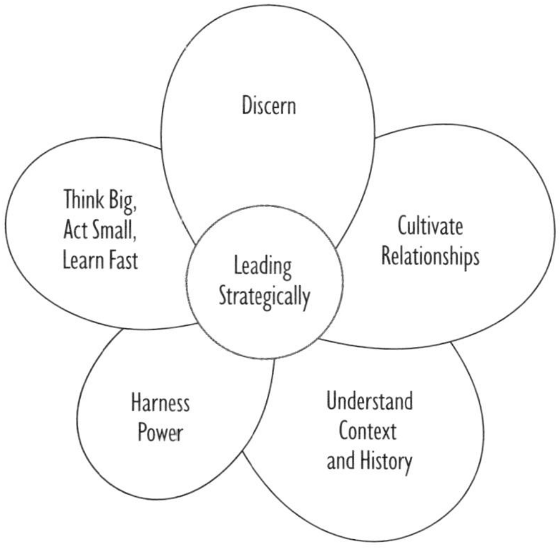

Figure 8.1 The Five Elements in Teaching a Leader to Fish

success in taking up many of the issues that she's raised. He formulates a set of questions in his head about these issues and tries to answer them:

- Which of the issues that Kendra raised could propel the system forward, really slow things down, or worse yet, jeopardize important work already underway?
- Where does Kendra have strong resources, capacity, or alliances to tap, and where is there little of that?
- Where is Kendra on the same page with her superintendent? Where may she need to manage up to build a shared understanding of a situation or a potential solution? And where are she and the superintendent in disagreement?
- What are the local politics, and how do they inform prioritization of the issues?
- Are there interrelationships among some of the topics (e.g., the school board thinks that it's time to move from a focus in math to a new topic, while Kendra is clear that the math work has not yet grown deep enough roots to be sustained without close attention)?

As Eddie is discerning, he draws on *context and history*, *relationships*, and *power*. He is trying to put Kendra's comments in a larger context to help him figure out which questions to ask to help her make a strategic decision about where to focus. The time that Eddie and Kendra have spent cultivating a trusting relationship over the last six months of working together is the foundation for this whole interaction. Her willingness to share all the things on her mind with him indicates that she is comfortable and Eddie has earned her trust. Eddie and Kendra are both Black leaders, which is something that Kendra looked for in her search for a coach. As she hoped, this shared identity has helped her feel comfortable sharing what's on her mind and heart and trusting Eddie to listen and understand her well.

Because Eddie has been coaching leaders for years, he does everything outlined here in his head in real time as Kendra tells him the things outlined in the second paragraph of this vignette. He's listening to her while scanning other data sources. This is discerning at high speed. When Eddie first started coaching, he asked himself fewer questions. He's layered additional things into his analysis over the years as he has built his capacity. He moves intentionally between understanding the complexity of a situation and reducing the complexity and focusing on simplicity by identifying a few manageable places to focus that have the potential for high impact.

What Eddie is doing is something that you can do with a friend, a colleague who comes to you for thought partnership or counsel, or someone you supervise. The power differential in a supervisory relationship may affect the level of vulnerability that the person being coached expresses and some of the moves that are made, but what is the same is the act of guiding them through a process focused on building the person's sense of agency and capacity to choose where to focus.

Supervisor Scenario

Imagine for a moment that Eddie is Kendra's supervisor. As her supervisor, his responsibilities extend beyond supporting her growth and development. He's ultimately responsible for her work. He likely has opinions about what she should do and how she should do it. And he doesn't have the same expansiveness of time that a coach has. As a result, it may be hard for him to not be more direct, telling her where he thinks she should focus, particularly if the stakes are high and time is short. The trade-off in doing that is that he misses the opportunity to build her capacity to discern. As a supervisor, Eddie's superpower lies in his ability to ask one or two carefully considered questions that help Kendra see and consider the big picture. She may come up with the idea that Eddie is holding in his head of where she should focus. Or she may come up with something else—maybe something even better. If not, then Eddie, as her supervisor, can be more explicit about his thinking and the rationale behind it, which is another way to model thinking and build Kendra's capacity. And, because there is a power dynamic between supervisor and employee, sometimes Eddie, as the person with more formal authority, will make the call.

OPT

Having sifted and sorted through all the data that he has to draw on, Eddie considers options for what he could say when Kendra pauses, and he senses that she is feeling some relief from expressing the jumble of things swirling in her head. He is *discerning to choose the right next action* to support Kendra in deciding where she'd most like to focus the coaching session. He could simply say, "Why don't we focus on the math issue?" But in doing that, he'd miss an opportunity to empower her and invest her in the conversation. Instead, he wants to support Kendra to build her capacity to discern the most important place to focus. This is a transferable skill that she can use in a variety of contexts, which builds her leadership capacity more generally. The gender dynamic between Eddie and Kendra adds to Eddie's vigilance about following Kendra's lead. In addition to believing that being directive as a coach is something to use very strategically and sparingly, he's aware of the power differential in him telling a woman what he thinks she should do.

After saying something like, "Wow! There are lots of things happening. Thanks for bringing me up to speed," there are several different ways Eddie can guide the conversation. Each route will invite Kendra to step back from the info dump that she has just done and *discern* where focusing would be most helpful. Eddie is modeling an approach to thinking and problem-solving that will support Kendra more broadly. His goal is that, over time and with less and less of his guidance, she will be able to take herself through this process anytime she's trying to sort through a variety of information. His job is to support her in building her capacity to do this herself. It reminds him of an adage: "Give a man a fish, and you feed him for a day; teach a man to fish, and you feed him for a lifetime."

The trick is for Eddie to distill all of his complex, layered analysis into a simple, clear question or two. Here are some of the questions that he considers asking to help focus the conversation:

1. "How are you feeling about the issues now that you've named them? Do any of them rise to the surface as most important or recede as less important?"
2. "As you were talking, I noticed that you seemed particularly animated when you spoke about the board and the superintendent. Are those places where you feel like taking action is critical, or are they places of great frustration but may not be your points of highest leverage?"
3. "I found myself wondering about the relationships between some of the topics. For example, how to talk with teachers about continuing the focus on math when you don't yet have all the support they need in place. And what that means for the conversations with principals. Does any of this resonate with you and feel worth exploring?"

4. "As you think about the next eight weeks before the school year starts, which of these issues feels time-sensitive and essential to kicking the school year off well?"

Stop–Opt–Go

- What questions do you prefer? Why?
- Is there another question that isn't listed here that you'd be inclined to ask? Why?

There isn't a single right next question. With whatever question Eddie asks, he is placing a bet about what will best help Kendra discern what's most pressing and choose a focus for the coaching session. And, once he asks the question, he will watch and listen to learn from what she tells him. This will then inform the next coaching move that he makes.

GO

Eddie decides to ask a combination of questions 1 and 4: "Are any of the issues you've named feeling particularly resonant right now? I know you're focused on ensuring that the new school year starts strong. Are any of the issues that feel most resonant also time-sensitive in terms of preparing for the start of the school year?" Eddie chooses that combination to try to support Kendra to tap into her gut instincts and inner wisdom as valuable sources of data when discerning, as well as to honor any urgency she may be feeling.

REFLECTIONS

What new insights do you have about your leadership after reading this mini-case?

9

RED LIGHT, GREEN LIGHT

SOFIA SIPS HER COFFEE, staring at the walls covered with chart paper and sticky notes. This is her favorite time of day—7 a.m., before anyone else arrives, when it's quiet enough to think. Her meetings today are virtual, but she still likes to come into the office at least three days a week. Otherwise, she feels disconnected from what she most enjoys about the work in the first place, which is the people.

Sofia took over as president and chief executive officer (CEO) of Cherry Children and Family Center (Cherry CFC) six months ago. She is the first person in her family to go to college. After she got her master's degree in social work, Sofia loved working directly with children and families, but she wasn't sure if she could sustain it for a full career. *¡Ya basta!* she thought at the end of each long day—*enough!* She wished she could put an end to all the challenges her clients faced, but she often felt that her efforts were *insuficiente*. So when a supervisor in a different organization where she worked told her that she had leadership potential and asked if she wanted to be assistant director of domestic violence and child abuse services, she said yes.

Later, she would wonder what it was about her leadership potential that her supervisor saw as most promising, or if there simply hadn't been anyone else to do the job. Either way, that started a string of leadership roles for Sofia over the last fifteen years, each one her attempt to help more people and to do something about the bigger forces that affected the people she served. That journey took her to a vice president role, and she thought she'd happily be a number two for the rest of her career. But then a recruiter called, and her boss encouraged her to apply.

Now here she is, president and CEO of a regional nonprofit serving several communities. Cherry CFC's region reminds her of home—rural farmland interrupted by a few small towns about thirty minutes away from one another. Like Sofia's hometown, most of the people who speak Spanish at home work on farms or at other low-paying jobs. Growing up, Sofia had seen strong Latina leaders in her hometown, but she had not seen a Latina leading in a professional role like president and CEO. Now in Cherry View, Sofia's presence doubled the number of Latina professionals in the local professional women's network. Faith communities are an important anchor for many people in this area, including for Sofia.

Sofia was hired when her predecessor didn't work out after a brief six-month tenure. So far as she can tell, the last person tried to bring in lots of ideas from his experience in another state, moving faster than the organization and board could tolerate. The board described this to her as "not getting what we're about." Sofia is the first woman and first person of color to run the organization—two facts that the organization seems both proud of and oblivious to at different moments. She is also from an area similar to Cherry View, unlike her predecessor.

STOP

Sofia sips her coffee again, trying to focus on the task at hand. Although the board wanted a strategic plan from her immediately, Sofia insisted on taking time to listen, knowing that she had lots to learn. *Humildad* is a core value in Sofia's family and faith tradition and is a big part of how she leads. She has found that leadership requires both humility and confidence, and she felt confident asserting herself on this issue. Even though she is still getting to know the members of the organization's board and how to work with them effectively, early conversations with her board chair convinced her that she had his support. And, given the short, failed tenure of her predecessor, Sofia knows that the board is committed to supporting her leadership and ensuring the organization's overall health. What she is less clear about is how supportive the board would be if she suggested substantive change.

She knows from her previous jobs that boards love strategic plans, but the plans often don't really reflect the community's priorities and tend to have much more in them than the already overstretched staff can manage. Plus, she doesn't see any real urgency for a new strategic plan. The longtime CEO before her predecessor, who had retired less than a year ago, established a strategy that seems to be working fairly well toward the organization's mission to "support children and families in the Cherry View region to be healthy and thrive."

Cherry CFC's strategy focuses on mental health, physical well-being, and developmental support. On one sheet of chart paper (see figure 9.1), Sofia has mapped Cherry CFC's current strategy, with the various departments.

The organization's work has expanded in each of these domains over the last few years due to both increased need and one-time boosts of federal and philanthropic dollars. The money is going away but the need isn't, and the community is now looking to Cherry CFC to continue meeting that need. The board described the organization to Sofia as "small but mighty"; last year, they served 5,400 clients with a $9.9 million budget and just under one hundred employees, who were a mix of full-time and part-time. They brought in $10.8 million in revenue last year, with $1.8 million from grant resources that are about to disappear.

On another sheet of chart paper (see figure 9.2), Sofia and her leadership team winnowed 100+ hours of listening across the community to a list of the five most promising areas for potential new services.

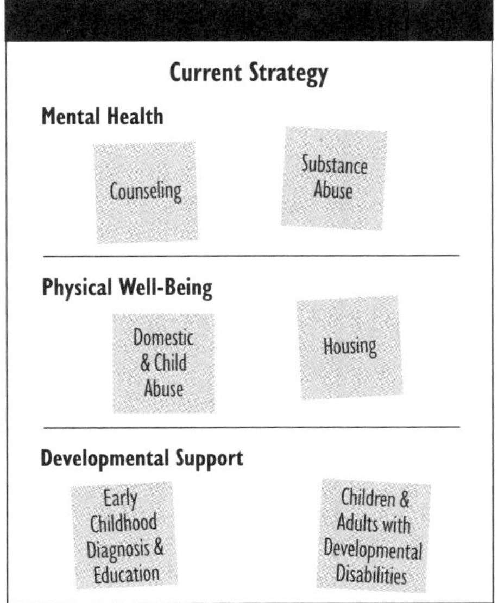

Figure 9.1 Current Strategy

Figure 9.2 External Feedback

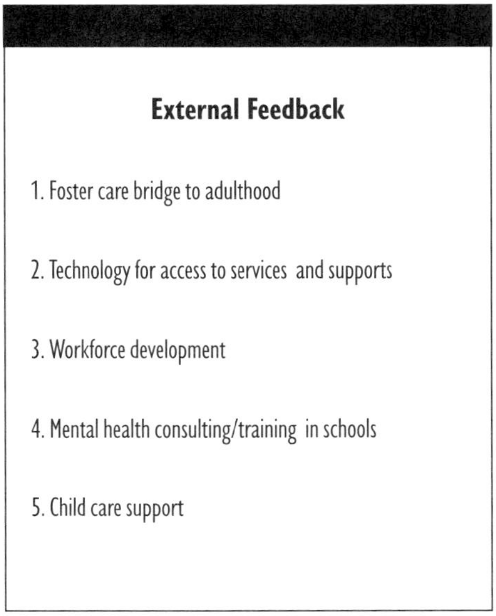

External Feedback

1. Foster care bridge to adulthood
2. Technology for access to services and supports
3. Workforce development
4. Mental health consulting/training in schools
5. Child care support

She knows that the organization can't do all these things well. She isn't even sure if they can do any of them well. And yet everything feels necessary. She runs through each of the items again in her mind; some of them are still fuzzy, while others are easier to picture.

- **Foster care bridge to adulthood:** This item is at the top of her list, mostly because of Angel, whom she met one night at a community event. Angel is seventeen, three months away from his eighteenth birthday, which means that he would soon be aging out of the government support system for foster youth, a process euphemistically called "emancipation." Angel seemed both worried and not worried about the coming changes: "My foster family said I could stay with them until I finish high school later this year. And then I guess I'll get a job and find a place to live." Sofia tries to imagine her eighteen-year-old nephew, Miguel, managing this transition—sometimes he seems like an adult, but sometimes he can't find his phone or his shoes. Sofia knows all the statistics: the fifty-six foster youth currently in their community; the twelve who will likely age out of the system in the next three years; the national statistics on high rates of homelessness, pregnancy, incarceration, and unemployment among recently emancipated young adults. . . . She has no idea yet how Cherry CFC might help foster youth, but she has a good sense of the problem, which seems aligned with the organization's purpose and worth solving.
- **Technology for access to services and supports:** Sofia is somewhat skeptical of this one, mostly because she thinks that technology is often positioned as a way to replace people in their very human work. Yet Theo and Ayumi, two twentysomething counselors who work in Cherry CFC's summer program for youth with developmental disabilities, are convinced that technology is key to engaging youth and their families in a low-cost, easily accessible way. They piloted a year-round way of staying in touch after the summer program and even enlisted two of the youth with developmental disabilities to be their assistants. They persuaded Claire, the director of programs, that this work is worth expanding, and Sofia figures that it would probably be easier to raise money for that than supporting foster youth.

- **Workforce development:** Sofia knows a lot about workforce development from her previous role, but she isn't sure what it means exactly in this context. It seems like a catch-all for trying to help both youth and older people in the community find well-paying jobs. Should they just focus on youth? Or on parents who are working multiple jobs to support their families? Or people emerging from incarceration? And who would partner with them?
- **Mental health consulting/training in schools:** Sofia and her team heard from both parents and educators in the community that the schools need help supporting the mental health of their students, with the needs increasing in the last several years. Teachers are expected to be everything to everybody and aren't trained to support mental health issues. Sofia knows from listening to teachers that they aren't sure how to handle recess conflicts or students who need more support than they can provide. Cherry CFC has lots of counselors who could provide a little training to educators and some bandwidth to help kids with the most urgent needs, but what is really needed is more trained mental health professionals working full time in and with the schools, and Cherry CFC doesn't have the resources for that.
- **Child care support:** This item is what parents said they need the most help with—after-school care is expensive, and any time the school has early-release days or weekdays off in the calendar, parents scramble to find a place for their kids to be. Sofia is sympathetic to this, but Cherry CFC isn't a babysitting agency. On the other hand, if they did provide this service, would it be a way to bring in people who otherwise aren't using their services, and perhaps extend Cherry CFC to some of the more vulnerable people in the community?

Then there is the list of priorities (see figure 9.3) that Sofia and her leadership team made after listening to Cherry CFC's staff. She smiles at the three items on this sheet of chart paper—*I'm starting to sound like all those consultants I've rolled my eyes about in my past orgs . . .*

- **Scale and replication:** This item is something that her board is really interested in, particularly as other communities reach out to Cherry CFC

Figure 9.3 Internal Feedback

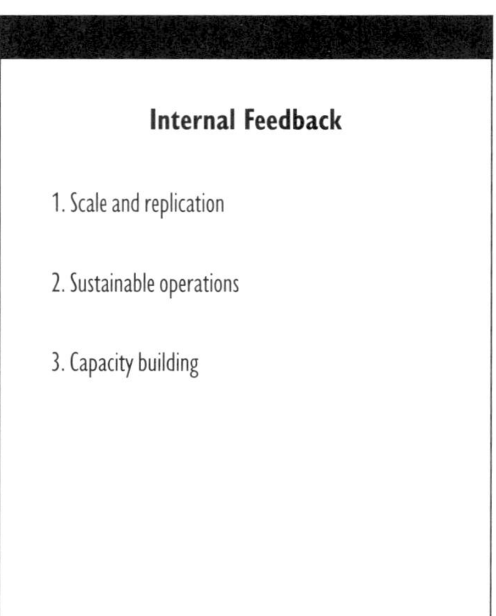

about either starting or helping them start a similar organization. Sofia isn't opposed to scale—wanting to have impact on a big scale was actually why she started down the leadership pathway to begin with—but she feels as though she hasn't put her finger on the most promising part of Cherry CFC's work to scale. And she isn't at all sure that the organization could support replication right now even if it wanted to—everything seems to live in the heads and hearts of the people working there. She mentally tables this one for another year.

- **Sustainable operations:** This item was clearly part of Sofia's charge when the board hired her. She needs to raise money, which is the newest (and most uncomfortable) part of the job for her. And she also needs to help the organization continue to establish systems that outlast people. The organization has grown enormously since it was started in the 1980s, and it has expanded services with a 20 percent increase in staff over the last ten years, but the financial systems and daily processes haven't caught up yet. As Sofia gets to know her senior team members better, she's seeing how the lack of consistent practices on things like meeting agendas, documentation of common processes, learning from work that is underway, and tracking its impact is limiting the effectiveness of individuals, teams, and the organization. She has talked with the chief operating officer (COO) about this one and thinks that he is ready to lead this effort before he retires in three years. Cherry CFC needs this in order to go after more complex funding sources like federal dollars and bigger foundations, but also to keep good people from burning out and to ensure high-quality leadership and work.

- **Capacity building:** From Sofia's point of view, this is the number one priority, although it isn't the sort of thing that is easy to raise money for. When she met with staff at multiple levels as part of her entry, she heard again and again how much they loved working at Cherry CFC—but how exhausted they all were. She has been trying to figure out why people are so tired beyond the nature of their work, and it looks to her like people are working really hard, and that hard work includes a lot of reinventing wheels. As she tries to learn how things work at Cherry CFC, she is directed to people to talk with; nothing seems to be written down.

  She also wants to develop leaders who can grow into more senior roles over time, but nobody in the organization has the bandwidth to onboard new employees who are doing some of the most emotionally demanding, client-facing work in the organization, much less to support and mentor more seasoned team members. Sofia sees that there is an important overlap between scale and replication and sustainable operations. And as she engages her senior team in strategy discussions, she's seeing that many team members are most comfortable thinking about their own department. Thinking expansively about the totality of the organization and its aspirations and programming and making decisions with that in mind are clearly unfamiliar tasks. There also seems to be a wide variance in team members' ability to ask questions and gather data and evidence that push the organization to think beyond business as usual.

Sofia moves the chart papers so they are all together (see figure 9.4). She stares at them, trying to think about how the pieces of the current strategy might fit together to have a bigger impact. She wonders if anything simply doesn't belong. Which of the new items on the feedback chart relate to the current strategy? What might be a good idea, but this isn't the right time for it? What might be key to unlocking other

Figure 9.4 Pieces of the Puzzle

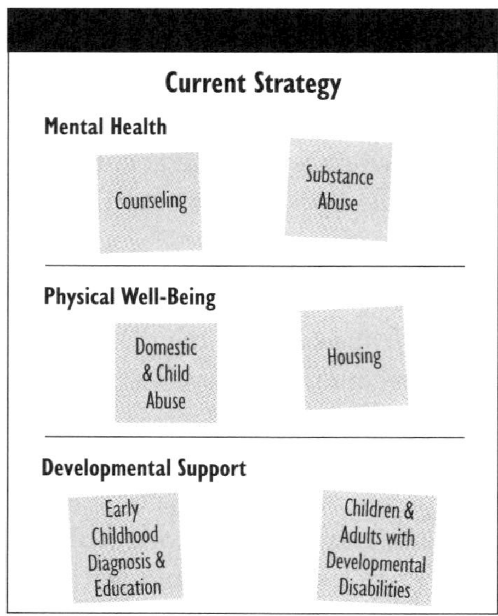

External Feedback

1. Foster care bridge to adulthood
2. Technology for access to services and supports
3. Workforce development
4. Mental health consulting/training in schools
5. Child care support

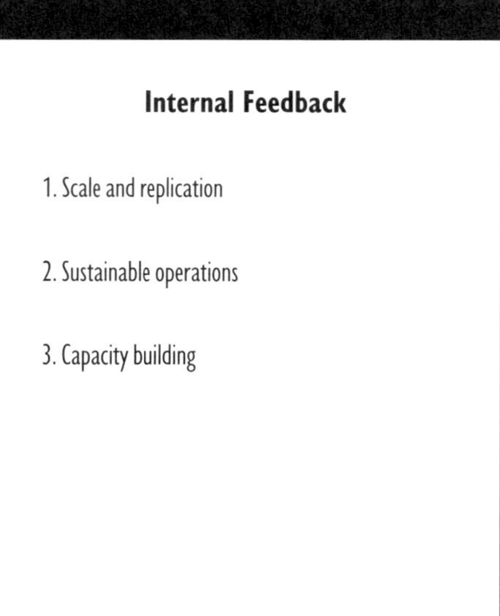

work? What might help the organization be more sustainable internally while supporting children and families to thrive?

Before adding programming or services, Sofia wants to see if there is anything that they could stop doing. She doesn't want to miss this opportunity to reconsider how things are done and to potentially free up some organizational capacity for other things that she is considering. She has been trying to assess the quality of the organization's various services, but it is tricky because most of their existing metrics are about quantity—like how many clients are being served, not how well they are being served.

Her sense is that the Early Childhood Diagnosis and Education Services division is struggling the most, but that seems to be because it is hard to get well-trained people to do that work at the salaries that Cherry CFC is currently offering. She doesn't want to cut Early Childhood because she knows that it is critical to catch kids early and give them support, but she can't afford to pay them more, and actually, Cherry CFC's salaries are competitive in the area. She also doesn't want to make her current staff across the organization worry about their jobs, so she is reluctant to cut any positions, much less a whole division.

There are so many needs in the community. She wants to show the community, her staff, and her board that she is listening to them without stretching the staff even more thinly.

Stop–Opt–Go

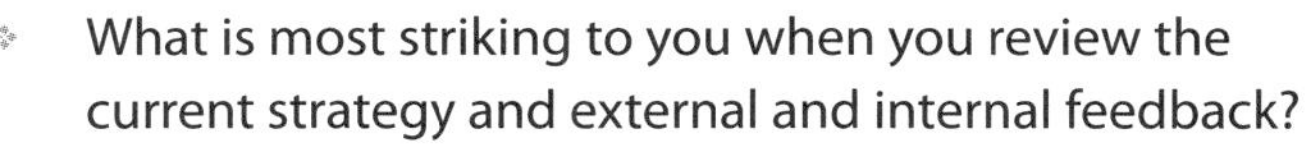

- What is most striking to you when you review the current strategy and external and internal feedback?
- What trade-offs is Sofia weighing?

OPT

Sofia thinks through her options. **Foster care** would have a direct impact on the fewest number of people, but it also would perhaps serve one of the most vulnerable populations in the community. Does this justify focusing on foster care? Sofia learned long ago that trying to make decisions by highest need and level of vulnerability is an impossible way to navigate painful trade-offs because there is inevitably something that you won't do and someone you want to serve whom you can't.

She has to have a different way of making hard decisions. Could she get a twofer or a threefer doing one thing that serves multiple purposes? Should she build off work that they are already doing or meet a need that they aren't yet meeting? Could she hold the duality of *short-term* needs and interests and *longer-term* thinking about the organization's potential and the capacity that she hopes to build?

She doesn't think that she can tell parents and the community that she listened to them, and then turn around and focus on **sustainable operations** and **capacity building**, which surfaced only internally. But she needs those things to do the outward-facing work well.

As she thinks about capacity building, she wonders about having her team work on playbooks, as she did in her last organization, to document the practices, priorities, and deep knowledge that she sees in pockets throughout Cherry CFC. That might be a small step to create some consistency of practice within the organization, address the "everything we need to know about *X* lives in one person's head" problem, build internal capacity, and potentially help with **scaling**. She floated that idea lightly to her leadership team, and there was some immediate hesitation about limiting flexibility and creativity while trying to centralize and automate human-centered work. But when she showed the team some vibrant examples that her last organization made in partnership with people in the community, including youth who had helped make the playbooks accessible and fun-looking, her team warmed to the idea.

Sofia could see Claire, the director of programs, as a future CEO at Cherry CFC or elsewhere, and she wants to figure out a way to help her grow. A natural move might be **expanding programming into another community in their region**, which her board would love, but Sofia is hesitant to expand right now. Maybe they don't need to do anything about **bridging foster care into adulthood**, and she could just follow up with that head of the local business organization whom she met a few weeks ago and see if he could help place **foster youth into jobs**. Or maybe she doesn't want that to be her first ask of the business community? Or maybe she should do something big and show everyone that she is meant to be in this role? But this job isn't about her. Yet she also doesn't want to tiptoe around big issues. . . . Sofia pauses as her mind spins in many directions.

Stop–Opt–Go

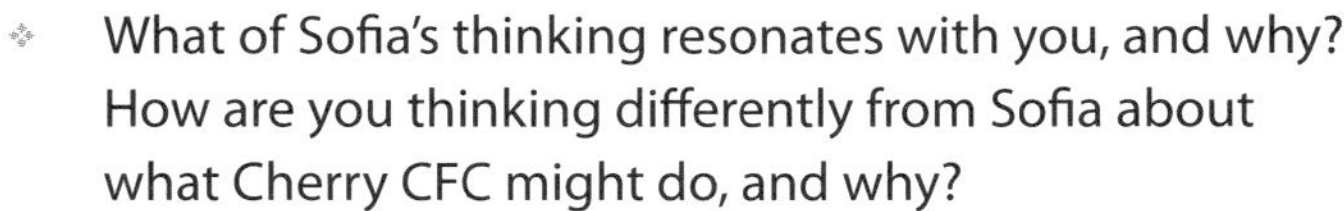

- What of Sofia's thinking resonates with you, and why? How are you thinking differently from Sofia about what Cherry CFC might do, and why?
- What questions or tools might she use to help her have her next conversations with her leadership team and board?

GO

Two days later, Sofia is meeting with her leadership team. Their task is to decide where and how to focus. She is scheduled to share their next steps with her board at their meeting next week. At the beginning of the meeting, Sofia models big-picture, strategic thinking by talking about the interconnections among different initiatives and looking for the thing to focus on that addresses multiple needs. Then she asks them to think together about a focus area that is both high priority and high leverage in terms of its potential for impact.

The team decides to focus on **sustainability**, and not just "sustainable operations," but sustainability for their staff and for their community. Embedded in their focus on sustainability is the idea of building capacity. Sofia is pleased to see how they're starting to think about the interrelationships among things in order to have more impact. Claire, the director of programs, has some questions about how to balance "this is the way to do it" with encouraging staff to adapt to clients and their needs. Sofia sees the duality of *flexibility and consistency* in Claire's remarks and pauses to both acknowledge it and also introduce the team to the bigger idea of dualities and how to manage them. Claire asks to talk with some people in Sofia's prior organization to learn more about how to navigate the tension between affording practitioners the flexibility needed to be responsive to needs and ensuring a consistent quality of service. To build on the team's work and push their thinking, Sofia asks, "What do you think we need to build into the design and implementation of this playbook to learn fast from the process and identify key contributors to its success, so we have good information to use if we decide to expand this work and develop additional playbooks?"

While the community and funders may not think that playbooks are important, playbooks will help Cherry CFC serve clients better in the near term, hopefully reduce stress and turnover among staff, and show the board that there is effort underway on the scale front without actually replicating anything yet. Sofia isn't sure that this will be enough to slow the board's urgency about spreading Cherry CFC's good work to other places, but she is sure that at this moment, the organization can't serve their current clients well and extend into other communities.

The leadership team also decides to do some **foster care work**, specifically focusing on youth who are aging out of the foster care system. Sofia met with Claire individually before the leadership team meeting to see what she might be interested in and have the bandwidth to lead. Claire thinks that focusing on a few foster care youth could be a good fit with their existing programming and might also offer an opportunity for Theo and Ayumi to use their tech ideas to stay connected with foster youth and provide support. Claire is worried that she is going to lose them to better-paying jobs and wants to keep them at Cherry CFC as long as possible. The leadership team thinks that all this makes sense, so long as they aren't doing technology for the sake of technology.

Back in her office, as she prepares for the board meeting, Sofia is thinking about how to share all this with the board. They aren't quite sure what the foster youth support will look like yet. She has planted some seeds of ideas like partnering with local employers to hire the youth in the summer during high school and then provide some ongoing training and support during college and/or full-time jobs if the youth decide not to go straight to college. In her effort to build her team's capacity to think both *short term* and *long term*, Sofia has been explicit about her thinking that this might be an opportunity for a twofer—trying some workforce development in a small way, which could develop in interesting ways over time.

Sipping her now-lukewarm coffee, Sofia thinks of her dad, who often reminds her that *la prueba del fuego* (trial by fire) is sometimes needed to move an idea forward—and she has lots of experience with learning by doing. She is ready to lead, knowing that she will make some mistakes in this new role but also sure that she can be purpose-driven, focused, and collaborative to serve her community well. Sofia prepares for the board meeting, ready to share the direction in which she and the leadership team want to go.

ANALYSIS

While all the elements of leading strategically are in play (see figure 9.5), and there is clearly a lot of *discerning* going on, Sofia is focused on *thinking big* (sustainability) and *acting small* (helping foster youth who are aging out of the system, developing a playbook, and developing Claire as a senior leader). The small pieces, if they get traction, could lead to other small pieces—more playbooks, more extensive foster care support, workforce development beyond foster youth, deepening work in domestic violence and child abuse services—and hopefully employee retention and reduced burnout, which will then increase overall capacity and individual and organizational well-being. They also could support her broader ambition to help the most vulnerable people in the community to thrive.

Sofia is also thinking about *relationships*—both the interpersonal relationships required to do the work well and the relationships among bodies of work.

Figure 9.5 The Five Elements in Red Light, Green Light

Working on supporting foster youth will require several parts of Cherry CFC to work together, which will be a new way of working for the organization and will provide some opportunity to support leadership development within the organization. Sofia is still developing the interpersonal relationships needed to support Claire, partner with community organizations, build a strong leadership team, and work with the board. She considers building relationships as key to her success as a leader and part of why she was hired. Now, in this particular context, she is learning to step into the positional *power* of president and CEO. To rise to the occasion, she harnesses all her sources of personal power, including being Latina from a working-class family, her twenty-plus years of professional expertise, and her faith. In Sofia's mind, these sources of power intersect with her strategic thinking at all times.

Sofia is nearing the end of this round of Stop–Opt–Go. First, she paused long enough to listen and hear many opinions and suggestions from outside and inside Cherry CFC, and then she narrowed down that list of options. Even though part of her just wanted to pick a place to start and go, she knew that would exacerbate her staff's exhaustion—and might not lead to more impact anyway. So she paused again with her leadership team, thinking through the trade-offs of multiple options and choosing a couple of "go" ideas. Now she prepares to discuss those ideas with her board. She is ready to go, and her job now is to help get the board and the organization to move in the same direction.

REFLECTIONS

What new insights do you have about your leadership after reading this mini-case?

10

STYMIED INNOVATION

MIRANDA IS ON CLOUD NINE as she walks out of the school board meeting on a balmy April evening. She had been so nervous about presenting the Teacher Innovator project that she'd been working on all year. She'd never spoken before the superintendent, the board, or a crowd like that. The slides that she'd labored over to describe the personal finance project she developed for her eighth graders explained it well. The quotes from her students about all they had learned and what they were left thinking about at the end of the project really brought it and its impact to life. As she walked down the hallway, she thought, *I like this teacher innovation stuff. It's hard, but it's fun to create new ways of doing things and new experiences for our middle-schoolers.* She saw Mr. Ramos, her principal, in the hallway and hurried over to him.

"Thank you for all your support as I developed the unit, and for your help in preparing for the board presentation, and being here tonight," Miranda said.

"It was my pleasure. You did a great job in the meeting. I could see board members' excitement about what you've done with your students."

"Yeah, they seemed pretty engaged. I wonder what happens next," Miranda said.

"I'm not sure what the plan is for year two. Do you want to teach the project again next year? I know you meet with the other teacher innovators regularly. Are you all talking about what happens with your innovations once the school year ends?"

"I'd definitely teach it again. I'm not sure if I'm supposed to help other teachers teach it, too. I don't know. We don't talk about that at our meetings much."

"Huh. The fact that they had you come talk to the board makes me think there's some bigger plan here."

"Maybe. I'll have to ask."

BACKGROUND ON THE TEACHER INNOVATORS INITIATIVE

The ten middle schools in Rutherford Public Schools have long been the system's Achilles' heel. They live in the shadows of a strong system of elementary schools and the allure of high schools, with all their offerings and opportunities. The academic programming consists of four core subjects, a foreign language, and one elective, which rotates between physical education/health, visual arts, music/drama, and technology/library. This, plus the fact that there aren't many extracurriculars, make for an anemic program that students seem to shuffle through, half-engaged. Students' weak engagement in their learning is juxtaposed with a fraught social scene: hundreds of students in the throes of early adolescence with access to social media and without the social-emotional skills to understand and navigate their feelings and the feelings of others. Over the last two years, there's been a citywide increase in middle-school bullying incidents and more referrals to counselors for social-emotional distress.

Wanting to make some progress on middle schools, the superintendent thought of the rock-star teachers he saw teaching in each of the schools during his school visits. He wanted to draw on their expertise. They likely knew firsthand what changes might help engage students more and offer a richer educational experience. Working with them directly could get a flywheel of improvement spinning. His goals were to empower middle school teachers to develop fresh approaches to common middle school dilemmas, and then to spread those approaches across schools to have a greater impact on students.

As the superintendent thought more about this, he remembered the recent grant that Jackson, his new director of innovation, had just received to support school-based innovation. *Ah, I'll ask Jackson to lead this work, and we can tap that grant to fund the effort, including teacher stipends. We can get to improvement through innovation.* This idea aligned with one of the system's priorities—recognize and empower educators—outlined in the new strategic plan. He knew that the union president would be enthusiastic, as she'd been asking about teacher leadership opportunities for months. The superintendent thought, *Innovating is definitely a form of leadership, and these teachers can become leaders among their peers and in their schools, maybe even in the system as a whole.* And, going straight to the teachers would mean that principals didn't have one more thing put on their plate. They were tapped out. The superintendent couldn't ask them to spearhead this initiative.

THE INITIATIVE

The superintendent's charge to Jackson was enticing and vague: "Something's got to change in the middle schools. I want you to disrupt the status quo by empowering and supporting our best teachers to innovate and see what you can get going." To get started, Jackson spent most of a month in middle schools across the system to understand the biggest issues limiting the middle school experience. He observed in classrooms, halls, and cafeterias and talked to students, teachers, and principals, both in focus groups and one on one. The principals helped him schedule listening sessions with families. In his meetings with principals, he asked for recommendations of their most successful teachers who demonstrated leadership skills; he then made sure to visit their classrooms to see their teaching and class cultures. If he agreed with the principals' assessment, he shared a one-pager about the Teacher Innovators Initiative, mentioned the stipend associated with the project, and invited the teachers to an information meeting.

Jackson saw clear themes about middle school issues across different stakeholders, which provided clarity about where to focus the innovation efforts.

Themes Regarding the Issues in Middle Schools

- Lack of engaging instruction
- Inflexible program limits students' options and engagement
- Lack of supportive relationships among students and teachers

Jackson attended one of the middle school principals' monthly meetings to share the themes and talk about the Teacher Innovators Initiative. Because of a brewing facilities crisis, Jackson's time with the principals was cut short. He shared the themes and described the Teacher Innovators Initiative, explaining, "We're inviting your most talented teachers to develop and experiment with innovations that address the three priority areas that grew out of the common concerns." He flashed a slide on the screen that listed the three priorities.

Priorities for Teacher Innovations

- Invigorate learning to engage students.
- Create some flexibility in the middle school program to boost engagement and ensure that students (and teachers) can try new things.
- Focus on building student and adult relationships.

Running out of time, Jackson handed out a one-pager about the Teacher Innovators Initiative, as he explained, "We'll identify the best work the teachers do and expand it to serve more middle schoolers." Disappointed that he didn't have more time with the principals, he walked out of the meeting with a small group of principals in hopes of continuing the conversation.

"So, there are going to be experiments going on in middle school classrooms around the system?" one principal asked.

"Yes. I'm drawing from your recommendations of talented teachers. We're shooting for forty teachers in this first round. We'll teach them how to use cycles of experimentation, culling their learning and then applying it to refine the innovation and try it again."

"What happens then?" another principal asked.

"At the end of the school year, we'll identify the most successful innovations that are relevant across schools and think about how to replicate and scale them in more schools and classrooms."

"Sounds exciting. I'll be curious to learn what the teachers do," said one of the principals.

"Yup. I'll come back to your meeting in a few months to update you on our progress and next steps," Jackson said as the principals started to scatter to their cars.

Shortly after this meeting, Jackson began designing a yearlong curriculum for the teacher innovators. He had come into his role after being a teacher in the system, getting a graduate degree focused on instructional and school improvement and innovation, and then trying to lead that work from the office of teaching and learning. The superintendent created the position of director of innovation last year, and Jackson was hired for it. With a passion for innovation, Jackson was excited to build a process from the ground up, while curating resources and creating tools and protocols to support the teachers in each step of the process. His boss, the special assistant to the superintendent, appreciated his thoughtfulness and careful planning, requesting periodic updates but otherwise leaving Jackson on his own.

Yearlong Curriculum for Teacher Innovators	
Month	**Focus**
August	Orientation and initial training
September	Developing innovation and experiments
October–November	Round 1 of experiments
December	Sharing feedback, results, and learning; plan for Round 2
January–February	Round 2 of experiments
March	Sharing feedback, results, and learning
April	Showcase of teacher innovations
May–June	Planning for scale and replication

THE FIRST YEAR OF INNOVATION

After all of Jackson's planning, the year started with great promise. Forty teachers, including Miranda, signed on as innovators, some as pairs and a few as teams. The energy and excitement at the kickoff planning and learning session were palpable. Teachers were thrilled to have the chance to address important issues, think creatively about both problems and solutions, learn about innovation, and be in community. The projects that they imagined ran the gamut, with many of them touching on more than one of the priorities, offering an integrated solution. Jackson thought that this was likely the key to success, rather than treating each of the three priorities individually.

Priorities for Teacher Innovations	Examples of Teachers' Innovations
• Invigorate learning to engage students. • Create some flexibility in the middle school program to boost engagement and ensure that students (and teachers) can try new things. • Focus on building student and adult relationships.	• A mini-course in leading a healthy lifestyle that includes students conducting an ad campaign and a school assembly for their peers • A mastery approach to learning piloted in several science units • An entrepreneurial makers' space where students develop ideas and plans for a small business • Personal finance unit taught (by Miranda) as an alternative to study hall • Partnership between social studies and English teachers to teach history through the lens of the news and the narratives created therein • Development of a social-emotional development inventory for students and an aligned badging system, which recognizes the ways that students develop these skills outside of school • Introduction of oral histories as part of the social studies curriculum, focused initially on learning from veterans about national service and war through a partnership with the local branch of the US Department of Veterans Affairs • A seventh-grade team of teachers, who share one hundred students, creating a six-week, interdisciplinary unit on extreme weather and its impact on habitats and migration

Within weeks, the teacher innovators were elbow-deep in their projects. They fleshed out their innovations and their design and execution and began their first experiments. While some innovators struggled to implement their ideas in the context of the existing school schedule and expectations, most of them figured out ways to skirt the school and system constraints, which included swapping out an existing curricular unit for the one that they developed; drawing on their relationships with the principal or their teacher colleagues to get help with creating the time, space, and supplies that they needed for their innovations; or implementing their innovations at the edges of the school day to avoid conflicts.

When the teacher innovators came together at the end of the first round of experiments to share their work and learning, there was a buzz of excitement in the room. Teachers reported that students were more engaged in their learning and taking more leadership of it, with great results, both in terms of their learning and students having an impact beyond the classroom. Innovators told powerful stories of teams of students supporting one another to ensure that they all got the badge toward which they were working; seventh graders making videos with their phones about the ills of a sugary diet and showing them at an assembly at the nearby elementary school; Miranda's eighth graders creating a *Top Ten Financial Tips for Teens* brochure (with accompanying TikTok videos) as a synthesis of their learning; and a student developing a business idea to provide meal-delivery services by bike for a restaurant in the neighborhood.

As Jackson listened to the teachers, he was impressed by all that they had learned from their experiments. Yet he could see how they struggled with improving their practices after studying the results of their early efforts. This issue had plagued the system's larger efforts at improvement. In preparation for the second round of experiments, Jackson built in scaffolds to help the innovators reflect together on their lessons, their implications for revisions or refinements to their projects, and the steps to take to make these improvements. Energy was high as innovators shared their plans for the second round of experiments and prepared for them. Jackson noticed that about 20 percent of the projects hadn't gotten up and running yet. He wasn't worried, though, given the typically high percentage of innovations that fail outside of education.

The tenor at the gathering of innovators at the end of the second cycle late in March was notably more subdued. The teachers seemed tired, which Jackson attributed in part to the usual late-in-the-school-year exhaustion. As he listened in on the small-group discussions among the innovators, he noticed some themes surfacing across the conversations. Regardless of what kind of innovation the teachers were involved in, there was frustration about constraints:

- They were unsure about how to move from success with one or two redesigned curriculum units to a reconceptualized seventh-grade science course.
- The time that innovators were spending on their projects, on top of their full-time work, was significantly more than their stipends covered.
- With so many innovations happening at the edges of the school day, student access was limited, with some students having no access, and the innovations weren't changing much about students' experience of the regular school day.

At one point in the meeting, Miranda said, "I couldn't do this without help. My principal is letting me use time in the day I wouldn't usually have access to in order to teach my mini-course, and he's given me a little budget. A couple of teachers who are friends are helping me fine-tune the curriculum. I'm not sure how to replicate that in other schools." Miranda's comment kept running through Jackson's head. The teachers were relying on their relationships and the power of their reputations and proven success to navigate around the entrenched structures and systems of their schools and the school system. Given that the goal was to scale and replicate the most promising experiments, Jackson worried that the current approach was neither sustainable nor the path to the broad-scale improvement the superintendent had charged him with achieving.

These thoughts were still on Jackson's mind as he watched Miranda present to the board in April and as he stood in a middle school cafeteria as the superintendent kicked off the Teacher Innovators Showcase in May. The innovators sat at tables ready to share their work with peers, alongside principals who appeared curious about the work happening beyond their schools. In the crowd, Jackson recognized some of his central office colleagues from the teaching and learning team, whom he had invited to introduce them to the work. As the superintendent spoke to the group, he kept using the words "teacher leadership." Jackson noticed that he emphasized the teachers as leaders in the system more than as innovators in their classrooms and schools, which was Jackson's primary orientation. The superintendent's remarks focused on replicating projects across some of or even all the middle schools, something that Jackson hadn't fully thought through yet, wanting to get some proof points worth replicating first.

After the superintendent's opening remarks, Jackson teed up the table sharing. As he walked around the room, listening in at tables, he heard a teacher who had come to learn about her innovator colleagues' work ask Miranda: "How could I learn how to replicate your project at my school across town?" After a long silence, Miranda said, "I'm not sure." As he kept circling the room, he heard a principal say, "This is a great project, but I can't see it scaling to touch many more students. The school schedule would have to be revamped to make that possible." Jackson felt a twinge of anxiety, as he sensed that the principal didn't see that as something he could or would do. Jackson realized that he had a serious problem on his hands that could jeopardize the whole initiative when one of the star teacher innovators said, "It was a great project and I'm really glad I did it, but I'm not sure I'd do it again. It was a lot of work."

Jackson retreated to the back of the room. As he chewed the inside of his lower lip, turning the comments over and over in his head along with the school board's enthusiasm for the initiative, the assistant superintendent who oversaw all of the middle schools joined him and said, "This is a great gathering. The teachers have done really interesting work. But I don't understand how these little boutiquey projects that they created are supposed to add up to improving the way we do middle school." Jackson looked at her blankly, wondering, *Can she read my mind?*

Stop–Opt–Go

- What are the critical issues in this case?
- Pretend that you're one of the actors in the case (e.g., Miranda, a principal, the assistant superintendent overseeing middle schools, or Jackson's boss). What would you need in order to realize the superintendent's goal?
- If you were Jackson, what would you do now?
- If you could turn back time and advise Jackson, what are a couple of things you would recommend he do differently? Why?

ANALYSIS

There's a lot going on in this case. As figure 10.1 illustrates, it touches on all the elements of leading strategically, which are intertwined in ways that make them

Figure 10.1 The Five Elements in Stymied Innovation

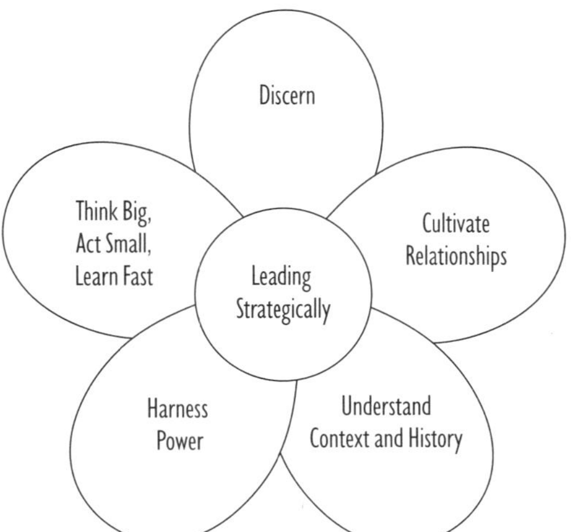

important to unravel to make visible the interplay between the elements. The issues around *relationships* and *power* are tangled together, as are those about *discerning* and *thinking big, acting small, learning fast*.

Relationships and Power

Looking at interpersonal relationships, one of the exciting things about this effort is the way that it supports relationship building among teachers. They are brought together by shared interests, and by sharing their work, they are deepening those connections and the collaboration that could happen among teachers in service of the initiative's success. In this initiative, very little attention is given to organizational relationships. How do the academic departments responsible for course creation need to be involved in this work? How do counselors and social workers and the central office team working on students' social-emotional development need to be engaged when teachers want to develop a badging system for students? How and when does the assistant superintendent of middle schools need to be engaged?

Given that the goal of the initiative is broad, systemic change that is transformational for students' middle school experience, teachers can't do this alone. Jackson appears to lack experience bringing work to scale successfully. He struggles to manage the duality of the *short-term* work of getting the experimentation up and running (his area of passion and greatest expertise) and addressing the *longer-term* investments necessary for bigger impact. Perhaps he overestimated how the superintendent's commitment to the initiative would solve the meaty issues of building buy-in and creating enabling conditions for the work in schools and across the system.

Jackson's lack of attention to organizational relationships is visible in how he doesn't nurture interpersonal relationships. He focuses most of his attention on the teacher innovators without continuing to nurture the relationships that he began to develop with principals and other stakeholders during his initial school visits. Principals are crucial to scaling the innovations, but Jackson does not have the strong relationships and/or credibility with them that would be needed to engage them in the next phase of the initiative. The fact that we first hear of the assistant superintendent overseeing middle schools at the May showcase tells us that Jackson did not appreciate how important a relationship with her was to supporting the scaling and replication of the innovations. It's not clear if Jackson has anyone in the system helping him think through these bigger issues; it doesn't sound like that's something his boss does.

The duality of *process and product* is at play here in an interesting way. Jackson is very attentive to the process that he's created for the teacher innovators, and he is clear the product is successful experiments. Yet he seems unaware of the attention that he needs to pay to the process of engaging the rest of the system in this first year of the initiative to build understanding and buy-in and create the conditions for its sustainability and broader impact.

The teacher innovators must draw on their personal power—the trust and respect that they've established with colleagues, students, and their principals. They have little to none of the positional power needed to move their small experiments toward the center stage of how middle schools' programming and scheduling are organized and run. That positional power is held by the principals and central office leaders who have been largely left out of the conversation, although they have the power needed to make scaling innovations impossible. Should they have been engaged early in this process? It's hard to know if that would have strengthened or constrained the nascent experiments, which needed gentle nurturing. Perhaps the long arm of the bureaucracy would have crushed early efforts with guidelines and requirements. Or maybe engaging them early, with clarity that their responsibilities were to identify key systemic considerations implicated by the innovations, would have created the conditions for replication and scaling. The fact that Jackson is startled by the different reactions at the showcase is concerning but not surprising, given his limited leadership experience and the trust without support that he is getting from his boss.

Discern and Think Big, Act Small, Learn Fast

The interaction of *discern* and *think big, act small, learn fast* in this case begins with the vision or purpose for the innovation initiative. When the superintendent asks Jackson to "disrupt the status quo and see what you can get going," he's clearly thinking big. His message is imbued with a desire for change, but without a vision of what the change will make possible for middle schoolers, the educators who serve them, and the system as a whole. He references improvement through innovation and teacher leadership but doesn't define what each of those things means to him. There is a lack of *discerning to identify purpose* that leaves the initiative on shaky ground before it's even begun.

The vagueness of the charge leaves the initiative without a clear, ambitious *why* to serve as the North Star that guides the work of Jackson and the teachers and grounds conversations and communications about the initiative. In the absence of that big *why*, Jackson relies on his expertise in innovation, prioritizing teacher innovation in three areas: (1) invigorate learning to engage students, (2) create some flexibility in the middle school program to boost engagement and ensure students (and teachers) can try new things, and (3) focus on building student and adult relationships. These things are *what* is to be done. At the point at which the *what* stands in for the *why*, the initiative loses some of its power and potential. Attention shifts from purpose to tactics, and the potential for transformation dims.

This challenge is compounded by a misstep related to *discerning to understand the problem*. Jackson starts strong, as he synthesizes issues identified by students, families, teachers, and principals. He homes in on the significant points of overlap among the stakeholders, figuring that those are high-leverage places to focus on. This is all very strategic. What happens next is a moment of huge missed opportunity. Rather than engage in root-cause analyses with educators to get beneath these symptoms of problems, Jackson simply reframes the symptoms as opportunities and names them as the priorities to be pursued. This results in vague statements of priorities that don't provide precision about where to focus the experiments. This is an incredibly common misstep.

Problems Identified	Priorities
• Lack of engaging instruction • Inflexible program limits students' options and engagement • Lack of supportive relationships among students and teachers	• Invigorate learning to engage students. • Create some flexibility in the middle school program to boost engagement and ensure that students (and teachers) can try new things. • Focus on building student and adult relationships.

The fact that the problems are described as "lack of," followed by a thinly veiled solution, is a flag that root causes haven't been identified. Without root-cause analysis, it's unclear if the problem of classes being boring is about teachers' skills, the quality of curricula, the time available for deeper learning activities, or something else entirely. Understanding which of those things are in play is needed to focus priorities on the points of highest leverage. Instead, there is a vague articulation of the priorities, which means that the whole initiative will be similarly broad and vague, and that will likely limit its usefulness. The diverse array of experiments the teacher innovators propose and pursue is indeed broad and vague. The variety of ideas being pursued is not a problem in and of itself. It is the lack of root causes to serve as a starting point for *discerning to choose right action* that puts the work on shaky ground.

With neither a clear starting point defined by root-cause analyses (rather than symptoms of problems) nor a clear purpose and vision for the effort, there is just the messy middle of teachers trying their best to do something productive that has a positive impact. This is haphazard, and while some promising experiments may grow out of the effort, their impact will be muted by the lack of these two essential things.

While the larger container in which the promising work is happening is not robust enough to maximize impact, Jackson does a great job creating the conditions for innovation and experimentation. Miranda and her teacher innovator peers get to exercise their creativity, *learn fast*, and improve, with some of them creating proof points and being recognized for their work. What's missing is the foundation needed for replication and scaling. This omission makes the sustainability of the initiative precarious. Equally important, it also has the potential to leave the teacher innovators frustrated and unsustained in their work.

REFLECTIONS

What new insights do you have about your leadership after reading this mini-case?

11

MANY COOKS IN THE KITCHEN

LEAFING THROUGH THE SLIDE DECK, Emily, the chief of high schools, says, "We're having a terrible time improving high school attendance. We've barely gained a percentage point over last year. If the kids aren't coming, all of our best-laid plans for what happens in schools are irrelevant. The things we are trying just aren't working."

"And the student survey data about the number of students who are feeling depressed or hopeless is really worrisome," says Laurie, the chief of student services.

José, the deputy superintendent, chimes in, "There's also a 5-percentage-point drop in students completing the FAFSA [Free Application for Federal Student Aid] form. What do we know about that? Is it about economics and kids needing to work immediately and forego college? Or do kids not understand that FAFSA is the gateway to grants and loans that can support them through college? We need to get a handle on that."

"We've done so much work refining our college and career pathways, yet 25 percent of our kids say they don't know what they're doing after graduation. What's happening that's letting them walk across the stage without a plan?" says Tom, the director of college and career counseling.

Sherise, the director of high school student support, chimes in, "Look at our ninth-grade on-track data: 87 percent on track to graduate. That's promising! But then look at the grade distribution in tenth grade: 50 percent of students are failing a class. It seems like our support for ninth graders is paying off, but then things deteriorate in tenth grade. And when we disaggregate the data, we see that performance among students with the lowest socioeconomic status [SES] is flat across ninth and tenth grade. Disaggregation also shows us that Black students made the greatest gains on ninth grade on-track, and they are represented disproportionately in the group of students failing a class in tenth grade."

The Elroy Public Schools superintendent convened this group to look at the end-of-year high school data. She was hopeful, given the school system's investment in this work over the last few years, that they would see substantial improvement. High school transformation is one of the pillars of the system's strategy. There is the "Portrait of a Graduate," which was created with broad-based support and sets the vision for what students should know and be able to do when they graduate. In every high school, there are strong partnerships in place that support pathways to college and careers. A new school-based counseling and advising coordinator role has been recently introduced into the schools, and several of the people in these roles are already beginning to reshape how counseling and advising work is done in schools, realizing promising early results.

Despite all these investments, the data are not what the team hoped they would be.

The superintendent leans forward in her chair and says, "Given all of ours and the community's investments in high schools, these data are concerning. I need you to get beneath the numbers and identify the underlying problems and their root causes. Once we're clear on that, we can identify a couple of things to focus on tightly next year to reverse these trends. Emily, I want you to lead this work, working closely with Sherise and Tom and keeping Laurie in the loop. José, please keep me updated—I want to review a plan that responds to these data in eight weeks." For context, here is the organizational chart for Elroy Public Schools (figure 11.1).

At the end of the meeting, Emily, Sherise, and Tom linger to talk about next steps. Emily says, "I think we need to talk to some students, maybe also teachers and principals, to get a better sense of what's going on in the schools. Tom and Sherise, I want the two of you to work on this together. Make sure that the people you talk to reflect the diversity of the system so we can see if experiences and perspectives vary by gender, race, ethnicity, income, students with disabilities, multilingual learners,

Figure 11.1 Organizational Chart (related to high school advising and counseling)

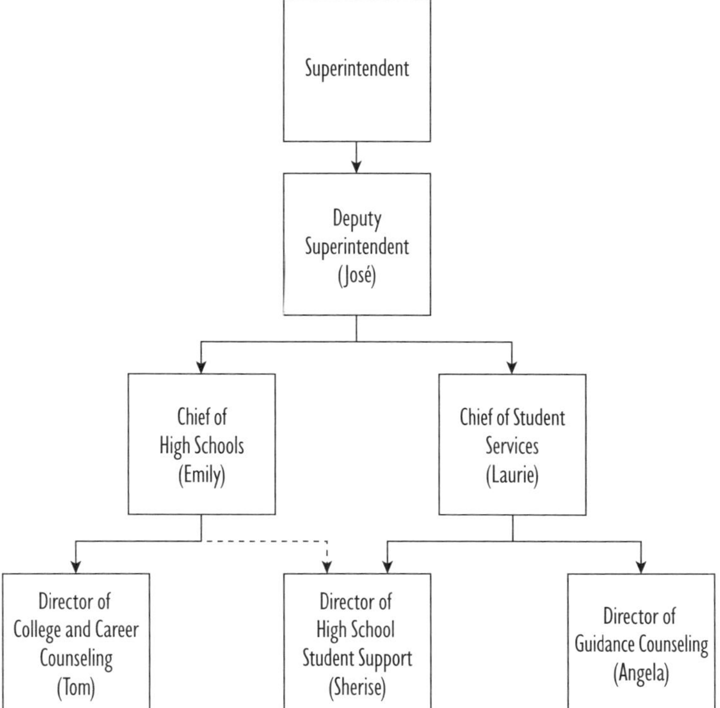

and more generally, students who are being academically successful and those who are not realizing success in the current environment. We need to hear all voices. And, Sherise, I know you've only been here a year, but your experience in your last district building a counseling and advising system is going to be critical. I will talk with Laurie to fill her in."

DISCERNING TO UNDERSTAND THE PROBLEM

Two weeks later, Sherise and Tom observe a focus group that one of Sherise's counselors is facilitating with students from across the district's high schools. The students reflect the diversity of the student body across multiple dimensions. The focus of the conversation is on their high school experience.

"I'm not sure if I have the credits I need to apply to college," says a junior who was recruited for the focus group because after a shaky start in ninth grade, his engagement and performance in school improved steadily. His progress has made him think that college is a possibility.

A sophomore who is doing well and hoping to go to college with some college credits already under her belt, sighs, "I don't know who to go to for what. I have a guidance counselor, a counselor in my college-prep pathway, my homeroom/advisory teacher. . . . It's confusing. Luckily, I have a cousin who is already in college, so she told me what I need to do and keeps checking in to make sure I'm doing it."

"High school has been great," says a senior. "I love my health-care pathway and am on track to graduate with a Medical Assistant certification. My pathway advisor helped me get a summer internship, and there's a chance that I can get a job after graduation at the place where I'm interning."

A junior with a learning disability says, "I haven't been able to participate in a pathway because the schedule of those classes conflicts with me receiving the services outlined in my IEP [individualized education plan]. I really want to explore STEM [science, technology, engineering, and mathematics] careers, but I can't, which makes me worry about what I'm going to do after high school."

A senior chosen because she was missing key credits required for acceptance at an in-state college says, "Tenth grade was really rough. I had a good year in ninth grade, but then my mom got sick. I failed two classes, and I didn't know who to turn to for help."

"I feel stuck," says a junior who had hoped to graduate with an industry certification that would help him get a good-paying job right out of high school. "I chose a career pathway in ninth grade. By the end of tenth grade, I figured out it wasn't right for me, but they told me I couldn't change it. I'm afraid I'm going to graduate and not be able to get a decent job. I can't afford college, so I need a job."

After listening to the students, Sherise and Tom debrief. Tom says, "We've done so much on developing robust pathways to both college and careers, but students don't seem to be reaping the full benefits of that work. There are so many more counseling and advising supports than there were when I started in the district as a counselor twenty years ago. Yet students sound confused about what they need to do or are having trouble getting the right support based on their individual circumstances."

Sherise agrees, saying, "I know, and, based on this focus group, it looks like our Black and brown and low-income students are more frequently unsure about what supports are available and how to access them. I think we need to talk to the high school counselors to understand what's happening in the schools."

"Well, I'm not sure we need to include *my* people," Tom says, referencing the college and career advisors.

After an awkward pause, Sherise says, "I think it's important to have all the different counseling and advising roles represented."

"Okay, if you say so, but I think we're all good on my end," Tom replies.

At the counselor focus group that Sherise sets up, a guidance counselor says, "I'm responsible for helping students and their families complete and submit their FAFSA forms. Given that I have a load of four hundred students, I focus on the students who are in a college pathway. I assume that the students in a career pathway are going directly into jobs after graduation."

Sherise clasps her hands together in her lap to keep from exclaiming, *But we've committed as a district to making college accessible to all. The research is so clear how many more opportunities and increased earning potential college graduates have. We can't make career pathways and college mutually exclusive. That will disproportionately affect low-SES students and Black and brown students negatively. We have a long history of thinking that college is for middle class students and white students.* As she sits quietly, she wonders how a guidance counselor with a load of four hundred students can be expected to do more.

"I work with students and their families to get the FAFSA completed," says an AVID [Advancement Via Individual Determination] program counselor from another school, who works with students over the four years of high school to get them ready for college.

A ninth grade on-track counselor chimes in, "I have no idea what happens after students leave me at the end of ninth grade. I sometimes feel like I'm sending them out into the wilderness. I particularly worry about the students who struggle in ninth grade and need ongoing support. I don't think there's a structure or system to ensure that happens."

"We do things differently at my school," someone else says. "I'm one of the people in the new counseling and advising coordinator role. I'm bringing all the counselors and advisors together at my school regularly to talk about their work and to focus us all on our top priorities. Right now, we're all working with ninth and tenth graders on their course selections for next year to make sure they stay on track to graduate and meet their pathway requirements. We also identify students with needs that aren't being met and develop individualized supports."

Sherise asks the group, "How many counselors or advisors are there in your school?"

The responses pop like popcorn around the conference table: "I don't know"; "There are two other counselors I see in the hallways"; "I think there are four or five, but I don't know them all or what they each do"; "Ditto"; "I work on ninth grade and do a handoff to three pathway counselors who work with my students from tenth to twelfth grade." Sherise tries to jot down the answers and the schools from which they come.

After the focus group, Tom and Sherise walk out to the parking lot together. Sherise says, "I heard the same confusion among counselors and advisors as we heard among the students. It's not clear which counselors do what. It varies from school to school. And the counseling services within schools are not being consistently coordinated. We have to sort this out."

Tom replies, "I think the confusion may just be among the people in the focus group. I'm not sure it's a broader issue than that. I make sure that my counselors are on the same page."

"Well, it's great if all your college and career pathway counselors are on the same page, but do you know how they're working with the other counselors and advisors in their schools?" Sherise asks.

"Not really. I don't focus on that much 'cause we have plenty to do on our own. I think it's easier if each group focuses on its own work," Tom replies. Before Sherise can respond, her phone buzzes. Looking down at it, she says, "I need to run to my next meeting. Let's talk more about this." As Sherise drives to her next meeting, she thinks, *Tom and I are not on the same page. This could get messy. What do we tell Emily?*

Stop–Opt–Go

- What do you think are some of the key problems and their root causes in this case?
- What do you want to understand better?

Two weeks later, Sherise and Tom meet with an ad hoc work group that they've pulled together. It includes a couple of high school principals, a few high school counselors who are leaders among their peers, and two of the people in the new school-based counseling and advising coordinator role. They step back from the

Figure 11.2 Related Root-Cause Analyses

Symptoms of Problem
Students are confused about what they need to do to progress toward graduation and how to access counseling and advising support.

WHY 1
Students don't consistently know the indicators of progress toward graduation.

WHY 2
The indicators are not shared with them OR they're not shared in ways that stick.

WHY 3
There isn't a clear process for advising students through each year of high school to ensure they are on track to graduate.

WHY 4
The system hasn't defined a high school counseling and advising curriculum and scope and sequence and aligned all counseling and advising to it.

Symptoms of Problem
There is inconsistency in the work of counselors and advisors (C&A) with overlaps in job responsibilities.

WHY 1
Decisions are made at the school level about what counselors and advisors do.

WHY 2
Schools need to respond to students' needs, and the current C&A roles and responsibilities don't fully respond to those needs.

WHY 3
School-based staff weren't involved in defining the C&A roles and responsibilities AND students' needs are changing rapidly.

WHY 4
Central office departments define C&A roles and responsibilities, and they're not best positioned to track changes in students' needs.

WHY 5
Defining roles and responsibilities is thought to be the work of the central office.

WHY 1
New C&A roles have been added in the system and layered on top of the existing roles, creating overlaps and gaps in services.

WHY 2
Grants and partnerships are underwriting new roles, and the C&A work isn't being coordinated.

WHY 3
Counseling and advising come out of different central departments that don't work together.

WHY 4
There are neither structures for nor expectation of cross-department communication, collaboration, or coordination.

WHY 5
The system functions in a siloed manner, and systems and structures reinforce that.

chart papers on the wall (figure 11.2), which capture the root-cause analyses that the group just completed.

Sherise rubs her temples as she says, "I look at this and think that while we have lots of advising and counseling happening in the high schools, there is not a system of counseling and advising." She starts sketching the images shown in figure 11.3 on a whiteboard. She says, "The picture on the left is what we have. The picture on the right is a system." There's a buzz of recognition in the room. Sherise continues, "We haven't defined *what* needs to happen in counseling and advising, holistically and

Figure 11.3 Random Acts versus a System

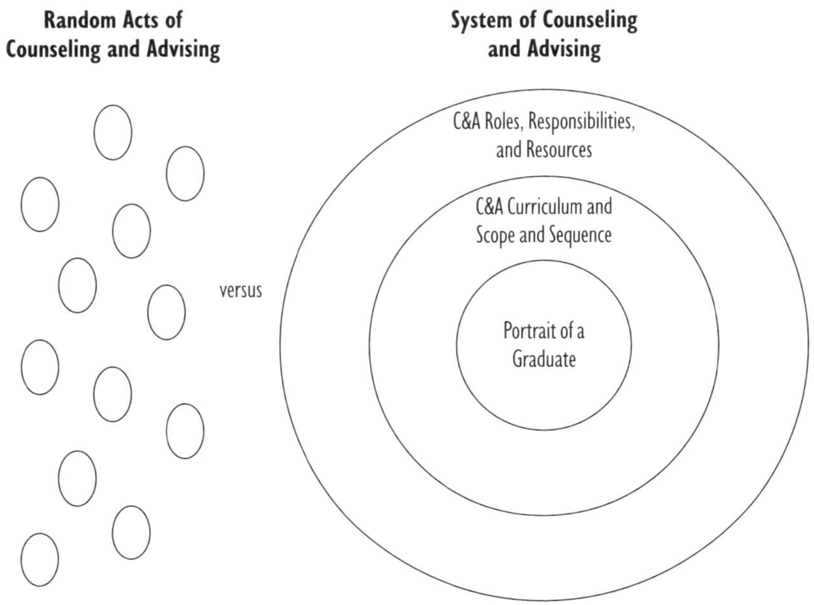

at each grade, based on the portrait of a graduate (*why*). And, we haven't defined *how* we'll do it."

A principal speaks next: "The stuff we uncovered about structural problems with *how* counseling and advising roles and responsibilities are defined and overseen resonates with me. We (principals) don't have much input on the front end, so we adapt on the back end, which is contributing to incoherence. We're going to have to figure out how to give us principals a voice in the process and ensure some consistency."

A counselor speaks up: "Counseling and advising efforts are being managed by multiple central office departments that aren't working together. This plays out in my school, too. I don't even know who the people are in some of these roles."

Sherise interjects, "I think these two problems are related. Without a scoped curriculum, there's nothing consistent to guide the work of counselors and advisors or to use as a vehicle to break down silos and foster collaboration and coordination. It's creating incoherence and confusion."

Another counselor speaks up: "Yeah, but the good news is that Elroy seems to have lots of resources to draw on, much more than the system I came from."

Sherise turns to Tom, who has been pretty quiet through the root-cause analysis and discussion. "What do you think, Tom?"

"I'm not sure. This feels very complicated. Maybe *too* complicated," Tom replies.

A well-respected counselor who has been sitting quietly says, "I think we need to look at some of the job descriptions for counselors and advisors and any curriculum they're using to guide their work. We need to get a better handle on how the jobs are defined and what resources we have to draw on."

By the end of the conversation, the group decides to disaggregate student data by school, and also by student demographics, to see if there are variances or inequities that need to be explored. And they agree to talk to everyone in the central office who is overseeing any form of high school counseling or advising.

When the work group comes back together two weeks later, they share these key findings with each other:

- The school-based counseling and advising coordinators were introduced in every school this year to coordinate the work of the different people doing counseling and advising. The coordinators meet one day a month to share what they're doing in their schools and to problem-solve both common and unique issues that they're facing. They were hired after the "Portrait of a Graduate" was written and are unfamiliar with it.
- Some principals named counselors' beliefs about what students are capable of achieving based on race and class as a serious impediment to building a system of counseling and advising that ensures access to opportunities for all students.
- The system recently received a grant to support the training and development of counselors and advisors.
- Angela, the director of guidance counseling, who's been in the system thirty years, feels like her team's work has been sidelined as the focus on career pathways has increased. In response, she has isolated herself from the other counseling and advising efforts and encouraged her staff to do the same. She has not been invited to any of the meetings that have happened so far on this topic.
- A few principals have set up their master schedules to include regular student advisory sessions led by teachers. The leading indicators of student

success and well-being at some of these schools are better than at the other high schools.

- There is one school at which the college-going rate is high and consistent across students, regardless of race and class.
- Some schools have broken down silos so college and career pathway counselors are collaborating with ninth grade on-track counselors and guidance counselors to ensure a seamless transition of support for students as they move from one grade to the next.

Stop–Opt–Go

- What strengths and opportunities do you see?
- Where would you focus your attention? Why?

DISCERNING TO CHOOSE RIGHT ACTION

At the work group's next meeting, Emily, the chief of high schools, joins the group. After the group gives her a quick update on their deeper analysis, she says, "I love how you're getting beneath the surface, disaggregating data, looking for proof points, and learning from students and the educators who support them. The time you're taking to figure out what's really going on and why will make it easier to pursue the actual improvements quickly because we'll really understand the issues and what's most needed. I think it might be helpful to develop a power map."

"What's that? How do we do it?" Tom asks.

"Given the complexity of this issue and how many different counseling and advising roles there are and the different departments managing them, we need to figure out who the key players are; points of shared, complementary, or competing interests; and the resources we have and need. Understanding this will help us choose and prioritize what we want to do. A power map helps us do that," Emily explains.

"Let's do it," says Sherise.

"It's important to acknowledge that people around this table will be in the power map we develop," Emily says. There's a little awkward laughter in the room. She continues, "So, when we get to roles where the people in them are in the room, let's have them start by sharing their interests and the resources they have for this work and their needs. Then, if others of us have thoughts, we can share them. How does that sound? And, of course, for everyone on the map, this is just our best thinking at the moment. We can always add to it or adjust. The goal is to give us a sense of where there are some interesting synergies and opportunities."

There are murmurs of assent, and the group starts the process. Table 11.1 shows the map that they developed.

Table 11.1 Power-Mapping Interests and Resources

Key Players	Interests/Values	Resources That the Key Players Have	Resources That the Key Players Need to Address Their Interests/Values
Deputy superintendent (José)	• High school student outcomes	• "Portrait of a Graduate" • Money • Ability to make policy • Influence and authority	• Buy-in • Expertise
Chief of student services (Laurie)	• Coherent system of student support, K–12, that meets student needs	• Budget for guidance counselors	• Authority to develop the high school advising and counseling curriculum and scope and sequence
Chief of high schools (Emily)	• Holistic system of counseling and advising	• Monthly half-day meeting with high school principals • College and career readiness (CCR) counselors and the AVID counselors • Reviewer of high school budgets and staffing	• Authority to develop the high school advising and counseling curriculum and scope and sequence • Cross-functional collaboration with other departments (e.g., counseling, student support, diverse learners)
Director of college and career counseling (Tom)	• Strong pathways • Student success in pathways	• CCR partnerships • Grant money • Advising staff in every high school	• Access to teachers, principals, and employers
Director of high school student support (Sherise)	• Robust student support system • Student success and well-being	• Expertise regarding counseling and advising systems • Counselors in every high school • New school-based coordinators (and monthly, daylong meetings with them)	
Director of guidance counseling (Angela)	• Desire for recognition and to be included	• Historical perspective • Three to five counselors per school	

Table 11.1 (Continued)

Key Players	Interests/Values	Resources That the Key Players Have	Resources That the Key Players Need to Address Their Interests/Values
Principals	• High-functioning school • Student success • Clear, manageable expectations from school district • Autonomy	• School schedules • Assignment and supervision of all school-based staff • Supervision of coordinators • School budgets	• Involvement in decision-making that affects schools
Principal supervisors	• Clear expectations from school district re: priorities • Autonomy • Ability to differentiate based on school needs	• Supervise principals • Convene principals and provide professional learning	• Involvement in decision-making that affects schools
School-based counseling and advising coordinators	• Responsive, high-functioning, school-based counseling and advising • Clear expectations • Ability to apply their expertise • Thriving students	• Access to all school-based counselors and advisors • Insights about what is or is not working and how things could work better • Early efforts at coordination and what they're learning from them • Conduit of information from the system to schools and vice versa • Direct contact with students	• Access to counselors • Access to central office leaders working on counseling and advising • Time

"We've got some empty boxes here," says one of the counselors.

"I know. I think we may need to engage a broader group of people in this conversation, or at least talk one on one with some folks, like the principal supervisors," says one of the principals.

"That's a great point. The principal supervisors need to be on board. They tell us what to do. If they don't care about this, nothing's going to happen," says another principal.

"Tom and Sherise, how are you feeling about what we've included for each of you?" says another counselor.

"Mine is fine," Tom says.

"I'm still thinking about the question of resources that my team needs," says Sherise.

"I'm worried that we may have left someone important off this chart," says a counselor.

"It's a good question to ask. We can always add people. There are no external partners listed, which may be something we need to address." Emily replies.

"This is a lot to take in. What do we do now?" says another principal.

"Well, we could use one of those Ease-Impact matrixes Emily likes so much to synthesize the complexity of all the data we have collected into something simple that helps us identify a few things we can do that will have a big effect," says Sherise. She continues, "One of the things I'm thinking about is the expertise needed to address some of the systemic issues we identified, like the curriculum and scope and sequence. I'm not sure whether we have that in house."

"That's a great point. We need to think about when we need to build internal capacity and when it's a better idea to hire in expertise. Let's factor that into where we put things in terms of ease and impact. We may want to visit some other districts or talk to experts in counseling and advising," one of the principals says.

"I'm guessing we have all the expertise we need in house," says Tom.

"Well, why don't we take a run at mapping out Ease-Impact knowing that these variables are in play? Also, we may figure out in the process that we need more input from other people. So let's think of this as a first cut. How does that sound?" says Emily. Everyone around the table nods in assent.

Figure 11.4 shows the Ease-Impact Matrix the work group developed.

Figure 11.4 The Ease-Impact Matrix of the High School Work Group

High Impact, Hard	**High Impact, Easy**
Build a 4-year curriculum and scope and sequence for counseling and advising to guide everyone's work Develop handoff for advising and counseling as students move from ninth to tenth grade Improve communication among counseling and advising staff within a high school	Focus the coordinators on coordination Communicate about our vision for counseling and advising and the different players and their roles in the work
Low Impact, Hard	**Low Impact, Easy**

Stop–Opt–Go

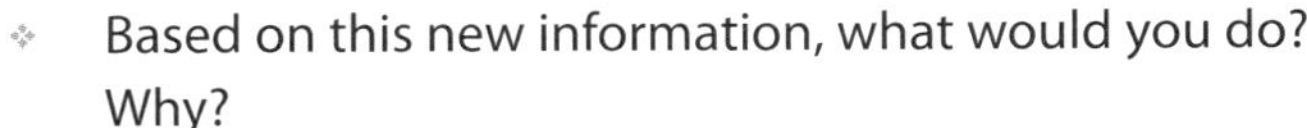

- Based on this new information, what would you do? Why?

As Sherise drives home from the work-group meeting, she thinks, *Emily charged Tom and me with this early work, but Tom doesn't seem to want to get involved. I've got to go back to the power map to see if we have shared interests that might provide a foundation for collaboration. We're all too busy to champion this work, and while the work group is great, it's not going to drive implementation. Should I try to help with the whole thing or carve out a piece where I can use my resources? The new coordinators come out of my budget. Maybe I should just focus on them and partner with the principals to see if we can build on their early work. Or maybe I need to see if I can work with Emily and Laurie to get more authority and take the lead on the whole effort.*

ANALYSIS

The Elroy work group is on a promising path. It has embraced the duality of *action and reflection* by developing a rhythm of action and reflection that is moving the work forward and ensuring that it is thoughtful. The root causes offer a strong starting point, and the subsequent work has surfaced nuances about turf, power, relationships, buy-in, resources, context and history, and promising efforts underway

Figure 11.5 The Five Elements in Many Cooks in the Kitchen

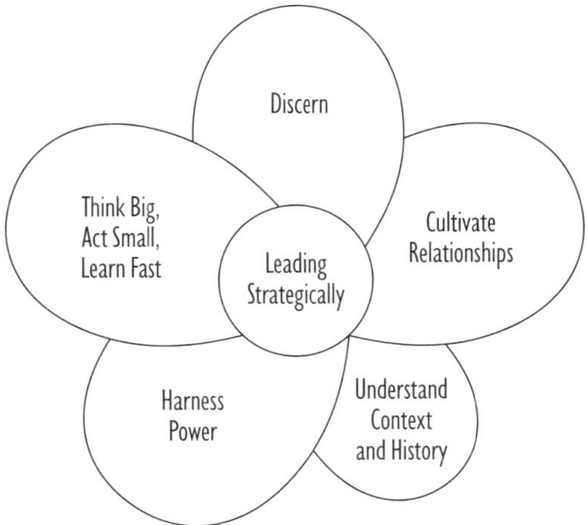

that are important to consider as they *discern to choose right action*. Team members are embracing the duality of *complexity and simplicity* as they explore the complexity of the issue in order to ensure that they fully understand it, and then try to simplify as they think about actions to take. It's already clear that some things are long-term investments, while other things could surface some quick wins that could be scaled.

Part of the calculus of what to focus on relates to how to *think big, act small, learn fast*. The "Portrait of a Graduate" is an important resource that reflects Elroy's *thinking big* and *discerning to identify purpose*. There is a need to backward-map from it to define the counseling and advising system with a curriculum and a scope and sequence, rationalize school-based roles and responsibilities, and articulate cross-functional foci for the central office. This is the *big thinking* needed. Developing it is a heavy lift that will take time and significant organizational capacity.

Meanwhile, the team has surfaced promising small efforts underway in schools around curriculum, advisory, and collaboration, which the new coordinators and principals are leading. Pursuing a combination of small things could be manageable and impactful. Small experiments underway could be tracked, learned from, and considered for scaling. They could also inform the design and content of the counseling and advising system. Integrating these small pieces into the whole of the advising and counseling system is part of what will make this work strategic and impactful.

What's tricky is that while it will take time to develop the larger system, its direction needs to be clear enough to inform the choice of small things, and also be early enough in development to be informed by the small successes that result from experiments. The interplay and synergy between the small things and the big thing is where the greatest promise for impact lies. This means that the group may need to continue to meet and serve as the team that thinks about short-term moves and how they set direction for longer-term work. To realize this potential, group members need to anticipate how things will play out, any likely bumps in the road, and the future implications of decisions made now. They also need to figure out how they will learn along the way and apply that learning to adjustments.

Elroy has a lot of resources to draw on as it tackles this issue: money, staff, additional grants, promising work happening in schools, new coordinators who are trying to organize counseling and advising efforts and staff, and principals who are demonstrating leadership in this work and having success. This is a great context for taking up this work.

Some things that the Elroy work group members might consider as they move forward in *choosing right action* include:

- How to make the "Portrait of a Graduate" widely owned and understood to maximize its power as a North Star,
- How to center students' experience in whatever they do,
- The potential value of bringing in outside expertise versus freeing up or building more internal capacity to support curriculum development efforts, and
- Ways to incentivize cross-functional collaboration in the central office.

With these considerations in mind, there are different approaches Elroy could take that could yield promising results. There is no single right action, but instead options to weigh and well-informed bets to place.

REFLECTIONS

What new insights do you have about your leadership after reading this mini-case?

CONCLUSION

WE HOPE THAT YOU ARE EXCITED about the possibilities of leading strategically and your head and heart are fully engaged as you think about how to apply the ideas that we have introduced in this book.

As we bring this book to a close, we come full circle, returning to our why for writing it. It is our why that guided us through the conceptualization of the book, the writing process, and the moments of uncertainty. Our *why*—aka North Star—is about two interrelated things: effectiveness and sustainability. We want to support you to do complex, ambitious work that contributes to the world. As you grow as a strategic leader, you increase your capacity to create and support the kind of learning, process, and outcomes that the people in schools, organizations, and the communities they serve deserve. Your application of the elements of strategic leadership helps you focus and reduce the noise and constant whirl of unfocused and ineffective action. This supports both effectiveness and sustainability. It helps you work smarter rather than harder, realize a bigger impact, and feel your power and efficacy. And all of that will make you hopeful about what is possible and what you and the people you engage with are capable of. That combination is deeply sustaining.

Throughout this book, we have been holding *simplicity* and *complexity* in tension. We delved into five complex elements of leading strategically—(1) discern, (2) cultivate relationships, (3) understand context and history, (4) harness power, and (5) think big, act small, learn fast—and we provided simple tools you can use

Figure C.1 The Five Elements of Leading Strategically

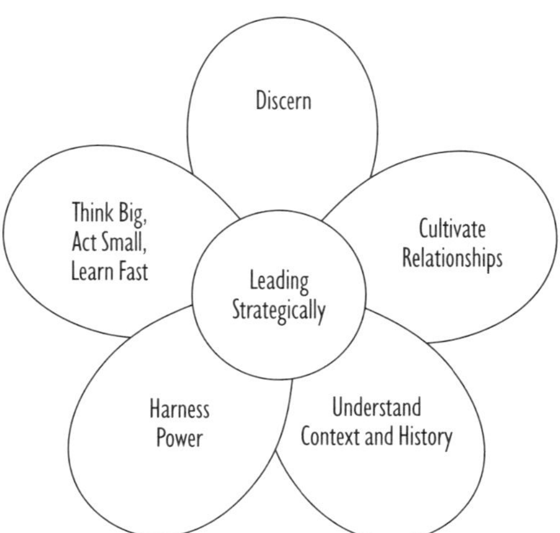

to apply those concepts in your life and work. We introduced a set of dualities that exist in the world, your work, and your life that you must be aware of as a strategic leader. These dualities are nuanced and complex. The simplicity lies in not needing to resolve them. You must simply be aware of them and make conscious choices about when you emphasize one aspect of the duality over the other and when you want to shift that dynamic. Finally, we shared a number of mini-cases that illustrate how the elements and dualities of strategic leadership show up in real life and offered analyses designed to simplify the complexity by homing in on crucial issues.

We hope that the five elements will anchor you and help you to consider your own real-life messy challenges and opportunities. We want to embrace the *simplicity-complexity* duality one last time by sharing a tool that is our best effort to distill the complex ideas and many questions in the book into a few simple questions—which we call the Essential Eight—that you can ask in any situation to help you lead strategically. These questions come from our own practice—they are what we ask in multiple situations and contexts, and also what we hear other strategic leaders ask.

The Essential Eight are a shorthand to keep at the ready to guide you with a specific situation or action item in the moment or to provide an entry point to more complex, long-term work. Depending on what you are working on and the opportunities and pain points that you have identified, you can use the questions as a bundle or focus on an individual question or a subset of the eight. You can prompt others to consider these questions as you build their capacity for strategic leadership, and you can also use them for personal reflection. These questions serve an emerging leader as well as they do a seasoned veteran.

The Essential Eight

1. What is your ambition for this work?
   - *Be clear about the larger why.*
2. What's the problem you're trying to solve?
   - *Get beneath the symptoms to the root causes.*
3. Who cares about this work, and why?
   - *Identify key stakeholders and their relationships, interests, and resources; pay particular attention to the stakeholders who are often overlooked.*
4. What will success look like?
   - *Define the indicators of success.*
5. What will you focus on to make progress?
   - *Identify a few high-leverage things to do that will lead to success.*
6. How do current conditions and past successes and failures inform this work?
   - *Consider what currently supports or constrains this work; identify previous work (and learnings from it) to build on.*
7. What are the trade-offs?
   - *Assess the risks, opportunities, and synergies of both what to do (or not do) and how to do it (or not do it).*
8. How will you measure progress and learn from your efforts?
   - *Collect a variety of data and evidence regarding implementation and impact and use what you learn to continuously improve.*

Strategic leadership is something we all continue to develop over our lifetimes. There is no promised land we get to where we are fully formed strategic leaders. None of us are the same leaders we were five years ago. And if we keep learning, in five years none of us will be the leaders we are today. Every day, life offers us opportunities to learn and grow in both our personal and professional lives. There are personal examples of the elements throughout the book because noticing and practicing strategic leadership in our personal lives help us to exercise the same leadership in our professional lives and to be authentic, healthy, whole people. That is a powerful model with the potential to be transformative for ourselves, the people we work with, and the organizations and communities of which we are a part.

The happiest, most effective strategic leaders we know are healthy, whole human beings who bring that wholeness to their work. We wish that for you, too.

APPENDIX: TOOLS FOR LEADING STRATEGICALLY

DATA TRACKER

Overview

The Data Tracker provides a simple template to track what you're collecting when gathering information to better understand a problem, the status of work underway, or the impact of efforts. Completing the Data Tracker helps ensure that your data are rich and varied, have integrity, and provide you with the information you need.

Steps

1. Choose a problem that you want to understand more deeply.
2. List your sources of information in the appropriate box of the template (next).
3. Review your lists to make sure that you're not overrelying on one or more of the categories of information at the expense of the others.
4. Rebalance your information-gathering approach as needed to get a good variety of information.
5. Once you've filled out the template, step back and look at it holistically. Consider the questions here:
   a. What are your observations?
   b. Does the chart reflect a range of perspectives from stakeholders implicated in or affected by the problem?
   c. What gaps and/or overlaps in information collecting do you see? How well do the data locate problems in systems versus reinforcing a deficit mindset about people and communities?
   d. What additional data sources are most essential to deepen your understanding of the problem and challenge common narratives and assumptions? Or, conversely, what data sources are least essential for understanding this problem? (An opportunity to *not do* something!)

   e. How much time do you have for this inquiry, and which data sources are most essential?

6. *So what?* With all this analysis in mind, the final question to ask is: *What do we need to do next?*

Data Tracker				
	Count	See	Hear	Feel
Satellite data (high altitude; illuminates patterns)				
Map data (medium altitude; identifies gaps)				
Street data (low altitude; describes the experiences of individuals proximate to the problem you're trying to solve)[1]				

Tips

- **Be promiscuous with data sources:** Gather data from a variety of sources. Doing that enriches your understanding of the problem and gives voice to different kinds of data and information.
    - You don't necessarily have to have a data source in every box, but pay attention to how the data sources sort into the chart. For lower-stakes or less-complex issues, you may have a smaller array of data sources. For higher-stakes or more-complex issues, you may want a richer array.
- **Get proximate to data sources:** Get close to the problem that you're trying to address and the people who understand it most intimately (often students, teachers, and families).
- **Get perspective:** Talk to a variety of stakeholders as part of your data collection to get different perspectives and to build trust, relationships, and buy-in.
- **Ensure data quality:** Think critically about the quality of the data sources (e.g., if you know that a certain kind of data is not collected and/or reported consistently, effectively, or with integrity, it's not a good source of information).
- **Be curious:** Be open-minded as you consider data sources and review the data, rather than looking for confirmation of what you think.
- **Do this with other people** who bring different perspectives.

2X2 MATRIX

Overview

The 2x2 Matrix (figure A.1) is a versatile tool to assess actions that you are considering, using two factors in relationship to one another (e.g., ease–impact; risk–reward; importance–urgency). The assessment can guide strategic decision-making about *what* work to pursue, *how* to pursue it, and *why*. It also helps with *when*, as you prioritize and pace and sequence the pursuit of the actions. Examples of the 2x2 Matrix in action can be seen in figures 1.2, 5.2, and 11.4.

Steps

1. Decide what two factors you want to consider in relation to one another. Label the axes accordingly and how the two factors present themselves in each quadrant (e.g., low A, high B; low A, low B).

2. Identify the array of different actions that could be pursued given the root causes identified and the vision articulated. This can be done most effectively with a group of people who understand the work under consideration and/or are on the ground where implementation will occur.

3. Use sticky notes (one per action) to map each action under consideration onto the four-square matrix. This step will likely require some discussion to ensure accurate placement.

Figure A.1 2x2 Matrix

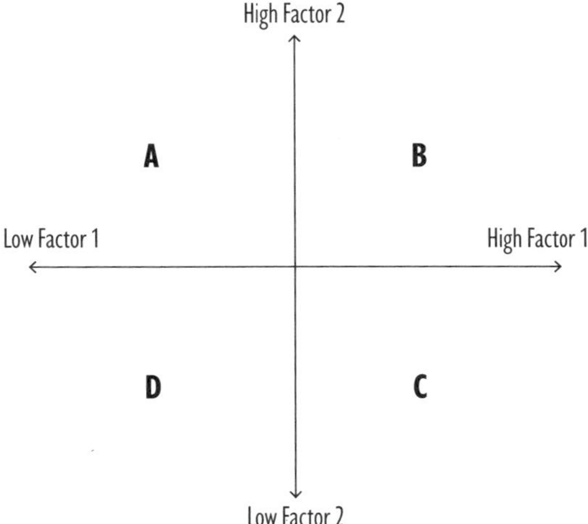

Figure A.2 Ease-Impact Matrix

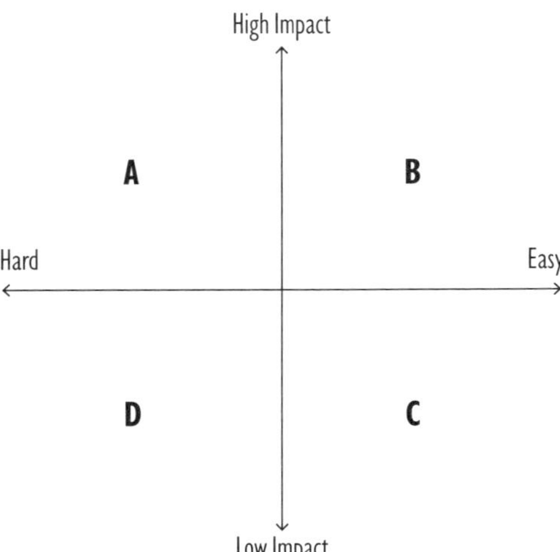

4. Step back and see what the matrix tells you. Your analysis will depend on what factors you choose for the axes. Take, for example, an Ease-Impact 2x2 (figure A.2).

5. Work that falls in quadrant B (Easy, High Impact) is a great place to start. This is the quadrant of low-hanging fruit and quick wins. Starting here can help build momentum, capacity, and a sense of efficacy. Discuss which of the options here you could start with and why, and what else that work might set you up to do.

6. For work that falls in quadrant D (Hard, Low Impact), discuss what you can stop doing. If there are reasons (regulations, political considerations) why you must do things listed in this quadrant, focus on finding the easiest, least labor-intensive way to address them or revise them to give them a higher impact.

7. For work that falls in quadrant C (Easy, Low Impact), consider the following: what you can keep doing but adjust your approach to add more value; what isn't worth continuing; and which things you want to keep doing (e.g., because the risks of not doing them are too great) but, based on their limited value, you can devote less time and energy to. There may be items that seem important, but have an indirect connection to the particular impact you seek, in which case you can ask: "What are the impacts of each of these things? Do we value them enough to keep doing them?" Be careful about doing many things in this quadrant because cumulatively, they take capacity.

8. Quadrant A (Hard, High Impact) is often crowded with lots of ideas. For this quadrant, ask questions like these: "Do we want to do all these things? Do we have the capacity to do everything in this quadrant well?" If the answer to one or both of these questions is no, then the next question is, "How do we prioritize, pace, and sequence the work over time, and what can we *not* do?" Individual/organizational capacity is a key consideration in prioritization, pacing, and sequencing.

9. *So what?* With all your analysis in mind, the final questions to ask are: "What's possible? What will be most useful? Where do we start? And what do we want to get to over time?"

Tips

- Create the 2x2 Matrix with a group or team to yield a more accurate assessment, tapping on different people's information, experience, and expertise. Including the people who will be charged with implementing the prioritized actions can be invaluable both for the input they provide and the buy-in that emerges.
- Share a 2x2 Matrix that you have created on your own with someone whose perspective (and expertise) you trust to get their feedback on where you placed things on the matrix.
- In the Ease-Impact version of the 2x2 Matrix, common elements that affect how easy or hard implementation is include:
    - Internal and external capacity to do the work required (e.g., knowledge and skill, operational and managerial capacity, partnerships)
    - Stakeholder engagement (e.g., who needs to be engaged in the decision-making, design, and implementation for substantive and/or political reasons)
    - Change management (e.g., how many people need to make how big of a change in the way they work, and how hard will that feel to them)
    - Resources (e.g., time, people, money, and technology)
    - Opportunities (e.g., grants, policy that can support and accelerate the work)
    - Political will (e.g., within the system and the larger community)

RELATIONSHIP MAPPING

Overview

Relationship mapping is an easy way to visually lay out the people, departments, and/or organizations implicated in specific work, the relationships that exist among them, and any critical gaps that need to be addressed to ensure success. This can help you determine how to pursue the work.

Steps

1. Write the name of the issue/priority that you want to address in the center of a sheet of paper and circle it.
2. Write the names of people, departments, and/or organizations that need to be part of responding to this issue/priority on sticky notes (one per sticky note). Place those most closely connected to the issue nearest to the center circle and those most peripherally involved farthest away.
3. Map the relationships between people, departments, and/or organizations by drawing lines and arrows between the sticky notes.
4. Step back and reflect and discuss with others what is most striking to you about the map. Some things to consider include the following:
    a. Where do expertise, capacity, resources, and political influence reside? How much of each is there relative to how much may be needed? Are there different ways to think about these four things?
    b. Which current relationships can support your purpose and goals? Which relationships need to be built?
    c. Are traditional dynamics of power and privilege reflected? If yes, are there ways to shift those dynamics?
5. *So what?* Consider the implications of your analysis for how you address the issue/priority and any necessary groundwork that needs to be laid.

Tips

- Do this with other people, particularly people with different roles, experiences, and relationships than yours; they often bring broader perspectives that add to the richness of the analysis.

- Think about the interrelationships among individuals, teams, departments, and organizations as you map the relationships (e.g., a nonprofit board member who knows a potential funder for work that the nonprofit is considering; and a team that has relevant experience but has a new leader who was not part of that experience).
- Think about expertise, capacity, resources, and political influence in relationship to one another. Is there lots of political influence but little expertise? Strong resources but little capacity? These nuances need to inform how the issue/priority is addressed.

SETTING UP A CROSS-FUNCTIONAL WORK GROUP FOR SUCCESS

Overview

Setting up a cross-functional work group for success guides you through key considerations when establishing a work group. By "work group," we mean *a cross-functional group of people brought together to tackle a specific issue*. The group's work is likely time-bound. The considerations are designed to ensure several things: that there is a clear and compelling *why* for the group, and that the membership, design, and process of the group are aligned with it.

Steps

1. **Why:** *What are we trying to accomplish? What problem are we trying to solve?* Getting very clear about this can inform how you shape the structure and participants.
2. **What:** *What is the charge to the group?* This should be related to the why question, but it may be more grounded in accomplishing specific things that will lead to the why.
3. **When:** *How often will the group meet?* Does it require a consistent schedule of meetings over three, six, or twelve months, or could a lot be accomplished in just a couple of meetings?
4. **Who:** *Who are the right people to get involved given the stated why and what?*
    a. What is the mix of expertise, experience, authority (formal and informal), power (or access to it), political acumen, proximity to the work under consideration, and relationships to other key players that is needed to set up the group for success?
    b. Which combination of people will ensure interdependence and that the group will tackle complex and meaningful work?
    c. What group size will ensure that everyone's voice is heard and the group doesn't become unwieldy?
    d. Who will champion this work to the leaders of the organization?
    e. Who will lead the daily work of the group?
5. **How:** *How will the group function?* There are a number of dimensions to consider:
    a. **Facilitation:** *Is there a logical person inside the organization to facilitate the group, or do you need to look to an external partner for facilitation support?* The answer to this question should consider skills, relationships, and capacity.

b. **Norms:** *What are the norms to which all group members will abide?* Norms are something on which group members need to agree.

c. **Building community:** *What culture needs to be built within the group to support its effectiveness?* This can include doing a work styles clarification exercise to build awareness among group members about their own and their colleagues' skills and needs. Also, group members can share with one another their connection to the work that the group is charged with doing and their related experience.

d. **Momentum:** *How frequently will the group meet? What will happen between meetings? Who will be responsible for making those things happen?* In answering these questions, a crucial issue is who is doing this work on top of all their other responsibilities versus who has time carved out of their schedule to do this. If no one has time devoted to the group's work, it will be hard to make progress.

e. **Decision-making:** *What decision-making authority does the group have?* Groups may *make* decisions, *advise* someone else on decisions, or provide information to *inform* decision-making done by others. It's possible that a single group will do more than one of these things. While the group's level of authority matters, what matters more is that everyone in the group is clear about the level of authority. Lack of clarity can lead to frustration and loss of trust.

f. **Organizational learning:** *How are the team's efforts and what you learn from them about supporting cross-functional work going to be captured and shared with the larger organization to help future efforts?* Be intentional about how the group will facilitate and document its learning and then feed that learning back into both current and future work.

Tips

- Before convening the work group, get very clear about the *why* of the group to inform how you shape the structure and choose participants.
- Develop a one-sentence statement about the purpose (*why*) of the group to use when recruiting people to work with you and build buy-in for the idea of a work group.
- Take into consideration potential group members' individual contributions, their personal tunings and temperaments, the politics of including/excluding particular people, their time availability, and how well they play with others.
- Build and regularly use mechanisms to check in on group process and progress (e.g., Plus-Delta at the end of meetings, a work plan to track work, benchmarks).

LADDER OF INFERENCE

Overview

The Ladder of Inference is designed to help you slow down your brain's natural desire to process quickly, create meaning, and make decisions.[2] It helps you notice when you do things like the following:

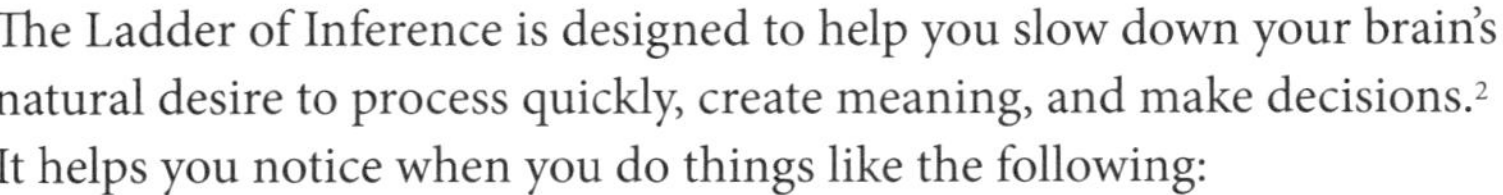

- Interpret what is happening through the lenses of biases, experiences, and beliefs;
- Make assumptions and generalizations and draw conclusions based on these biases, experiences, and beliefs; and
- Take action based on assumptions and generalizations rather than reality.

Steps on the Ladder of Inference

7. You take *action* guided by your beliefs.
6. You adopt *beliefs* based on your conclusions.
5. You draw *conclusions*.
4. You make *assumptions* based on the meaning that you've made.
3. You *add meaning* to the data that you collect based on your biases, experiences, and beliefs.
2. You *select specific data* from what you count, see, hear, and feel.
1. A wide array of data is available.

Example of Moving up the Ladder of Inference

Janet walks into the shared kitchen at her office at 8:55 a.m., desperate for a cup of coffee. She didn't sleep well the night before and is feeling tired and grumpy. Alone in the kitchen, she notices dishes in the sink. Irritated, she thinks, *I hate when people leave dirty dishes in the sink. This has been happening more and more frequently. People are ignoring the kitchen rules. It's so disrespectful. Maybe we should institute a fine for anyone caught leaving dirty dishes in the sink. Who should I email about this?*

Once Janet has filled her mug with coffee and taken a few sips, she realizes that she's gotten all hot and bothered about the dishes in the sink and may have rushed to judgment and jumped to conclusions. To slow down and bring herself down the Ladder of Inference, she looks around the kitchen. She opens the dishwasher and sees that it's full of clean dishes. She remembers that there's an all-staff meeting at

9 a.m. and wonders if someone put dishes in the sink as they hurried to the meeting. Her phone pings with a message that Maria, the administrative assistant, is out of the office today. She wonders if maybe Maria's the one who usually unloads the dishwasher. Walking back to her office, Janet realizes that instead of sending an angry email, she could give herself a few minutes of peace and calm with her coffee. And, maybe, when she returns her empty mug to the kitchen, she'll just unload the dishwasher herself if it hasn't already been done.

Steps

1. Notice and state that you have jumped to a conclusion and, perhaps, are ready to take action.
2. Move back down the ladder by making explicit what you saw, heard, or experienced that led you to your conclusion or belief (there is usually a mix of something observed and beliefs in play) and inviting others to do the same. Ask, *What am I thinking? Why? What did I see or hear that made me think that? Is my thinking sound?*
3. If you identify faulty reasoning, revisit it.
4. Go back to the facts of the situation, gathering additional data if you identify that your original facts were incomplete.
5. Start your thinking process again, moving slowly and consciously up each rung of the ladder.

Tips

- Speaking in absolute and/or broad terms (e.g., *everyone thinks that the new performance management system is a disaster*) is a sign that you may be climbing the Ladder of Inference. Using descriptive language (e.g., *five people have expressed concerns about the self-reflection section of the new performance management tool*) keeps you low on the ladder and supports understanding what the actual data are before deciding what to do about the situation.
- Don't get overly focused on going down the ladder, one rung at a time. What's most important is to identify the assumptions that you made and whether you missed any important facts that were present.
- Build a habit (for yourself and in groups) of naming when people are operating in a high-inference/judgmental space (e.g., "That sounds up the ladder to me," or "I know I'm going up the ladder here . . ."). This can help socialize the Ladder of Inference as a valuable tool and make this common behavior discussable.

BRUTALLY HONEST TRUTHS

Overview

Brutally Honest Truths (BHTs) involve an *IF . . . BUT . . . THEN* statement that you can develop to understand the current state of affairs regarding a situation, a body of work, or the totality of an organization's efforts (it can also be used to look at your individual efforts, personally or professionally). Developing BHTs makes hard truths discussable by drawing the connection between the actions that you're taking and the results that you're achieving.

Examples of Brutally Honest Truths

IF we build a strong home visit program to build relationships with families and improve student attendance, *BUT* students still experience instruction as boring and disconnected from their lives and don't feel a sense of connection and belonging in school, *THEN* we won't succeed in keeping students in school and improving their learning.

IF we invest in a variety of instructional coaches who provide direct support to teachers, *BUT* the coaches are managed by different central offices, do different things with teachers (sometimes with the same teachers), and do not communicate or collaborate with one another, *THEN* teachers and principals become confused and we have fractured, uncoordinated, and potentially misaligned coaching that has less impact than it could.

Steps

1. Identify the situation or body of work that you are trying to understand better.
2. Describe what (good, bad, and otherwise) is currently being done (or, if you're thinking prospectively about work to be done, name the things that you are planning to do) related to the things that you identified in step 1. Put an *IF* in front of the description of helpful things being done.
3. Then add a *BUT* and include the things that are in place (or that you anticipate could happen, if you're thinking prospectively) that could or would compromise the effort.
4. Describe the results being achieved through the work described. Put a *THEN* in front of this description. This is the brutal reality (or the anticipated result, for prospective work) that you would not proudly proclaim.

5. Put the statements together and read them aloud. What do you notice? What does it tell you about what needs to be considered to ensure maximum impact of the effort? It should feel both "ouchy" and true—it should make you cringe and then exhale.

6. *So what?* What needs to be reconsidered to address impediments to success?

Tips

- Brutally Honest Truths are most powerful when they are developed collaboratively by a group of people who are actively engaged in the work under discussion.
- The *IF* is often something that you would proudly proclaim—it might be on your website, in your strategic plan, or in frequent conversation. It reflects all your/the team's/the organization's smart thinking and hard work.
- The *BUT* captures the wrinkles in the plan or implementation. It is most powerful when it implicates the people doing the Brutally Honest Truths exercise (more mirror than window/finger-pointing) and is within your sphere of control or influence rather than about what other people are doing or not doing. There may be systemic things outside your control, but they are seldom the sole source of the challenges.
- When doing this in a group, it often helps to invite people to write one or two Brutally Honest Truths individually, and then share them in pairs or trios before bringing the whole group together and inviting everyone to share. Applaud people's bravery when they do share. This process can be both scary and cathartic for people and organizations, so it's important to make it as low risk as possible for people to share. In some contexts, that may require making the truth-sharing entirely confidential (e.g., in a survey or shared document with anonymous inputs; or write suggestions on index cards, put them all in a hat, and have people draw one and read it aloud).
- If you're familiar with the idea of theory of action or theory of change, this is a variation of that idea. The *IF* might be exactly like what you would say in a theory of action. The *BUT* is the twist that describes points of challenge, conflict, and/or misalignment. The *THEN* is not what you would put in a theory of action (in theory of action, the *THEN* is the aspirational outcome). Here, it is the actual or anticipated reality.

IDENTIFYING VALUES, INTERESTS, AND RESOURCES

Overview

Identifying Values, Interests, and Resources is a tool you can use to understand better what people in a given situation care about, what resources they bring to a situation, and any resources they need to ensure that their interests are met. By building your understanding of these details and laying them out, you can identify ways to draw on the resources that people have, respond to their interests, create synergies, and prioritize collaborations, alliances, and power-sharing to maximize the likelihood of success in addressing the issue at hand.

Steps

1. Fill out the template to identify the values, interests, and resources of each of the key players in a situation that you're curious to explore. Be sure to include yourself. Add rows as needed.
2. Step back from it and see what you notice about the following points:
   - The values and interests that are shared *or* in conflict
   - The resources that people bring to this situation (Where do you see resources that could support people's interests and build power?)
   - The places where persuasion or coercion may be necessary to move forward
3. What new understandings do you have about the situation?
4. *So what?* What do your new insights suggest about how to address the issue?

Identifying Values, Interests, and Resources			
What are you trying to accomplish?			
Names of Key Players	Their Interests/Values	Resources They Have	Resources They Need and Who Controls the Resources

Tips

- As you think about whom to put on this chart, think broadly. Maybe there is someone who organizationally may be only peripherally connected to the work under consideration but has a personal interest that could be tapped to good effect, or someone with lots of resources but limited interest (how might you build their interest?).
- If you're unable to answer these questions for the people who are involved in the project or could be involved, talk with them, people around them, and/or others who have insights into their interests and resources. Triangulating information from a couple of sources, particularly for the most influential people on your list, can sometimes be quite helpful in capturing nuances.
- Look for synergies (e.g., who has resources that someone else needs, where are there shared values and interests, where might challenges arise due to differences in values and interests, where can resources be combined to increase impact?).

POWER MAPPING

Overview

Power Mapping uses a 2x2 Matrix (figure A.3) to identify support and opposition, as well as where power lies among stakeholders relative to what you're trying to accomplish. It invites you to draw connections between the stakeholders based on their relationships, which provides insight into opportunities to build alliances and to have stakeholders with power exert their influence.

Steps

1. Identify the key stakeholders for whatever you're trying to accomplish.
2. Place each of them on the map based on your sense of the power that they can exercise and their level of support for or opposition against what you're trying to accomplish.
3. Use arrows to map the relationships between the stakeholders to reflect where there are shared values and/or interests, people or organizations that can bridge the divide between supporters and detractors, and other interesting dynamics at play.

Figure A.3 Support-Power Matrix

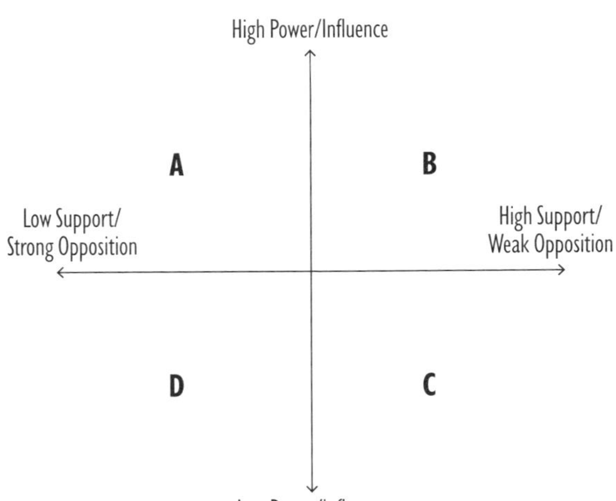

4. Reflect on the map to see what it can teach you about the following:
   a. Where the opportunities lie for using power in service of your goal;
   b. Where stakeholders can persuade or coerce in service of your goal; and
   c. The extent to which the distribution of power is aligned with historically dominant groups and/or groups to which you are aligned, how that might help and/or hurt you, and where you may need to build alliances to accomplish your goals.
5. *So what?* Identify next steps to take based on your analysis.

Tips

- Stakeholders can be people, departments, and/or organizations and are often more than one of these things.
- Relationships can be based on friendships, affiliations, like-mindedness, and past collaborations and partnerships.
- Do power mapping with other people to ensure that the map reflects a variety of networks and perspectives.
- Use sticky notes with different people or organizations listed on each so you can move stakeholders around on the matrix while you discuss them. This will let participants try to align on how they see power flowing.
- Run the map by a stakeholder with a different perspective who will honestly share it with you. This might be someone who is a boundary spanner, can see multiple perspectives, and has a good sense of the interests and resources of each side; understands the opposition's perspective with empathy; has a much better understanding of *context and history* than you do; or opposes you on this particular issue but is trustworthy and shares a broader purpose with you. You want this person to tell you if you're missing key players you need to win over, underestimating or overestimating the power that a particular person or group holds, or misunderstanding what the people in opposition care most about.

NOTES

Introduction

1. Rachel E. Curtis and Elizabeth A. City, *Strategy in Action: How School Systems Can Support Powerful Learning and Teaching* (Cambridge, MA: Harvard Education Press, 2009).

Chapter 1

1. *Oxford Languages*, s.v. "discern (*n*.)," accessed August 4, 2024, https://www.google.com/search?q=definition+of+discern.
2. Lewis Carroll, *Alice's Adventures in Wonderland* (1865), https://www.gutenberg.org/files/11/11-h/11-h.htm.
3. Kathryn Parker Boudett, Elizabeth A. City, and Richard J. Murnane, eds., *Data Wise: A Step-by-Step Guide to Using Assessment Results to Improve Teaching and Learning* (Cambridge, MA: Harvard Education Press, 2005).
4. Shane Safir and Jamila Dugan, *Street Data: A Next-Generation Model for Equity, Pedagogy, and School Transformation* (Thousand Oaks, CA: Corwin, 2021), 54–58.
5. Anthony S. Bryk et al., *Learning to Improve: How America's Schools Can Get Better at Getting Better* (Cambridge, MA: Harvard Education Press, 2015), 57.
6. Bryan Stevenson, "4 Rules for Achieving Peace and Justice," speech at Harvard Kennedy School, January 31, 2019, https://www.youtube.com/watch?v=9vI7UPuCUrE.
7. Chimamanda Ngozi Adichie, "The Danger of a Single Story" (TEDGlobal, July 2009), https://www.ted.com/talks/chimamanda_ngozi_adichie_the_danger_of_a_single_story.
8. john a. powell, Stephen Menendian, and Wendy Ake, *Targeted Universalism: Policy & Practice*, Othering & Belonging Institute at UC Berkeley, May 2019, https://belonging.berkeley.edu/targeted-universalism.

Chapter 2

1. *Oxford Languages*, s.v. "relationships (*n*.)," accessed August 4, 2024, https://www.google.com/search?q=what+do+relationships+mean&oq=what+do+relationships+mean.
2. Donna Hicks, *Leading with Dignity: How to Create a Culture That Brings out the Best in People* (New Haven, CT: Yale University Press, 2018), 15–27.
3. Ross Gay, *The Book of Delights* (Chapel Hill, NC: Algonquin, 2019).

4. C. Otto Scharmer, *The Essentials of Theory U: Core Principles and Applications* (Oakland, CA: Berrett-Koehler, 2018), 26.

Chapter 3

1. Peter Senge et al., *Schools That Learn: A Fifth Discipline Fieldbook for Educators, Parents, and Everyone Who Cares About Education* (New York: Doubleday, 2000), 68–71. The Ladder of Inference builds on the work of Chris Argyris and Donald A. Schön; see, for example, Chris Argyris and Donald A. Schön, *Theory in Practice: Increasing Professional Effectiveness* (San Francisco: Jossey-Bass, 1976).
2. Success Analysis Protocol, https://www.schoolreforminitiative.org/download/success-analysis-protocol-for-individuals/.
3. This question generates a response that is similar to a Strengths, Weaknesses, Opportunities, and Threats (SWOT) analysis, a widely used organizational analysis tool. For more on SWOT analysis, see https://www.mindtools.com/amtbj63/swot-analysis.
4. Marsha A. Green, "Take Five: Tips for Uncovering Bias," Campus, Working@Duke, March 18, 2013, https://today.duke.edu/2013/03/takefivediversity.
5. Green, "Take Five: Tips for Uncovering Bias."

Chapter 4

1. *Oxford Languages*, s.v. "power (*n.*)," accessed August 4, 2024, https://www.google.com/search?q=definition+of+power.
2. Dolores Huerta, interview by Erica Gunderson, WTTW (PBS), February 25, 2023, https://news.wttw.com/2023/02/25/92-activist-dolores-huerta-still-fight.
3. Bertram H. Raven, "The Bases of Power and the Power/Interaction Model of Interpersonal Influence," *Analyses of Social Issues and Public Policy* 8, no. 1 (2008): 1–22; "French and Raven's Five Forms of Power," by the Mindtools Content Team, Mindtools, accessed August 9, 2024, https://www.mindtools.com/abwzix3/french-and-ravens-five-forms-of-power. Many thanks to Christine Ortiz and Kofi Taha of Equity Meets Design, who shared with us the Raven and Mindtools articles and Equity Meets Design's work about "positional" and "personal" power building from those sources.
4. Srilatha Batliwala, "All About POWER: Understanding Social Power & Power Structures," Creating Resources for Empowerment in Action (CREA), accessed August 4, 2024, 13, https://creaworld.org/wp-content/uploads/2020/07/All-About-Power.pdf. Italic added for emphasis.
5. Leading Change Network et al., "Organizing Guide: People, Power, Change" (2014), accessed August 9, 2024, https://commonslibrary.org/organizing-people-power-change/. Marshall Ganz, "Marshall Ganz' Framework: People, Power, Change," modified by Jacob Waxman, accessed August 9, 2024, 3, https://wcl.nwf.org/wp-content/

uploads/2018/09/Marshall-Ganz-People-Power-and-Change.pdf. See also Marshall Ganz, *People, Power, Change: Organizing for Democratic Renewal* (New York: Oxford University Press, 2024), 19–23.

6. Batliwala, "All About POWER."

Chapter 5

1. Shane Safir and Jamila Dugan, *Street Data: A Next-Generation Model for Equity, Pedagogy, and School Transformation* (Thousand Oaks, CA: Corwin, 2021).
2. Katharine C. Briggs, *Myers-Briggs Type Indicator. Form G* (Palo Alto, CA: Consulting Psychologists, 1987); "Compass Points: North, South, East, and West—an Exercise in Understanding Preferences in Group Work," Center for Leadership & Educational Equity, accessed August 4, 2024, https://www.schoolreforminitiative.org/download/compass-points-north-south-east-and-west-an-exercise-in-understanding-preferences-in-group-work/.

Part II

1. See https://zonesofregulation.com/how-it-works/ for the original Zones of Regulation® curriculum.

Appendix

1. Shane Safir and Jamila Dugan, *Street Data: A Next-Generation Model for Equity, Pedagogy, and School Transformation* (Thousand Oaks, CA: Corwin, 2021).
2. Peter Senge et al., *Schools That Learn: A Fifth Discipline Fieldbook for Educators, Parents, and Everyone Who Cares About Education* (New York: Doubleday, 2000), 68–71. The Ladder of Inference builds on the work of Chris Argyris and Donald A. Schön. See, for example, Chris Argyris and Donald A. Schön, *Theory in Practice: Increasing Professional Effectiveness* (San Francisco: Jossey-Bass, 1976).

ACKNOWLEDGMENTS

THIS BOOK OWES MUCH TO MANY.
It reflects much of what we have learned about leadership over our combined sixty-plus years in education, leading and supporting and developing other leaders. We thank the leaders who have shared their stories, their hopes, their challenges, and their questions with us over the years. We hope that you all see yourselves in this book, and that this book will help you continue to grow and reach your audacious goals.

Part I of the book benefited greatly from the thoughtful, strategic practitioners who gave us feedback on emergent drafts. We thank the following leaders for their counsel during "Feedbackapalooza": Akeshia Craven-Howell, Amy Briggs, Andie Corso, Anthony King, April Wang, Babak Mostaghimi, Dana Roseman, Dia Bryant, Donna Lynn Phillips, Ellen Winn, Emily Glasgow, James Hilton Harrell, Joan Dabrowski, Joy Delizo-Osborne, Karla Baehr, Laura Meili, Leslie Patterson, Mark Odsather, Michele Caracappa, Regan Kelly, Sharon Foley, Shirley Vargas, Steph Frenel, Tassan Sung, and Tiffani Curtis. What a gift to have wise colleagues who were enthusiastic and told us what they really thought!

Chapter 4, "Harness Power," also benefited from early feedback from staff and alumni of the Leadership Institute of Nevada, as well as Liz's graduate students in her classes on "Leading Strategically" and "Driving Change." Thank you for the powerful conversations.

Part II's mini-cases were enriched by the perspectives of multiple leaders. We thank Chris Horan, Karen Mapp, and Melanie Edwards-Tavares for their help with some of our early thinking. Special thanks to April Wang, Dia Bryant, Miho Kubagawa, Paola Peacock-Villada, and Simone Wright for their keen eyes and thoughtful feedback on later drafts.

And then there are the generous souls—Chong-Hao Fu, Kofi Taha, Sarah Fiarman, and Shayne Spalten—who read the complete manuscript draft for us. We are so thankful for the extraordinary gift of their time, expertise, commitment to our vision for the book, and loving nudges to make it even better. Each of these readers also made a special contribution for which we are grateful. Chong-Hao urged us to go deeper on *cultivating relationships*. Kofi expanded our view of *power* and reminded us to center on people. Sarah helped us consider our own identities and their impact on the experiences and lessons that we've written about. Shayne encouraged us to be more explicit about building others' capacity as a core act of leading strategically.

Additionally, Liz thanks the hundreds of students who have taken a course on "Leading Strategically" with her at the Harvard Graduate School of Education (HGSE) since May 2020 and shared their strategic challenges, questions, and learnings. Liz also thanks Erin

Simmons, Keri Randolph, and Rebecca Grainger for the conversations about leading strategically; the Holdsworth Center for hosting her as a Scholar-in-Residence to work on this book; and HGSE's Dean's Office for providing time to work on the book.

Rachel thanks the Aspen Urban Superintendents Network members who constantly strive to lead strategically and continually teach her about the possibilities and complexities of that work. Thanks to Ann Clark, Gene Pinkard, and Ross Wiener, her colleagues at the Aspen Institute's Education and Society Program, for their continued thought partnership on many of the ideas in this book. And, finally, thanks to the senior school system and educational nonprofit leaders whom Rachel teaches and coaches for keeping her anchored in their lived reality and showing her so many ways to be strategic leaders.

And then, of course, there are all the people who helped turn the manuscript into a book! We thank Heidi Gross for her invaluable editing and for catching all the little things. Thanks to Lisa Andrews for helping us render our wordy ideas into simple graphics. And thank you to all the people at the Harvard Education Press (HEP) who have supported us along the way: Molly Cerrone, our editor; Jess Fiorillo, executive director of HEP; and the whole team behind the scenes who turned all our words into an actual book.

Our final words of thanks go to our families, who have supported us along the journey of writing this book, whether by simply asking how it's going, encouraging us to keep going, or blessedly distracting us from writing. A special thanks goes to the children who love us and remind us every day why we do this work. Liz thanks her children for their patience with her many hours writing the book, as well as for telling her to turn off the computer and go play backyard soccer or bake delicious treats. Rachel thanks Violet and William for having absolutely no awareness of or interest in the book and offering endless giggles, delights, and hugs. We love you.

ABOUT THE AUTHORS

Elizabeth A. City helps educators improve systems of learning, teaching, and schooling through leadership development, strategy, and practices of improvement. Liz has served as a teacher, instructional coach, principal, and consultant, in each role focused on helping all children, as well as the educators who work with them, realize their full potential. She is currently senior lecturer on education at the Harvard Graduate School of Education, where she is executive director of Reach Every Reader and previously served as director of the Doctor of Education Leadership (EdLD) program.

Her coauthored and coedited publications include *Meeting Wise, Strategy in Action, Instructional Rounds in Education*, and *Data Wise* (2005 and 2013 editions). She holds a doctorate of education in Administration, Planning, and Social Policy from Harvard University.

Rachel E. Curtis helps educators, as well as the partners who support them, in their pursuit of a richer vision of teaching, learning, and schooling through strategy, leadership development, and systems of professional learning. She is currently director of the Urban Superintendents Network at the Aspen Institute and a consultant and leadership coach to superintendents and senior leaders in public school systems and educational nonprofits. Her work is profoundly informed by the decade she spent in the Boston Public Schools, where she was most recently assistant superintendent for teaching and learning.

Her coauthored and coedited publications include *Teaching Talent, Strategy in Action,* and *The Skillful Leader II*. She holds a master's in education in leadership and organizational development in the context of standards-based K–12 education from Harvard University.

The authors can be reached at elizabeth_city@gse.harvard.edu and rachelecurtis@gmail.com.

For more on leading strategically, see www.leadingstrategically.org.

INDEX